Also of interest

Richardson's *Clarissa* and the eighteenth-century reader

TOM KEYMER

Clarissa is one of the undisputed masterpieces of eighteenth-century literature and the English novel. Recently it has also become central to poststructuralist, psychoanalytic and feminist debate. This book, whilst benefiting from recent theoretical studies, restores *Clarissa* to its largely neglected eighteenth-century context. Reading the novel against a variety of literary, historical and cultural backgrounds, it pays particular attention to the problematic relationship between Richardson's didactic intentions, the complexity of the text itself, and the diverse reading experiences of its first audience.

Cambridge Studies in Eighteenth-Century English Literature and Thought 13

The literary importance of letters did not end with the demise of the eighteenth-century epistolary novel. In the turbulent period between 1789 and 1830, the letter was used as a vehicle for political rather than sentimental expression. Against a background of severe political censorship, seditious corresponding societies and the rise of the modern Post Office, letters as they were used by Romantic writers, especially women, became the vehicle for a distinctly political, often disruptive force. Mary Favret's study of Romantic correspondence re-examines traditional accounts of epistolary writing, and redefines the letter as a "feminine" genre. It also reconsiders a central concept of Romantic poetry in historicist, feminist and prosaic terms, by asking us to question the categories of gender and genre which determine our sense of Romantic literature.

The book deals not only with fictional letters which circulated in the novels of Jane Austen or in Mary Shelley's *Frankenstein*, but also with political pamphlets, incendiary letters and spy letters available for public consumption. Mary Favret argues that the travel letters of Mary Wollstonecraft and the foreign correspondence of Helen Maria Williams disturb any simple notions of epistolary fictions and the "woman of letters" by insisting on the democratizing power of correspondence. At the same time, the history of correspondence promoted by the British Post Office deflects that democratizing power by channeling letter-writing into a story of national progress.

Cambridge Studies in Romanticism

ROMANTIC CORRESPONDENCE

CAMBRIDGE STUDIES IN ROMANTICISM

This series aims to foster the best new work in one of the most challenging fields within English literary studies. From the early 1780s to the early 1830s a formidable array of talented men and women took to literary composition, not just in poetry, which some of them famously transformed, but in many modes of writing. The expansion of publishing created new opportunities for writers, and the political stakes of what they wrote were raised again and again by what Wordsworth called those "great national events" that were "almost daily taking place": the French Revolution, the Napoleonic and American wars, urbanization, industrialization, religious revival, an expanded empire abroad and the reform movement at home. This was a literature of enormous ambition, even when it pretended otherwise. The relations between science, philosophy, religion and literature were reworked in texts such as *Frankenstein* and *Biographia Literaria*; gender relations in *A Vindication of the Rights of Woman* and *Don Juan*; journalism by Cobbett and Hazlitt; poetic form, content and style by the Lake School and the Cockney School. Outside Shakespeare studies, probably no body of writing has produced such a wealth of response or done so much to shape the responses of modern criticism. This indeed is the period that saw the emergence of those notions of "literature" and of literary history, especially national literary history, on which modern scholarship in English has been founded.

The categories produced by Romanticism have also been challenged by recent historicist arguments. The task of the series is to engage both with a challenging corpus of Romantic writings and with the changing field of criticism they have helped to shape. As with other literary series published by Cambridge, this one will represent the work of both younger and more established scholars, on either side of the Atlantic and elsewhere.

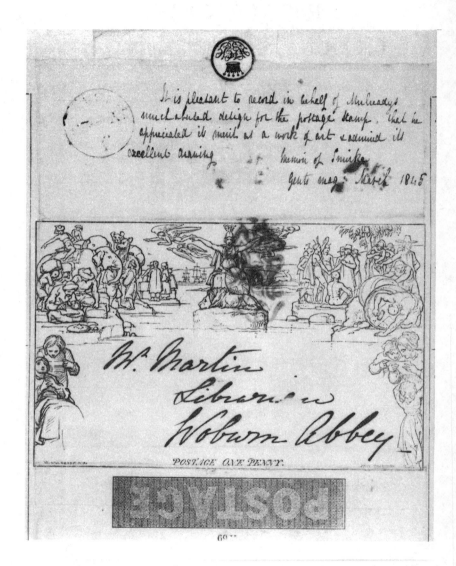

William Mulready, Allegorical representation of the British Post Office for the first approved postage stamp. Engraving by Thompson, 1840. London, The British Library.

ROMANTIC CORRESPONDENCE

Women, politics and the fiction of letters

MARY A. FAVRET

Assistant Professor of English and Adjunct Faculty in Women's Studies
Indiana University

CAMBRIDGE
UNIVERSITY PRESS

Published by the Press Syndicate of the University of Cambridge
The Pitt Building, Trumpington Street, Cambridge CB2 IRP
40 West 20th Street, New York, NY 10011–4211, USA
10 Stamford Road, Oakleigh, Melbourne 3166, Australia

© Cambridge University Press 1993

First published 1993
Reprinted 1994

Printed in Great Britain at The Ipswich Book Company, Ipswich, Suffolk

A catalogue record for this book is available from the British Library

Library of Congress cataloguing in publication data

Favret, Mary A.
Romantic correspondence: women, politics, and the fiction of letters / Mary A. Favret.
p.   cm. – (Cambridge studies in Romanticism)
Includes bibliographical references.
ISBN 0 521 41096 7
1. English letters – Women authors – History and criticism.   2. Women authors, English –
Correspondence – History and criticism.   3. Politics and literature – Great Britain –
History – 19th century.   4. Politics and literature – Great Britain – History – 18th century.
5. Women and literature – Great Britain – History – 19th century.   6. Women and
literature – Great Britain – History – 18th century.   7. Epistolary fiction, English – History
and criticism.   8. Romanticism – Great Britain.   9. Letters in literature.
I. Title.   II. Series.
PR911.F38   1993
826′.7099287 – dc20   92-4491   CIP

ISBN 0 521 41096 7 hardback

215838

Contents

Illustrations

All illustrations are reproduced with permission.

Acknowledgments

This book, now read with rear-vision, seems the logical product of two concerns: the question of whether individuals can ever understand one another and the necessity, nonetheless, of trying to communicate. In these concerns I have been educated by my friends, family and colleagues, whom I would like to acknowledge here. Yet in an acknowledgment, the pressure of these concerns bears down with remarkable force. Most of my gratitude therefore will not find expression in these pages.

This study of correspondence would never have been realized without the support of a number of exceptional readers. To Barbara Gelpi, Herbert Lindenberger and George Dekker, who helped shape the initial version; to Steven Kruger, Elizabeth Hagedorn Cook, Deirdre Lynch, Elizabeth Bohls, Jean Kowaleski and Ellen Weinauer, who commented at various stages of revision; to Donya Samara, who rescued this project at the eleventh hour; and especially to Marilyn Butler, James Chandler, Kenneth Johnston and Andrew Miller, whose advice and questions pushed the manuscript into its final form; to these readers I am indebted for more than words.

I am grateful for the resources and the collegiality provided me by two institutions in particular – the English Departments at Indiana University and Stanford University. Grants from both these universities, as well as from the Mabelle McLeod Lewis Foundation, supported me during various stages of writing. The kind assistance of Josie Dixon at Cambridge University Press also demands my gratitude.

Chapter 6 appeared in an earlier version as "The Letters of *Frankenstein*," in *Genre* 20 (Spring 1988); the material is used with the publishers' permission.

If only for my own sake, I would like to recognize here the several places where I worked on the various parts of this book. Each site left its traces on the pages: the libraries and studies of Bloomington, Stanford, Berkeley, New Haven, Vancouver and London; and the homes that welcomed me in these various places, especially the Enthoven, McGeer, and Holden homes. I owe even more perhaps to the places of rest, and especially to Walnut Hills in Pennsylvania. Therefore, to those ultimate hosts and faithful correspondents, my mother and father, I would like to dedicate this book.

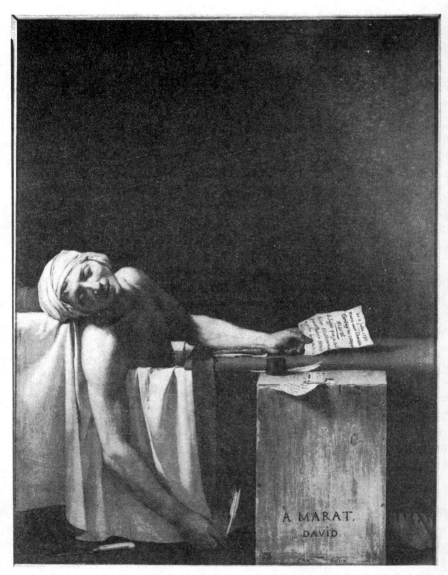

Figure 1 Jacques Louis David, *Marat Assassiné* (*The Death of Marat*), 1793.

Introduction: *the public letter, or* la lettre perfide

I will ask you to direct your gaze away from the head of the martyred hero in the portrait, *Marat Assassiné*, and toward the letter in the hero's hand (fig. 1). This move upsets the composition a bit: the artist has so carefully balanced the face of the dying man with the letter he seems to have just read. Yet our adding weight to that letter compensates for the extraordinary attention which, ever since the portrait was first displayed, has been awarded to the "Marat" half of *Marat Assassiné*. Acknowledging that the dying hero alone is not the *central* figure of the painting, we can then legitimately place Marat to one side. The figure already appears detached from its audience, in a separate time and space. The closed eyes and muted features convey a distant and timeless quality: the hero is immortalized, and beyond our world. More succinctly: he is dead. The letter, on the other hand, has a life of its own. It balances this transcendent image and reminds us of the historical context – the turbulence of Paris in April 1793, when Marat, the rabble-rousing "Friend of the People," was murdered in his bath by a young woman, Charlotte Corday. The letter introduces us into its world and intrudes upon our own.

I draw attention to this image in order to stress the value of the letter not as a literary vehicle – the epistolary form – but as a figure from everyday life. Furthermore, I want to suggest that the historical, material role of the letter in the late eighteenth century was every bit as forceful in the art and literature of the period as was the formal epistolary tradition. The very idea of the letter, in David's painting and elsewhere, produced representations that threatened to disrupt the sentimental tradition which promoted it. The emblem of isolation and vulnerability found itself in a powerful, public space.

To return to the painting: unlike the serene face, the letter – like the hand, the knife, the bath and the breast – is marked with blood. In contrast to the soft, composed features of the face, the written

characters of the letter seem stark, almost too real. The black
"Marat," underlined, opposes its dying referent: the written name
stands in the middle of the page, but off-balance. In fact, the entire
letter knocks the viewer off-balance. It tilts at an unsettling angle,
mirroring the drooping head, but pulling away from it and toward its new audience. By means of the angle of presentation, the
letter becomes public property. The clarity of the writing insists that
you read the message. But to read, you must move – change your
position, and tilt your head according to the angle dictated by the
paper. By disturbing the viewer/reader, the letter upsets a portrait which would otherwise remain silent, immobile statuary. Thus
the letter moves its audience to confront historical, even violent
change.[1]

Parisians viewing the portrait on display in the Louvre, six months
after the assassination, would have known the more sensationalized
circumstances of Marat's "over-dramatic and over-publicized end."[2]
They would also have recognized the duplicity behind the cryptic –
and ironic – words of the letter. Translated, it reads: "From the 12th
of July, 1793, Marie Anne Charlotte Corday to the Citizen Marat. It
is enough that I be unfortunate to have a right to your benevolence
[or kind protection]." The face value of this letter is not to be trusted:
what takes the form of deferential language hides the murderous
intentions of Charlotte Corday. Baudelaire labelled it *la lettre perfide*
– the treacherous letter – since, in at least one sense, the letter caused
Marat's bloody death. Corday had written to Marat, offering to
serve as a double agent and betray to him the names of counter-
revolutionaries. In agreeing to meet with her, Marat fell victim twice
to the letter's duplicity.[3]

Compare the letter to the other items in the composition : Corday's
knife, the pen she used, the bathtub, the inkwell, the head-wrappings,
the banknotes on the writing-stand, the stand itself. These mundane
articles have been transformed, as one critic puts it, into a still-life of
"holy relics."[4] David has merged and transcended what, in his day,
would have been contradictory traditions – the neo-classical and the
Christian – but he has also created a saint out of everyday elements,
and faithful to the daily newspaper accounts. Marat has become "the
icon of a new religion" for revolutionary France.[5] But our attention
has shifted from the disturbing letter. Strangely enough, the letter
remains off the critic's list of "holy relics." Perhaps because of its
duplicity, perhaps because of its invitation to be reread, the letter

defies the process of canonization. It reminds us that flattery and supplication can be treacherous, and that transcendence denies historical fact. In the face of the painting's tranquillity, Paris would have seen tension and ambivalence surfacing in the letter.

What Charlotte Corday had written was not only deceptive, it was lethal. Marat's own pen has fallen quietly, like a dying bird, dividing the painting into two areas: that of the immobile martyr and that of the written word. A second pen, however, defies the division he tries to establish. It mimics the bloody knife and, poised like a dart, threatens to attack the martyr's breast again.

David intensifies the conflict between hero and assassin by adding a different sort of duplicity: he selects a small portion of the woman's *lettre perfide* and renders it in his own handwriting. Perhaps he intended to restore the note's tribute to his hero, to erase the irony and transgression; but the feminine adjective remains highly visible – *malheureuse*, unfortunate. Charlotte Corday now appeals to the viewer through that letter. Both the duplicity and the irony are redoubled. Corday silences Marat and David silences Corday, but the letter calls to its viewers/readers for the last word.

One transcription is not enough: the artist overrides – or underwrites – the unsettling letter with an alternative one. Flush with the surface of the canvas, David's tombstone-like inscription makes a directed letter of the entire still-life:

A MARAT DAVID L'AN DEUX

The upright roman capitals fight for an unchallenged immortality – upfront, direct and immediate. Like the flattering letter, the memorial inscription has a hidden agenda: in this case, to unite Marat and David in a correspondence which defies mortality. Nonetheless, like the letter, too, it cannot escape the stains of its history. When David invokes *L'An Deux* of the Jacobin calendar, he calls attention to the dating of the *ancien régime* used by the Girondiste Corday. The "sanctified" immobility of the still-life and the unshadowed inscription must meet the challenge presented by that tilted letter, the challenge of change and difference. David's neo-classical ideal thus calls up the mortal realities of contemporary conflict. For the letter of the *malheureuse* maintains the upper hand. Along its political slant, *la lettre perfide* introduces a context which the art historian, concerned with classical and Christian iconography, virtually ignores: how the letter represented certain imaginary relationships, or "fictions" in the revolutionary period, which were public, political and powerful.

In *Marat Assassiné*, the art historian easily spots the allusions to classical and Christian models: the Ecce Homo of classical sculpture and the Christ-figure from baroque depositions and *pietàs* are Marat's forefathers.[6] Across the intersection of classical and Christian traditions however, David adds a third dimension: the popular dimension of sentimental appeal. We see this appeal on the right side of the canvas – in the woman's letter, the journalist's banknotes for a widow and her children, and the tombstone inscription.[7] We should recognize that these stock items of the age of sentimentality have become politically charged in the painting.

In one sense, I am asking you to read the epistolary fiction creeping out from behind the image of *Marat Assassiné*. We normally associate the letter tradition of the eighteenth century with sentimental heroines, seductive villains and long, tortuous romances. David himself read and admired Richardson's *Clarissa* and Rousseau's *Julie*.[8] Moreover, he would have been familiar with an epistolary tradition in painting, where letters indicated interior spaces and female vulnerability, especially sexual vulnerability (see figs 2 and 3).[9] In the face of such a tradition, I am asking that you read in this piece of revolutionary propaganda, the popular epistle made explicitly political. Charlotte Corday's letter offers more than a figure of the melodramatic: it shows that the melodramatic covers over and yet gives shape to the contemporary realities of class conflict, sexual violence, social upheaval and civil war. Despite the victim's composure in this portrait, France is in turmoil. The familiar letter of sentimental fiction has been unhinged, just as formal matters in France – customs, institutions, definitions – have been jolted out of alignment.

In its appeal to a heterogeneous audience, *Marat Assassiné* replaces the heroine of sentimental fiction with a political hero. Whereas the letter of the sentimental novel could invade the domestic and sexual privacy of its heroine, the letter of this painting brings the viewer into the private bathroom of the hero. In both cases, the letter serves as a letter of introduction: it gains us entry. Here, however, the woman deceives and the man dies, in a reversal of familiar convention. Note how Marat, with his exposed, vulnerable body, is feminized in his status as victim. His bath becomes a bleached version of Clarissa's coffin, his own public sepulchre. And like Rousseau's Julie, Marat

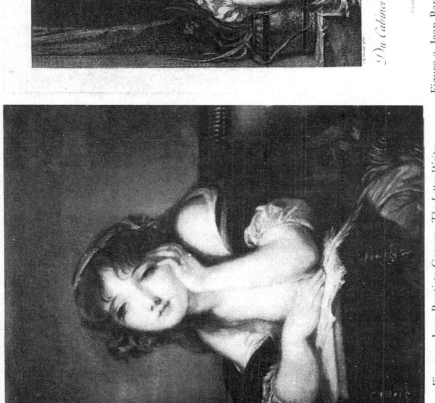

Figure 2 Jean-Baptiste Greuze, *The Letter Writer.*

Figure 3 Jean-Baptiste Greuze, *The Kiss,* or, *Une Jeune Fille qui envoie un baiser par la fenêtre, appuyé sur des fleurs, qu'elle brise.* Engraving by Augustin de St Aubin.

finds martyrdom in a watery grave, surrendering life for "the good of the public."[10] Entering along the lines of Charlotte Corday's overtly conventional, but ultimately contentious letter, then, is the reality of the contemporary, popular imagination. And the contemporary slant of the letter introduces, across the two-dimensional plane of the classical/Christian icon, ideological and political conflict.

Ronald Paulson characterizes this third dimension of revolutionary art as evidence of an emerging subculture, "graffiti on the borders of the official."[11] The woman's letter and the sentimental appeal do not rest easily beneath the formal regularity of salon-sanctioned or party-sanctioned art. They introduce not only popular culture, but the very voice of the masses who would view the portrait – the same disruptive mobs which could rise up to overthrow their own heroes. In a very particular sense, the letter carries the voice of a people capable of rebellion and murder, but held at arm's length from the sanctified individual. Few contemporary viewers of the *Marat* would have failed to find parallels between this assassination and the regicide performed only three months earlier.[12]

The letter, unsigned, speaks not only for Charlotte Corday, the fanatic bourgeoise Girondiste who murdered the republic's benefactor; it also speaks for the crowd of anonymous "unfortunates" who called on Marat's aid, and who called, more vociferously, for the bloody execution of so many public officials. This very public dimension, introduced into Marat's private bath, topples the authority of the heroic image. Anita Brookner writes that:

To appreciate its incredible power, one would not need to see the Marat in a museum... as an icon, an Ecce Homo, a Pietà or Deposition, but hanging in some kind of public tribunal, behind the speaker of the day, to impress upon him and his audience the extreme precariousness of his calling.[13]

Brookner's comment suggests that the painting does not canonize Marat at all, but rather calls into question the relationship of the hero and the crowd, a relationship I see figured in the tension between the head and the letter. What makes the painting radical is not its nominal hero, the dying Marat, but rather the idea that no single hero can respond to the demands of the public – or the open letter. Transcendence will never satisfy historical reality. The official representation, even if dictated by the most radical of revolutionary committees, will always be interrupted by unofficial voices, the voices of the "other."

We see, for example, how the artist seeks to have the final word himself: ultimately the painting presents itself as a gift from the artist to the hero, from one man to another, in a moment which creates its own history: "A MARAT, DAVID – L'AN DEUX." The roman capitals want to remain as aloof from the mob as the figure they salute.[14] But the competing letter from the *malheureuse* interferes in this auto-referential myth-making.

Behind the art of David's *Marat* stands "something other" which is volatile and public, but also private and female. When the artist seeks to smooth over the violent bloodbaths caused by the unholy mobs, he replaces them with the crime of a single woman. He then moves to recast the feminine intrusion by rewriting Charlotte Corday's letter in his own hand. When the journalist Marat sends money to a grieving war widow (the banknotes pictured on the wooden writing-stand), he attempts a similar silencing: both these gestures aim to make violence intimate and personal, even as they point to public violence – assassination and war. The revised *pietà* that David creates, with Marat as the new martyr for humanity, implies a crucifixion, a public execution; but it gains its impact from the moment between mother and child (see fig. 4). Then, with the violence properly under sentimental wraps, the woman is erased: David removes the grieving, eloquent Madonna. We move from a public to a private, "feminized" moment, from which the woman herself has been removed. Only in the background of that vast, silent, blank wall can we perceive a crowd of women, marked by violence.[15]

And that is why I have chosen to concentrate on the letter, rather than the hero-artist, in the literature of the period following the French Revolution. David's painting offers a convenient example of how the volatile politics of the moment appropriated the strategies of the sentimental tradition. Politics walked through the private, domestic sphere and, dressed in feminine terms – La Liberté or La Guillotine – unleashed violence. At the same time, however, women writers used the familiar letter for entry to the world of politics: Charlotte Corday was not alone. In the mind of late eighteenth-century Europe, the letter fused the world of epistolary romance, the domestic tragedies of *Clarissa* or *Julie*, with the world of political revolution.

Politically charged letters in England and France appeared in innumerable pamphlets sold to the public under the guise of "An Open Letter to George III," "A Letter to a Noble Lord" or, in the

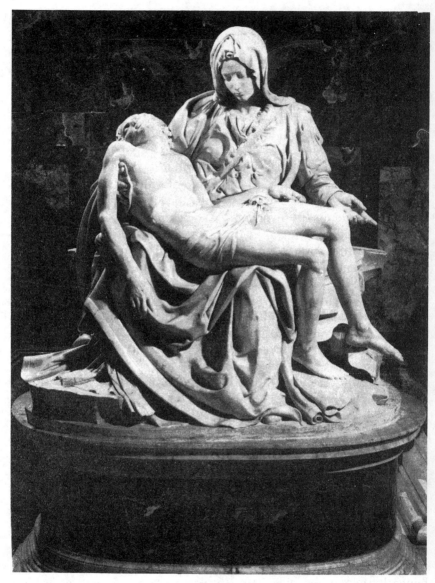

Figure 4 Michaelangelo, *Pietà*.

case of the feminist Olympe de Gouges, a bold "Letter to Citizen Robespierre." It is generally assumed that Manon de Roland penned the letter of protest to Louis XVI which resulted in the downfall of the Girondist ministry. And Helen Maria Williams' *Letters from France*, published serially from 1790 to 1796, provided some of the most widely read pro-revolutionary propaganda in England. Even the debate between Edmund Burke's *Reflections on the Revolution in France* and Thomas Paine's *Rights of Man* was waged primarily in the form of letters sent back and forth between very public individuals. Despite his apology that "a different plan" might have been "more favourable to a commodious division and distribution of his matter," Burke recognized the advantages of an "epistolary fiction" for circulating his less-than-private *Reflections*.[16] In the struggle over symbols, both pro- and counter-revolutionary groups recognized the value of the letter: the French monarchy's *lettre de cachet*, the hidden letter of absolute law, became a symbol of tyranny, in contrast to the "open letter," symbol of representative government and evidence of a tolerant, equitable system of justice – and of communication.

The letter had, in fact, become a phenomenally useful political tool, available to anyone with a pen. Politics provided the fuel for the incendiary letters peasants sent to oppressive landlords and magistrates, a terrorist tactic common during this period which became more pronounced in years of extreme class tension. Political activity was the cause and effect of the letters of the London Correspondence Society, founded in 1792 as the first working-man's political organization in England, and outlawed by 1794 as a treasonous conspiracy. When letters carry the seeds of organized rebellion or "conspiracy," we discover *les liaisons dangereuses* inside and outside the realm of sentimental romance.

A crucial change occurs at this time: the political force always latent in, or extracted from the letter of fiction, takes over the public image of the letter. When the disturbing power of the letter comes to the fore, as it does in *Marat Assassiné*, it not only challenges the formal order of "official art," but, more radically, suggests turbulence beneath the surface. The letter in Romanticism hints at a correspondence between public and private experience, and that correspondence continually revises – and disrupts – fixed images or narratives. What the individual writes, the masses read; experience is translated from the private to the public domain, and back again. The woman and the mob are co-respondents in the realm of social upheaval; both are figures for the suppressed voice of the other which challenges the official word. As the letter of *Marat Assassiné* indicates, the figure of the letter subverts the deferential language which would substantiate the heroic individual and his transcendental status; it moves outside of static representation in its appeal to history, mortality and the public. The disorienting tilt of the letter communicates to its audience a message from the oppressed, the *malheureuses*: a message of social inequities, of bloody uprisings, fanaticism, violence. It challenges, and stands above the exchange of immortality between public artists and public officials. It interrupts canonization.

This book attempts first to revise the familiar fiction of the letter in literature and, second, to demonstrate how the sentimental fiction of letters disguises, in part, a revolutionary politics. This fiction dresses the letter in feminine robes and scrutinizes the private spaces, the physical and emotional vulnerability, that such robes shape and define. We accept too readily the notion that the letter allows us a window into the intimate, and usually feminine, self. Feminists have celebrated the letter as a form of expression which validates female experience, a form which allows unregulated fluctuations of thought and feeling at the same time that it documents the minutiae of domestic life. Conversely, feminist scholars have read the letters of epistolary fiction as emblems of a social trap, which either locks the woman into marriage (as in *Pamela*) or betrays her into death (as in *Clarissa* or *Julie*). Recent studies of epistolary writing by feminists lament that "the one genre with which women have been persistently connected has specialized in narrowing the range of possible inflections for feminine expression."[17] Patricia Meyer Spacks, while discussing the power strategies which fuel the letters of Jane Austen's *Lady Susan*, nevertheless concludes that "however angry or despairing" epistolary fictions may be, they still "reinforced the status quo by assuming it."[18]

But other fictions of the letter are and have been available. Few scholars have studied letters as tools for political agitation or propaganda in a particular historical moment defined by revolution, reaction and Romanticism. Few ask why *Marat Assassiné*, for example, places the letter from his female assassin in the hand of the Revolution's martyr.[19] And few have contemplated the connection between Romanticism's appeal to correspondence – from Edmund Burke's *Reflections on the Revolution in France*, which originated "in a correspondence between the Author and a very young gentleman in Paris," to the "correspondent breeze" of William Wordsworth's *Prelude*, to the letters from "friends" which interrupt Samuel Taylor Coleridge's *Biographia Literaria* – and the epistolary genre, which has been "persistently connected" to the feminine. I propose another look at the letter, one which takes into account its shifting politics within Romanticism, and the ideological drapery which has obscured those politics and that history with the fiction of the sentimental woman and her love story.

CHAPTER I

History and the fiction of letters

In the late eighteenth century, under the pressure of revolutionary activity and political upheaval, the practice of correspondence produced subversive and contradictory effects. Conventional literary history tells us that the genre of the familiar letter was able to reduce experience to discrete, contained units. It tells us, moreover, that the epistolary tradition in fiction drew upon the familiar letter in order to define – if not actually establish – the individual's identifiable and proper place in society. The letter typically registered private, interiorized moments – domestic details, closed circles of family and friends, the inner workings of the mind.[1] In the Romantic period, however, we "discover" that the epistolary novel no longer seemed viable, and these typically feminine spaces appeared suddenly to dissolve. The world represented by such a feminized letter evidently seemed outmoded in the major literature of the Romantic period. Yet this limited notion of the genre does not account for many types of letter that remained quite familiar to Romantic writers and readers.

Throughout the eighteenth century, the letter's ability to define and confine personal experience had already been subject to a centripetal force which carried the private into the public realm, offering the individual's most intimate self for mass consumption. Epistolary fiction invaded, then shattered, the closed areas of home, family and personal identity. This literary form, which developed alongside the eighteenth century's growing faith in the value of personal – and especially feminine – experience, grew in time to betray the very individualism it promoted. By the time the epistolary novel achieved its apotheosis at the end of the century, it had revealed that individualism to be a deathtrap, a box-like identity into which society forced women and men. Pamela's marriage, Julie's beatification and Werther's suicide all effectively silenced the individual's voice. Meanwhile, other fictions of the letter as a "feminine" genre emerged to contest the belief that a letter expressed only private, individual desires. At the same time that the fiction of private correspondence was being dismantled in these novels, the epistolary form was acquiring a public voice: the stories of these fictional individuals and others were the topics of public debate; epistolary characters entered the discourse of the age and became the property of cultural history. This transition from private expression to published property pulled the letter out of its fiction of individualism and complicated its "feminine" identity.

The practice of correspondence was fused, to a certain degree, with the practice of literary production; both were seen as feminizing processes. In regard to David Hume, for instance, Jerome Christensen has argued that the mid-eighteenth century saw collaboration and specular imitation between the practices of the Post Office and the publishers' monopoly, or Conger; a connection which "disabl[ed] the hypothetical distinction between correspondence and publication."[2] The publishers used the up-graded postal system to transmit their merchandise and to center the publishing industry in London; the postal system was underwritten by the increased traffic in books. This coordinated system for circulating both private messages and published works "impoverished whatever notion of intention or privacy the man of letters would cling to and protect from...commercial exchanges."[3] To enter the world of letters, then, was to admit "Infirmity," as Hume does in a letter to his publisher, who had circulated material from Hume's private correspondence without Hume's consent.[4] To be published was to participate, Christensen suggests, in a "self-castration" that "brings [the man of letters] into line with a dominant system of reproduction [commercial exchange]," a symbolic order that can be "endlessly repeated" at the expense of the writer's claim to self-representation.[5] In short, Christensen finds Hume imagining the exchange of letters in the eighteenth century – via the post or via the publishing house – as a threat to feminize the man with the pen. "It is with books as with women," writes Hume: both must sell themselves to succeed. "The good fortunes of a book, and that of a man," therefore, "are not the same."[6]

Of course, Christensen himself imagines Hume, the eighteenth-century "man of letters," within the structures available to a postmodern literary critic. Jacques Derrida adopts these same structures in his fiction of circulating letters for the late twentieth century, "Envois": "the letter, the epistle...is not a genre but all genres, literature itself," he writes.[7] For Derrida, the movement of letters (the "Post") is the system which produces and determines privacy: private identity and feminine spaces (*privés*) only reinforce public exchange. Publication needs and reproduces endless fictions of privacy, secrecy, individual desire:

I [the letter-writer] am the *privé* [the private, the deprived one], more than anyone else henceforth. And I can hear you:...so then the *privé* of everything, and of all women, the *privé* of these ladies? No, I was speaking of the desire to pose or post myself in a kind of absolute privatization...The secret without measure: it does not exclude publication, it measures publication against itself.[8]

The letter-writer displays a deliberately elliptical rhetoric here and throughout "Envois": he intimates that we know his references at the same time that he excludes us from that knowledge. Deprived of knowing our own position in this correspondence, we become the "ladies" he abandons in order to speak of his own desire. Within his words of deprivation, of self-castration, Derrida's letter-writer reveals the cry of the transcendental subject: "more than anyone else" in history, "absolutely," "immeasurably," the letter-writer masters his effeminization by feminizing his public.

Both Derrida and Christensen introduce a distinct role for the feminine in the realm of letters, and consequently, a distinct fiction about letters and the feminine. Their version of the feminine shares not a concern with interiority and individual, sincere expression, but rather with the masculine "posing" as feminine in order to be "posted/positioned" within a fixed system of public circulation and exchange. For them, a correspondence based on symbolic castration links the practice of letter-writing with the world of letters/literature; the figure of the feminine makes possible that correspondence. The feminine, like the letter itself, serves them as a vehicle or form without specific content.[9]

Yet what of the woman of letters, whose privacy was already repeatedly violated in epistolary fiction in the eighteenth century, whose position in the network of publication and exchange was (and remains) easily appropriated by male writers? Her self-castration would appear unimaginable (or redundant) in this system. Could she so neatly connect the practice of letter-writing with the production of literature? What were the potential effects of exhibiting her "infirmity" in letters? Like Derrida, could she twist deprivation into privilege?

Derrida's epistolary work and Christensen's treatment of Hume as a "man of letters" rely on an identification between literature and letters which does not acknowledge the woman who writes letters. This identification also slides over the complicated history of the letter between the eighteenth and the twentieth centuries, a period during which the structure and practice of personal correspondence were repeatedly rewritten through political and social change. As the "treacherous" letter of *Marat Assassiné* demonstrates, the correspondence between the "unfortunate" woman's letter and the unpredictable reading public writes an alternative fiction of the letter's femininity, one that endangers fixed symbolic economies. Thus the woman writing letters in the period of revolution and reform has the potential to upset any simple or necessary correspondence between one closed economy (the monopoly of the Post Office or the publishing industry) and another (individual privacy or self-representation).

Rather than determine any single fiction of the letter's femininity, we should trace the historically specific tensions between publication and correspondence, between the Post Office and letter-writing, and between the epistolary novel and other representations of the letter. And we should ask how the woman writing letters situates herself within the field of connections between gender and genre. In other words, we need to analyze what Stuart Hall calls the "double articulations" of structure (publication/Post Office, genre/gender) and practice in order to understand how these articulations result in various and unexpected fictions about women and letters.[10] Nor can we ignore the political effects of these fictions, and their disappearance and recurrences in time. Christensen argues that the publishers' monopoly and the Post Office did jointly present a certain fiction of correspondence in the eighteenth century. Yet these economies of communication were neither hermetically sealed nor permanently compatible. By 1774, the courts and Parliament withdrew from the Conger its singular license to copy and regulate publications throughout the nation.[11] Nor could the government sustain mastery over the circulation of intelligence. The increasing number of readers and writers, as well as the variety of means of exchange, could not be regulated except by extreme measures which themselves were likely to produce new methods for disseminating intelligence.[12] Indeed, the growth of Post Office services between the eighteenth and nineteenth centuries raised "as a central issue the problem of the state operating within the [laissez-faire] market-place."[13] The circulation of letters was both an economic and political concern: where would the power of communication be located?

There were various ways of representing the relationship between contemporary politics and the exchange of letters. The introduction of the mail coach by Robert Palmer in 1784, for instance, exacerbated the problem of regulating correspondence by accelerating and proliferating the channels of exchange.[14] The mail coach invited new representations of the post, which now transported both letters and bodies; the sense of giddiness and danger offered to coach passengers quickly infected the public image of the Royal Mail. Lord Campbell, Chief Justice, recalls in 1798 the expectations surrounding his first ride by mail coach:

This speed [8 to 9 miles per hour] was thought to be highly dangerous to the head, independently of the perils of an overturn, and stories were told of men and women who, having reached London with such celerity died suddenly of an affection of the brain. My family and friends were seriously alarmed for me, and advised me at all events to wait a day... but I boldly took my place.[15]

The stories Lord Campbell relates about the mail coach's effect on the head and brain, not to mention its threat to the body, both echo and recast the conventional eighteenth-century response to much epistolary fiction. Consider the dislocating result of letter-reading upon one famous correspondent, Richardson's Clarissa: "My name is – I don't know what my name is!.... But I shall never be what I was. My head is gone. I have wept away all my brain."[16] With the underlying sense of epistemological confusion, with the too-rapid communication of intelligence/emotions/bodies, a technical inno-vation for the transport of letters (the mail coach) resonates with an earlier practice (epistolary fiction) and creates a new structure for understanding correspondence.

But I do not want to limit Campbell's story to these two registers alone. In the House of Commons, members of Parliament expressed outrage at Palmer's "impracticable and dangerous" innovations, decrying the "utter unsuitableness" of the mail coach as an emblem of the Royal Mail. The mail coach's speed and rapid schedule "would throw the whole correspondence throughout England, through London as well as the bye and cross roads, into the utmost confusion."[17] It was the duty of government to check and correct this confusion. Between 1784 and 1798, Palmer's mail coaches (originally a private enterprise) were brought under the supervision of the Postmaster-General. Palmer was made Surveyor and Comptroller-General of the Mails, independent of the Postmaster-General. In 1792, however, Palmer was dismissed and the mail coach system was consolidated with the other services of the Post Office; most of his proposals were ignored for another thirty years.[18] Though Chief Justice Campbell described a hair-raising event from the previous decade, he could, writing in 1798, now "boldly" call upon the contemporary political situation which asserted the stability, both institutional and rotary, of the English Mail. The confidence of the Chief Justice rides alongside the stories of danger and the echo of Clarissa's despair.

I invoke Campbell's anecdote about the mail coach to emphasize the variety of fictions which carry letters to us, fictions which rely on the intersection of specific historical practices. We will see the mail coach reappear later in Thomas De Quincey's "The English Mail Coach" (1849), in a significantly altered fiction. For now, however, I ask Campbell's story to exemplify my own use of Romantic correspondence, a discourse condensing specific political and social practices into a variety of fictions primarily about women and letters.

The fiction of correspondence suggested by the intersection of the topsy-turvy mail coach with the epistolary novel – two vehicles for letters – does not establish a neat system of regulated connections. The mechanism of movement does not remain prescribed and clearly addressed, without possibility for error. Within such a fiction of correspondence and communication (call it the ideal Post Office), writers and readers would be mapped into fixed and predictable locations. Nor does Campbell's mail coach convey an image of the fatal or "dead letter," lost between unknown origins and destinations, its directions illegible, its contents immaterial. Such an image insists that, in the absence of total certainty, necessarily no communication can be realized between two individuals, two positions or two distinct structures. Rather, the mail coach and the epistolary novel, brought together, allow us to imagine correspondence as both content and vehicle, neither entirely under control but both capable of reaching some, perhaps uncharted, destination.

This study will investigate a variety of fictions of the letter in British literature, during a period when the letter – public and private – became the focus of ideological and political struggle.[19] The ideological implications of the letter's form and conventions became apparent not only in the last great works of epistolary fiction, but also in journal correspondence, travel narratives and deliberately political writings – the partisan newsletters and the propagandist pamphlets which circulated in the last decades of the eighteenth century. Letters in literature, together with the everyday letters of British society, became explicitly political in this period in ways that produced new fictions of the "feminine" letter.

In my readings of various articulations of women with letters, I have ventured into the world of contemporary theory as into an epistolary novel or an ongoing correspondence, full of different, overlapping and sometimes contentious voices, terms and strategies. The following chapters adopt different critical discourses which, I believe, permit me to locate alternative, even contradictory, fictions of correspondence. For a secondary component of this study is concerned with the letter as a figure in the critical and literary imagination. Once constructed as different and distant from our own, the fictions of correspondence operating in an historical period (roughly, the England of the 1790 to 1840s) may, in fact, illuminate the contours of our conceptions of communication, especially as they find form in critical practice.

When we look at the language of contemporary literary criticism, we see that letters occupy a privileged position within the struggles of poststructuralist and feminist theory. Feminists offer epistolary discourse as a model for "radically anti-mimetic and profoundly political" expression. Epistolarity, according to Linda Kauffman, "subverts ... conventional dichotomies and explores ... transgressions and transformations."[20] More ambiguously, the letter "writes the female voice."[21] Jacques Lacan's seminar on "The Purloined Letter," with the reactions it provoked, and Jacques Derrida's *The Post Card* are other, more obvious manifestations of the letter's role in theoretical struggles.[22] Reflecting, therefore, on postmodernism, postrepresentation and feminist criticism, Linda Kauffman announces the ubiquity of the letter: "'The post-age' ... is upon us."[23]

While insisting upon a tension between letters in history and literary criticism, I have borrowed from these theorists. Yet I have also tried to resituate them within a critique of postmodernist theory, which Stuart Hall characterizes as a debate written in terms of correspondence. We need not, he suggests, think that meaning is determined by "the idea of a necessary correspondence between one level of a social formation and another." Nor must we follow the allegorical "slide" which produces "necessarily no correspondence," the resigned belief that "nothing really connects with anything else." Rather, we may admit that there is "no necessary correspondence" between these levels, without having to surrender correspondence altogether. There is no need to believe that, "under all circum-stances…[different discursive or social formations] can never be articulated together in any way [n]or produce a social force capable for a time of self-conscious 'unity-in-action'."[24] The fictions I examine do articulate connections between gender, genre and Romanticism in new ways, producing a social force which has yet to be measured. They help us recognize the possibility of "an articulation in terms of effects which does not necessarily correspond to [the] origins" of a theoretical position.[25] Our own letters, as well as the letters of Romanticism, may discover correspondents they never originally imagined.

PRIVATE LETTERS

Critical discourse has written for us a fiction of letters, a fiction which gives the letter the figure of the woman. Traditionally, the letter has not been read as having a public voice. Its literary history has been associated with a "feminocentric age" – the eighteenth century – and "a collective obsessing about an idea called 'woman'."[26] In the nineteenth century, when the more dynamic historical novel arrived with its "great bow-wow thing," as Walter Scott put it, the letter supposedly could not keep pace in a world concerned with political agitation, war and reform.[27]

An emphasis on the "private moment" expressed in letters tends to erase the outside world and ignore the structures of time and distance which, in fact, dictate the letter's form. Each letter becomes a private encounter with the writer, "where the life of the imagination [is] more important than lived experience."[28] A structuralist analysis of epistolary conventions in the eighteenth-century novel, for example, finds in the letter

a vortex that absorbs writers and readers into the narrative center…[where] the action of the novel is authenticated by (pseudo-)eradication of spatiotemporal distance between the narrated action and the writer, between the writer and the addressee, and ultimately between these two and the reader of the novel.[29]

In the language of deconstruction, the letter fiction is similarly private, yet voracious: "the letter contains both the word and the world; it substitutes the word for the world, substitutes writing for living."[30] Such language evokes a mysteriously intimate world, a world before the world, associated with the female body. It also echoes Lovelace's disturbing metaphor (in *Clarissa*) which finds the "events" of the epistolary plot "hidden in the Womb of Fate."[31] Letters, then, become the universal mother of fictions, as Jacques Derrida explains: "The letter, the epistle, which is not a genre but all genres, literature itself."[32] Read as tempting boxes of private experience, detached from "the world," letters become the repository for "private emotions," a confessional form whose "privacy, like virginity, invites violation."[33]

What produced this fiction which puts the letter at the mercy of a violent, intrusive and specifically male world? What made epistolary discourse itself into a conventional epistolary heroine, and fought to preserve a worldly innocence which was, itself, a fiction? No doubt, as for any fiction, we cannot locate an origin. We can, however, find voices which reproduce this fiction in critical discourse. We read, for example, a recent claim that the epistolary genre "cannot say on what authority it rests…whether or not the signatures to its individual letters are 'proper.' As a (feminized) genre, epistolary fiction can make no claim to its own purity, although that is one claim it insists must hold for its heroine."[34] In this fiction, the genre defines itself with the question of female chastity. Unsure of its propriety, insisting upon purity when its own has been sacrificed, the letter-novel is another Clarissa or Julie. Such an approach to the genre places irreconcilable demands upon the letter-novel, as upon the woman.

Jean-Jacques Rousseau has made one version of the letter–woman correlation legible to the reading public; with it, he attempts to keep women, letters and public in their "proper" place. Just as St. Preux instructs Julie via letters and creates Rousseau's ideal woman, so does Rousseau instruct readers in the prefaces to *Julie, ou la Nouvelle Héloïse*. In the correspondence between lovers, Rousseau informs the reader, a separate world is born:

finding nowhere a trace of what they feel, [the lovers] fold in upon themselves; they detach themselves from the rest of the universe, and, creating between themselves a little world different from ours, they create there a truly new spectacle.[35]

This picture of epistolary innocence, uncorrupted by contact with "our" fallen world, is central to Rousseau's political philosophy and to the social vision he creates in this "sentimental" novel. We should be extremely wary of Rousseau's manipulations in these prefaces: they instruct the reader regarding love, but hide the propaganda of the political philosopher. The fact that he presents this isolated "spectacle" to the public already questions the illusion of its self-contained purity.[36]

Although the limiting fiction of Rousseau's 'model" woman has long been recognized, we continue to accept Rousseau's "model" for reading letters. The prefaces explain the "true nature" of this *recueil de lettres*, insisting it is no fiction. At the same time, Rousseau naturalizes a manner of reading which, in fact, severely restricts the reader's perception of epistolary discourse. We have learned to repeat quietly Rousseau's formula that the letter is female, and therefore "not made to circulate in society [*le monde*]."[37] His Julie only accepts readers/lovers who leave *le monde* behind; who repudiate society, politics and philosophy; who withheld themselves "from business, big cities, and crowded social gatherings."[38] Rousseau wants his reader to experience these letters as a private affair, in the same manner that he, Rousseau, experienced the women in his life. "They are most useful," he advises," when one lives alone... one varies them less and meditates upon them more... their effect is less mitigated by outside influences." The impassioned letter will be more welcome when she/it is "loose, diffuse, all stretched out, in disarray, always repeating [her/]itself."[39] A quick glance at Rousseau's *Confessions* reminds us that the author advocated a similar strategy for "reading," and loving, women.[40]

We have adopted this fiction which insists that the letter be read as a feminine space, and that the feminine be detached from *le monde* of business and cities, untainted by discussions of politics and philosophy. The world of women and the world of letters form a pastoral paradise for Rousseau: they are not part of "our" fallen world. Yet, although the letters of *Julie*, like Julie herself, may be presented as objects of fantasy, they are nevertheless the instruments of a social order which Rousseau – and the critical tradition –

constructs.[41] In fact, in the face of Rousseau's propaganda, we can assert that the letter in eighteenth-century society was always already "fallen" into the realm of corruption. By the end of the century, the *petit monde* of the lovers could barely disguise the dangerous alliances letters had forged in the "real" world.

My language implies that literary criticism has written a plot for epistolary discourse, wherein the letter lives out the tragic destiny of an epistolary heroine: the innocent letter ventures out into the world, where she falls victim to manipulation, violation and finally, to literal or metaphorical death.[42] As a narrative technique, the epistolary form did attract great attention and many notable admirers in eighteenth-century Europe. The epistolary novel was the belle of the ball, her dance card signed by the literary titans of the age: Richardson in England, Goethe in Germany, Rousseau, Diderot and Laclos in France. Nor did she limit herself only to gentlemen: next to the closely related memoir-novel, she became the most popular and widely practiced fictional form in western Europe.[43]

But even without the accoutrements of the novel, the letter was attractive, inviting the talents of most of the literate population. On the one hand, popular letter manuals were "adapted to the tastes [and concerns] of all social levels"; on the other hand, the practice of serial publication made epistolary works affordable for all but the lowest levels of society.[44] At the same time, such manuals developed skills for a developing new medium: the expanding postal system. One bookseller advertised in 1740 a "Miscellanie" entitled "*Post-Office Intelligence: or Universal Gallantry*...a collection of love-letters, written by persons in all stations, from most parts of the kingdom."[45] Titles such as the *Universal Letter-Writer* and the *Compleat Letter-Writer* recur frequently, broadcasting the letter's claim to social comprehensiveness. The dedication of one popular letter guide marvels at the writer's range of material, covering "all Degrees" of society:

> The Scholar may learn curiously t'Indite;
> The Tradesman to his Correspondent Write,
> And to the plain Country-man his Sense Recite.
> To all Degrees you have your Style Addresst;
> As if the Words of all you had Exprest,
> As they themselves had form'd them in their Breast.[46]

Works as diverse as *The Young Secretary's Guide* (to letter-writing) and *The Letters of George I* indicate that the class distinction bridged by the fictional Pamela and Mr. B was minor compared to some of the social bridges over which the familiar letter travelled.

Fiction writers did their best to promote the wide-ranging potential of correspondence. The *History of the Matrimonial Adventures of a Banker's Clerk* (1761), for example, reveals the social mobility of the man and woman who write letters. The clerk corresponds with "a Pretended Lady Anne Frances Caroline Boothby, otherwise Sister to the Duke of Beaufort, otherwise Miss Trevor, otherwise Miss Scudamore, otherwise Mrs. Errington."[47] In 1784, the year *Les Liaisons dangereuses* appeared in English (as *Dangerous Alliances*), one could read not only the intrigues of French aristocrats, but also the letters of *The Bastard* and *The Virtuous Villagers*, as well as *Original Love Letters Between a Lady of Quality and a Person of Inferior Station*. Epistolary transgression violated more than simple social and economic boundaries. Letters between dead and living celebrities remained popular throughout the century.[48] Some, such as the 1786 series of letters between "Lucifer" and "The Right Honourable Lord President of the Stygian Council at Pandemonium," carried transgression and mobility to new extremes.[49]

In fact, as we survey the activity of the published letter in eighteenth-century society, we notice that it did seem a bit naive or "familiar" in its travels, willing to believe its own fiction of surmounting social and formal barriers. "Many a young woman has caught from such works as *Clarissa* or *Cecilia* ideas of delicacy and refinement which were not, perhaps, to be gained in any society she could have access to."[50] Thus one fiction about epistolary fiction saw young women moving up the social ladder into the confines of the high and mighty, as Anna Letitia Barbauld suggests; but another imagined them descending to the netherworld of Lovelace's whores, or of Evelina's vulgar cousins. Even though individual collections of letters and most letter-novels managed to restrict correspondence to a defined social group, the conflicting fictions overlapped in the public imagination. The letter had become promiscuous in the writing of the day, ranging through all levels of society, and lending itself to anyone with a pen.

Even the form of the familiar letter seemed to loosen as the century progressed, acquiring a "negligent charm" attractive to an "enthusiastic public, as distinguished from a choice audience of scholars."[51] The English public especially broke from the classical models of the ancients and the elegant conventions of the French, and moved toward "an increasing negligence of form, extremely loose ...colloquially expressed, and thoroughly British."[52] The primary regulating mechanism for personal correspondence – the guidebooks, *Familiar Letter-Writers* and *Young Men's Secretaries*, which developed in the course of the eighteenth century – sought to "socialize" what was a potentially volatile form of expression. When common consent granted the letter the power to convey "passion" in language, it also accused the letter of a lack of intrinsic control. Letters were imagined as fluid, spontaneous and unregulated. Letter-writing, more than most forms of writing, might encourage the writer to abandon all sense of propriety. In the words of a 1780 rhetoric book, the letter allowed its writer "to be at his ease and give vent occasionally to the overflowings of his heart."[53] At the same time, the rhetorician felt obliged to rein in the antisocial impulses of any correspondent:

The liberty, besides, of writing letters with too careless a hand, is apt to betray persons into imprudence in what they write. The first requisite, both in conversation and in correspondence, is to attend to the proper decorums which our own character and that of others demand ... when we take the pen into our hand, we must remember, that "Litera Scripta Manent" ("letters, once written, remain fixed").[54]

Even as popular letter-writing promoted a flowing, "natural" style, the law of epistolary discourse aspired to be writ in stone.

The letter played a feminine role, for only women "possessed the easie Negligence of stile which is particularly required in letters," along with the gift of "Expression more from the Heart than from the Head."[55] We will see, however, that once "looseness" and "negligence" were known to lend themselves to politics, letters could not easily resume a respectable place in the literary market. They were tainted goods.

FAMILIAR LETTERS

"Looseness," not surprisingly, made the familiar letter the most significant instrument for political propaganda during the years of revolution. Earlier in the century we find Alexander Pope's tightly composed "Epistle to Dr. Arbuthnot" (1735), in which the letter device, borrowed from Horace and Seneca, locks the poet and his friend in an intimacy which rescues them from a threatening mob. Pope's epistle begins:

Shut, shut the door, good John! fatigu'd I said
Tye up the knocker, say I'm sick, I'm dead,
The Dog-star rages! nay, 'tis past a doubt,
All Bedlam, or Parnassus, is let out.[56]

At the other end of the century, however, a loosely defined and broadly discursive letter "to a young friend" barely contains Edmund Burke's fiery *Reflections on the Revolution in France* (1790) or Thomas Paine's uninvited response, the rabble-rousing *Rights of Man* (1792). With the twists and turns of political rhetoric, the letter was rerouted via the "threatening mobs" and popular political societies of the 1790s. Whereas, in Pope's day, the epistle belonged to a classical tradition of male scholars – Cicero, Pliny, Horace and Seneca – in the latter part of the century the letter rested in less respectable hands. The classical *epistolae ad familiares* collided with a new determination of friendship and familiarity. The collision yielded a new sense of whom and what correspondence could represent.

When Edmund Burke adopted the guise of the familiar letter for his *Reflections on the Revolution in France,* he seemed unaware of the compromises then emerging in the genre. These "Reflections," he writes in a foreword, "had their origin in a correspondence between the Author and a very young gentleman at Paris."[57] Burke's epistolary opening apologizes for personal sentiment and private opinion:

I will not give you reason to imagine, that I think my sentiments of such value as to wish myself to be solicited about them. They are of too little consequence to be very anxiously either communicated or withheld. In the first letter...I wrote neither for nor from any description of men; nor shall I in this. My errors, if any, are my own. My reputation alone is to answer for them.[58]

Here Burke coyly suspends his letter between public and private, between solicited exposure and diffident restraint. Writing under the pretense of a letter "intended to be sent" to a young friend in Paris, Burke can present himself as the experienced mentor instructing a wayward student. Of course, the friendly letter "intended to be sent" has been deflected into publication and public debate: Burke now speaks for England, his correspondent is now cast as the "very young" spirit of France. "You are young; you cannot guide, but must follow the fortune of your country."[59] Burke can thus insinuate that British history should provide the corrective model to the present waywardness in France (and England). The "friendly letter" writes itself as political allegory.

Burke's use of this conservative, didactic epistolary mode suggests a fiction, like Pope's "Epistle to Dr. Arbuthnot," based on the classical virtues of "consistency" and "equipoise," on stable interpretive structures and on a smooth transition between generations.[60] "Hereafter," he writes, "[my sentiments] may be of some use to you, in some future form which your commonwealth may take."[61] Simultaneously, however, Burke invokes the rhetoric of erratic individualism: "My errors, if any, are my own." Breaking through the predictable structures of the didactic epistle come the rhythms of excess, the emotional immediacy, and the unregulated diction allowed to sentimental fiction. The letter-writer's apology only draws attention to this rhetorical conflict:

> The Author...found that what he had undertaken not only *far exceeded the measure* of a letter, but that its importance required a more detailed consideration... However, having *thrown down* his first thoughts in the form of a letter, and indeed when he sat down to write, *having intended it for a private letter*, he found it difficult to change the form of address, when his *sentiments had grown into a greater extent*, and had received another direction. A different plan, he is sensible, might be more favourable to a commodious division and distribution of his matter.[62] (my emphasis)

Not just the Revolution but the *Reflections* themselves grow beyond all reasonable limits and intentions. Despite Burke's assumptions, the letter can obviously accommodate (and perhaps even promote) the excess of his sentiments. As Burke's critics were quick to point out, the devices of sentimental romance underwrite the lesson in political science. These simultaneously undermine the "rational" and "natural" fiction, born of "long observation and much impartiality," that Burke hopes to convey.[63]

Still other fictions of the "friendly letter" overdetermine Burke's rhetorical stance. On the one hand, Burke's open letter invited a rash of responding letters, thereby fueling the very discussion Burke wished to foreclose. On the other hand, in writing his political reflections in the form of a letter to a friend in France, Burke mimicked the practice of those organizations he singled out for attack – the London Revolution Society and the Society for Constitutional Information. The Revolution Society in particular had earned Burke's scorn for initiating an exchange of letters with the French

National Assembly, and more especially, for presenting these letters in a "corporate capacity" as a "public" and even "transcendent" entity. Not the content of the correspondence, but the fact that it gave the (hitherto obscure) Revolution Society political prominence irked Burke. "I should think it, at least improper and irregular, for me to open a formal public correspondence with the actual government of a foreign nation, without the express authority of the government under which I live." Insisting upon the personal nature of letters, Burke cannot conceive of the form as a vehicle for collaborative or "unauthorized general" expression.[64]

But that determination was literally out of Burke's hands. Though he pretends to write "in my individual and private capacity," Burke, too, speaks as a transcendental subject, addressing not one, but many nations in his *Reflections*. His mind, moreover, becomes the mind of Europe:

> I wish to communicate more largely, what was at first intended for your private satisfaction... Indulging myself in the freedom of epistolary intercourse, I beg leave to throw out my thoughts, and express my feelings, just as they arise in my mind, with very little attention to formal method... It looks to me as if I were in a great crisis, not of the affairs of France alone, but of all Europe, perhaps of more than Europe. In viewing this monstrous tragi-comic scene, the most opposite passions necessarily succeed, and sometimes mix with each other in the mind.[65]

To some degree, Burke struggles to maintain a fiction of the individual, private letter at the same time that he employs the letter in political psycho-drama. To understand the contortions exacted by such a maneuver, we should understand the political valence of the "friendly letter" in the early 1790s, especially as "friendship" and "correspondence" became the characteristic features of "unauthorized general" societies, associations and committees committed to parliamentary reform. In England, the "friendly societies" placed their own stamp on the familiar epistle.

With the rise to prominence of reform societies such as the Revolution Society and the Society for Constitutional Information, as well as the London Corresponding Society, manly "friendship" actually threatened the status quo as Burke imagined it. The "Friends of Liberty" became an umbrella term for the more than one hundred radical societies established in England between 1790 and 1797.[66] The "friends" embraced groups as wide-ranging as the Whig Association of the Friends of the People, the Borough Society of

the Friends of the People, the Constitutional Whigs Independent and
Friends of the People, the Stockport Friends of Universal Peace and
the Rights of Man, the Friends of Religious and Civil Liberty, the
Society of the Friends of Liberty, and the Committee of Friends of
Parliamentary Reform in Middlesex. Reformists addressed pam-
phlets to "Friends of Justice and Humanity"; "Friends of Reform";
"Friends of Freedom"; and "To Persons of Small Incomes and
Members of Friendly Societies." Toasts at club banquets hailed those
"friendly to the cause" of parliamentary reform, while popular
reformers, such as Horne Tooke, were labelled "true Friends of the
People." In the very speech which prompted Burke's *Reflections*, Dr.
Richard Price addressed himself to "all you friends of liberty and
writers in its defence!"[67]

Friendship, as Price suggests, was a literary activity, and most
especially, an act of correspondence. The "friendly societies" formed
a network throughout England, Scotland, Ireland and Wales
engaged in and devoted to the exchange of political discussion
through the mail. The earliest of these groups, the London
Revolution Society, set the precedent by passing a resolution on 4
November 1789, recommending the formation of similar societies
throughout England which, by corresponding with each other, could
establish "a grand concentrated Union of the true Friends of Public
Liberty, in order ... to maintain its [Liberty's] existence."[68] Friendship denoted not just sympathy and understanding, but a political
solidarity based on egalitarian principles and on correspondence
itself. The practice of the London Society of the Friends of the People
typified that of other societies. Members collected weekly at the
Freemasons Tavern, and spent the evening drinking, reading letters
to the society, approving letters written in response, and planning to
publish this correspondence "for the benefit of the public."[69] The
London Corresponding Society, founded in 1792, characterized itself
as a "friendly and well-meaning company" whose "object" was "to
correspond with individuals, and societies of men who wished for a
reformation, and to collect the opinion and sense of the nation as far
as possible by that means." Horne Tooke wrote to encourage the
project, "applauding their spirited conduct, ... [for] by these means
the eyes of the common people would be opened and all their desires
fulfilled."[70]

Produced within this network of radical correspondence was a new
sense of "Union," "nation" and "People" that thousands of men –

primarily working class – found exhilarating.[71] Thomas Hardy describes the powerful response of the fledgling Corresponding Society, when its members, London artisans and tradesmen, first received a letter from another radical society, the Sheffield Society of Constitutional Information:

> They were very much pleased with the Answer [to a letter penned by Hardy] and the printed Addresses which accompanied it – it animated them with additional ardor – when they were informed that others in a distant part of the nation had *thought* and *begun to act* in the same way with themselves – The communication being quite unexpected – they had not heard that any such Society existed at Sheffield at that time... The Society being so well satisfied of course I received their unanimous thanks for opening so important a correspondance [*sic*].[72]

The proliferation of corresponding societies encouraged communication between various "friends of the people," but it also forged a sense of shared identity and political purpose throughout the British Isles.[73] The "friends" found themselves represented collectively through correspondence, and represented on a national scale. Collective, however, did not mean uniform. The various societies insisted upon their local and often class-bound characters; they maintained distinct, but also overlapping agendas. Correspondence allowed them to imagine a wide network of groups, dispersed throughout England, Ireland, Scotland and Wales, participating in the same discussion. In other words, no one society (e.g. the Whig Association of Friends of the People, composed heavily of liberal MPs) could adequately represent or speak for the rest.[74]

Not surprisingly, the circulation of such letters threatened the current system of representation in several ways. First, as Burke noted, the "Friends of Liberty" dared to represent themselves to foreign nations. Letters were frequently sent to the French National Assembly as well as to French Jacobin societies in the years between 1791 and 1793; the leading groups combined to swear "inviolable friendship" and "friendly dispositions, etc." to the French.[75] Moreover, they gave their foreign correspondence public airing. The trend began in 1792, when *The Correspondence of the Revolution Society in London with the National Assembly in France and with Various Societies of the Friends of Liberty in France and England* appeared on London book stalls.[76] "Friendly" correspondence drifted very close to notions of "universal fraternity." More significantly, it threatened to replace – not just reform – representative government in England.

The 1794 Report from the Committee of Secrecy of the House of Commons on the LCS and SCI reiterates and intensifies Burke's "uneasiness" about the groups' representative power. Between the years 1791 and 1794, according to the report, the two societies had "by a series of resolutions, publications, and correspondence, been uniformly and systematically pursuing a settled design which appears ... to tend to the subversion of the established constitution." They had also been "endeavouring to establish a general correspondence and concert among the other seditious societies in the metropolis, and in different parts of England and Scotland, as well as in Ireland." The real danger, concludes the committee, rests not in the societies' attempt to reform Parliament, but rather the network's potential "to supersede the House of Commons in its representative capacity, and to assume itself all the functions and powers of a national legislature."[77]

The perceived influence of the corresponding "Friends of Liberty," their association with French political societies, together with their proposals for national reform conventions[78] accelerated the passage of the Seditious Practices and Treason Acts, the infamous "Two Acts" or "Gagging Acts" of 1794–5. (The Seditious Practices Act was introduced immediately after the 1794 Report from the Committee of Secrecy.) With these acts, the Pitt ministry produced a fiction of subversive, collective correspondence that, like the societies themselves, rewrote the letter's claim to privacy and individuality. The government fiction, however, tended toward a totalizing version of correspondence, one which denied debate and discussion. Against this revision, Samuel Taylor Coleridge, among others, complained vehemently:

Here lurks the snake. To promulgate what we believe to be truth is indeed a law beyond law; but now if any man should publish, nay, if even in a friendly letter or social conversation any should assert a Republic to be the most perfect form of government, and endeavour by argument to prove it so, he is guilty of High Treason.... [hence] All political controversy is at an end.[79]

Fictions of correspondence began to color political discourse itself. The genre of familiar epistle, from its roots in classical rhetoric, had emerged at the end of the century as the medium of collective political activity. But it also served as the emblem of such activity, an emblem which could be exploited by both liberal reformers and a reactionary ministry.

One notable example of the ministry's outraged response to the challenge posed by reformers' letters was its reaction to Charles James Fox's "Letter... [to the] Electors of the City and Liberty of Westminster." Fox's letter was published in January 1793, immediately after the announcement of Louis XVI's execution and England's subsequent move toward war with France. As leader of the opposition party in Parliament, Fox wrote a letter which was advertised, excerpted and hotly debated in all the major British newspapers.[80] Fox's message contained two central points, neither of which was calculated to ease the ministry's fear of a grand insurrection in England. First, Fox stressed the need to continue diplomatic ties with the provisional government in France. Communication, he urged, would heal the "insult" and "injury" between the two nations; war would only serve to harden the dreaded "French opinions" into "overt acts." His letter thus argued for correspondence between English and French "opinions," in the hope of securing "peace, harmony and confidence".[81]

Fox's second point undercuts the logic of his first. His letter argues to and for the people, rather than the king or the established ministry and Parliament. More radically, it places the power of the people above that of its representatives and its Constitution:

To declare war is, by the Constitution, the prerogative of the King... but to grant or withhold the means of carrying it on, is (by the same Constitution) the privilege of the People, through their Representatives; and upon the People at large, *by a law paramount to all Constitutions* – the Law of Nature and Necessity – must fall the burden and sufferings, which are the sure attendants upon that calamity. It seems therefore reasonable that they, who are to pay, and to suffer, should be distinctly informed of the object for which that war is made.[82]

Fox offers a version of the friendly societies' "law beyond law" which Coleridge also would invoke in his attack upon the Sedition and Treason Acts. By invoking a law beyond king and Constitution, Fox's "Letter" appeals to a disgruntled populace, already prone to express violent opposition to the policies of George III and Pitt.[83] This open letter, Fox's first published political pamphlet, reinforced his notion that authority rests, ultimately, with "the People." His letter took the same arguments that had proved ineffective in Parliament and addressed them to "the People at large." It thereby proposed to mobilize a political force outside the established walls of power. If

Fox had pushed this public appeal further, "there can be little doubt that... there would have been a rebellion against both the corruptions [in electoral representation] and the war."[84] But this "Letter" was Fox's last direct correspondence with "the People."

In response to the challenge of this public document, the ministry sought to represent Fox and his fellow "Friends of the People" as traitors; letters became the appropriate symbols of their treachery. Two ministerial papers, the *True Briton* and the *Public Advertiser*, "devoted whole issues to exposés of supposed correspondence between Fox and the French, or between the 'liberal' Lord Lauderdale and the French; and the Ministerial pamphleteers seemed to feel that Fox's opposition to the war was proof enough that such correspondence existed."[85] By casting Fox and his supporters as the Arch-Jacobin and his friends, the government deflected the issue of electoral reform, choosing rather to fuel the country's hostility toward France. An equation was being formulated by the ministry and before the eyes of the public: overt opposition equalled covert treason, and letters were the agents for both.

It is not difficult, therefore, to understand the symbolic significance of the Traitorous Correspondence Bill, introduced in March 1793. The government had prepared this move in the hope that it would generate a wave of francophobia, and excite support for the unpopular war. Both Fox and his ally Sheridan had complained, publicly, that their private letters had been "stopped at the post-office"; newspapers were told that the ministry was gathering incriminating correspondence which would expose untold plots against the security of the state.[86] Fox objected, with some indignation:

Is it not a situation of the country horrible to relate... that correspondence and conversation are to be pried into with such inquisitional jealousy, as to make it dangerous for them to commit their thoughts to paper, or to converse with a stranger, but in the presence of a third person?[87]

The Traitorous Correspondence Bill was meant to suggest to the nation that traitorous correspondence with the enemy did, in fact, exist. In a time of war, public security outweighed consideration for individual rights and privacy.[88] Use of the word "correspondence" was, however, a smokescreen: in spite of the press's interest in dangerous letters now held secure behind Post Office bars, the bill actually used "correspondence" only in the so-called "legal sense."

It would not "interfere with the exchange of letters," but rather prohibit commercial transactions between English citizens and the French army, or government.[89] Clearly, the reference to "correspondence" had little to do with the content of the bill, and everything to do with its public image. Fox and others fumed that the name was chosen for its effect on the people, "with no other view than to disseminate through the country false and injurious ideas of the existence of a correspondence between some persons and France."[90] The attention paid to this bill was merely a propaganda ploy, a clever fiction devised by Pitt. Advocates of the bill used the Opposition's complaints to murmur, loudly, that someone did protest too much. All in all, the debate surrounding the Traitorous Correspondence Bill had greater political impact than the bill itself. The fiction of the traitorous letter replaced that of the friendly epistle. It also took precedence over actual practice: the government never did produce actual evidence of treasonous correspondence.

The public debate surrounding Fox's "Letter," the ministry's response to the "friendly societies," and the subsequent Traitorous Correspondence Bill and Sedition Acts reveal the symbolic use of correspondence in England's reaction to the French Revolution. The fiction of political letters developed at least two functions. On the one hand, the fiction propagated by reformists, such as Fox, Paine and the "Friends of Liberty," depicted the letter as a gesture toward the will of the people, an appeal outside the structures of law and government. The letter was an open, democratic form, predicated on a belief in negotiation between disparate and multitudinous voices. According to this fiction, the letter became the most accessible, and consequently, the most public means of communication. The fiction generated by conservative forces, however, cast the letter as the tool of conspiracy, the epitome of deceit. For them, the letter represented a threat to the public weal: the safety of the country demanded that the state regulate all correspondence. Postal surveillance would act as that "third person" monitoring the potentially subversive conversation between two individuals. According to both fictions, correspondence was a political issue. For both parties, the fiction of the letter functioned as propaganda that simultaneously supported and betrayed them.

LOVE LETTERS OR SPY LETTERS?

The historical context helps to explain the political movements of the letter in literature after the rise and fall of the epistolary novel. But this story of the fall from grace – or shall we call it the delivery? – of the letter is set in the context of another story of innocence and experience: that of the French Revolution.

I am interested in the story of this "fallen" letter: not only how it lost its political innocence, but where it went when it became "marginalized" in literary practice, stigmatized by its history and its political involvement. Often, it kept up a formal pretence, presenting itself in all its conventional garb, as in Mary Shelley's *Frankenstein*, or Walter Scott's *Redgauntlet*. But the fiction of its respectability, or of its ability to coordinate friendly discussion, disintegrates in these novels and elsewhere. The letter's private life and representative power, having become public property, remain suspect in nineteenth-century literature. No longer would the letter inscribe the individual within a secure social order; no longer would it voice the heterogeneous will of the people; nor would it betoken the unregulated exchange of ideas and feelings. Nineteenth-century literature's fiction of the suspect letter thus depends upon a romantic illusion that a time existed when the letter was an open, innocent and decorous mode of expression – a virginal genre. The traditional canon of epistolary novels, which usually includes no novels written after 1790, reinforces this illusion.

Any innocence attributed to the letter in literature is achieved only after a more worldly history has been erased. Shari Benstock makes the point: "letters have been made to serve the law of literary genre," and that law does not want letters with a history.[91] The epistolary novel in England did not, in fact, begin with the unspoiled *Pamela*, come of age with *Clarissa* and realize its corruption in Laclos's Mme. de Merteuil, a French import. Such a "story" about the epistolary genre has been created and maintained through a careful selection of texts: *The Portuguese Letters*, "Eloisa to Abelard," *The Life of Marianne*, *Pamela*, *Clarissa*, *The Sorrows of Young Werther*, *Julie, ou la Nouvelle Héloïse*, *Dangerous Liaisons* and *Evelina*. Blockbuster hits in the marketplace, no doubt, and works of great literary merit, the books on this list all equate letters with love. With one exception, these books are written by men; with one exception, they place a woman at the center of the plot.[92] As a coherent tradition, they demonstrate no great engagement in "worldly events": in most cases, the characters are isolated not only from each other, but often from society as well.

This line of development in the literary canon isolates a certain "fiction" of the epistolary novel which, in turn, distorts the history of this genre. In fact, outside this fiction of the letter stand innumerable epistolary novels which do not emphasize the psychology of the love letter, do not target the woman as victim/heroine, and do not detach the world of letters from the world of political events. These works, the spy novels and travel novels of the eighteenth century, written as letters, have either been ignored by the canon, or placed outside the epistolary tradition. Aphra Behn's perennially popular *Love Letters from a Young Nobleman to His Sister* (1684–7), combining incest, erotic fiction and political *roman à clef*, is a scandal to the epistolary genre.[93] Montesquieu's *Lettres Persanes* (1721) are, perhaps, too philosophical and worldly to be classified with *Pamela*. Goldsmith's *Letters from a Citizen of the World* (1762) create a too-glaring contrast with *Julie, ou la Nouvelle Héloïse* (1761). Smollett's *Humphrey Clinker* (1771) rests one foot in the sentimental realm, while the other wanders in the picaresque. All these notable works are treated as anomalies in the epistolary tradition.

It is hard to remind ourselves that *Pamela* was an anomaly in its day. When Richardson began to write, the novel market was full of epistolary fictions dealing with court intrigue, international spying, social and political critique. Montesquieu himself, reflecting on *The Persian Letters*, admires "the form of letters... not dependent on any design or any plan already formed, [where] the author allows himself to add philosophy, politics and morality to a novel."[94] The extraordinarily popular *Letters Writ by a Turkish Spy* was first translated into English in the years between 1687 and 1694; this eight-volume work was continually reprinted throughout the first half of the eighteenth century, despite its high cost. Its offspring were as popular as the original, for the British reading public enjoyed spying on the machinery of government. *A Secret History of Whitehall* appeared (in letters) in 1697. Defoe "found" and published *Continuation of Letters Writ by a Turkish Spy at Paris* (1718). In the wake of the Turks and Persians, German spies, Chinese spies and Jewish spies reported their findings in letters in the 1730s. The trend continued throughout the century.

Nor were these clandestine analyses of government and court life the exclusive domain of male writers. Aphra Behn's *Love Letters*, Mary De la Riviere Manley's *Court Intrigue* (1711), along with Eliza Haywood's *Spy upon the Conjuror* (1724), and *Letter from the Palace of Fame* (1727) nourished a strong desire for books by women novelists. Their works indicate that the love letter and the spy letter were not clearly isolated from each other, at least not in the first decades of the eighteenth century.

We cannot deny that the popular plot of political intrigue, with its "spies, or leaders of cabals plotting in secrecy," did give way to tales of sexual intrigue, thwarted love, seduction and marriage.[95] In place of a nation's political security, a woman's physical and social security were the primary targets threatened by correspondence. Still, the cabalistic quality of intimate correspondence in the political works persisted both in the epistolary novel and in popular imagination, although it often remained hidden beneath the dynamics of "romance." In the fascinating yet corrupt machinations of Mme. de Merteuil and the Marquis de Valmont in *Dangerous Liaisons*, the letters between lovers surrender to the hands of spies and schemers. Laclos's novel underscores the Machiavellian potential within the sentimental fiction. The eventual downfall of these intriguing aristocrats, read in the waning light of the last years of Louis XVI's reign, comments directly on the corrupt politics of the French court. Sexual intrigue becomes a metaphor for political intrigue, reversing the trend of the previous forty years.[96] *Dangerous Liaisons*, read as political, rather than amorous letters, reveals the bias of a "safe" epistolary canon, which would rather spy on a woman's bedroom than look behind the closed doors of government.

Here again, we can invoke the example of *Marat Assassiné*. In the effort to elevate the martyr of epistolary tradition, criticism underestimates the subversive potential of the woman and the political collective ("mobs" and "friends"), which lurks behind the seemingly deferential form of the letter. If we look at the history of the letter in the eighteenth century, we can see why the accepted epistolary canon has perpetuated a "safe" fiction of the letter's "feminine" origins, and why it terminates the letter-fiction in the late 1780s.[97] The political letter, like the spy novel, has been neglected precisely because of its volatile tradition. Moreover, if we flip the equation, we find that the letters written and published by women in the early years of the century, either letter-novels or travel letters, were not at all limited to romance, domestic detail and personal introspection. In fact, by looking only at the examples of Lady Mary Wortley Montagu and Aphra Behn, we see that women's letters ranged far and wide over questions of war, foreign cultures and religions, law and forms of government. Their letters were well within the mainstream of popular literature; more importantly, they challenged the status quo of English society and government.[98]

The women's conduct-books/letter-manuals which emerged by the mid-eighteenth century can be read as an ideologically motivated check to such challenges. For example, Richardson's *Letters to and for ... Important Occasions* sought to define what was "important" in a letter, and thereby teach his public "how to think and act justly and prudently in the common concerns of human life."[99] Richardson's was the first letter manual to devote the majority of its material to women's letters.[100] But a tradition of women's less prudent *lettres du monde* surfaces throughout the century, and reappears in the 1780s and 1790s and well into the nineteenth and twentieth centuries, in the work of some of the finest travel writers and foreign correspondents in the English language.

The following chapters attempt to recover a history of letters by examining the epistolary writing and fictional work of several women writers of the Romantic period in England: Helen Maria Williams, Mary Wollstonecraft, Jane Austen and Mary Shelley. The careful negotiation of public and private expression, so critical in letter-writing, becomes a primary concern for these women. They confront one fiction of letters, which focuses on and finally silences the woman writer, with another fiction, wherein the letter represents a more democratic (and disruptive) potential. Stepping away from the "safe" and debilitating sentimental tradition, these writers develop an idea of correspondence which re-imagines epistolary form. The correspondence thus established between the woman writer and her public audience transforms the woman's relationship to her writing and to the society which would read them both.

CHAPTER 2

Letters *or letters? Politics, interception and spy fiction*

For an example of the political force registered in letters in the 1790s, we take a brief detour from the figure of the sentimental epistolary heroine and travel briefly with her unexpected masculine counterpart, the spy. Despite the evident disparity in their professions and histories, we can trace the movement of the spy, a movement inextricably bound to the idea of conspiracy and correspondence, and find ourselves once again confronted with the dangerous destiny of the woman of letters.

EPISTOLARY FICTIONS AT THE HOME OFFICE

Samuel Turner, one of the government's most successful agents in its fledgling network of spies, was a well-placed member of the United Irish Society and Britain's most useful informant about the activities of the Irish rebels between 1796 and 1804. While living in Hamburg and infiltrating the Irish community in exile there, Turner struck up a correspondence with Lady Pamela Fitzgerald, wife of Lord Edward Fitzgerald, the leading figure among the Irish insurgents. Through this clandestine correspondence, Turner gained a privileged intimacy with the Irishmen's projects, including the plans for the 1798 rebellion. As Lady Pamela Fitzgerald's "confidant," Samuel Turner could, simply by writing letters, create and shape the documentary evidence he needed for the Home Office. He would be protected, moreover, by his correspondent's desire to keep any epistolary exchange between them thoroughly private. Inspired by Lady Fitzgerald's first name and his own, the British spy signed his letters to her as "Richardson." Throughout his intrigues in Hamburg, "Richardson" or "Mr. R." remained his code name, both in his relations with his female correspondent and in his communiqués to the Home Office. So valuable a spy was Turner that not even parliamentary committees on secrecy were given his real identity. He was the nearly anonymous author of this exchange in letters, a fiction created on demand for the government.[1]

What do we make of this espionage conducted as epistolary fiction? Perhaps we ought first to ask how the workings of British Intelligence encourage us to imagine the author's relationship to his heroine. The role of Mr. R., the author/editor of epistolary fiction, seems to blend the role of Richardson with that of Mr. B., Pamela's scheming and intrusive master. In the letters of espionage, "The line between the spy and the 'agent provocateur' was indistinct."[2] *Pamela*'s influence provides a legitimating fiction for the informant's rerouting of Lady Pamela's missives into government business. Or does government business retrospectively distort Richardson's business?

When British fears about invasion and insurrection were at their height, legal prosecution of seditious activity relied on the interception and confiscation of the rebels' correspondence. "In a sense," writes E. P. Thompson, "the Government *needed* conspirators, to justify the continuance of repressive legislation which prevented nation-wide popular organisation."[3] The combination of various legislative maneuvers – the Alien Act (1793), the creation of the Alien Office (1794), the Traitorous Correspondence Act (1793; extended in 1798), the "Two Acts" against Treasonous Practices and Seditious Meetings (1795), and the Newspaper Act (1798) – allowed both the Home Secretary and the Foreign Secretary, as well as the Post Office itself, to scrutinize, appropriate or restrict any written material circulating in and out of England.[4] Like the editor of an epistolary novel, the Home Office accumulated bundles of letters written by suspects such as Thomas Hardy and John Bone, or letters sent between other members of the London Corresponding Society, the United English and the United Irish Societies.[5] When such correspondence became inaccessible, agents such as Turner worked to create supplementary correspondence (beyond that which was intercepted) that would yield the desired evidence – in this case, via a woman.

Consider, however, that Lady Fitzgerald was not the final object of either Turner's or the Home Office's surveillance. The new Pamela served rather as a meeting-point for two systems of secret correspondence. She facilitated the transfer between a government spy network and a treasonous conspiracy: the former, an unpopular and necessarily covert institution, the latter, an elusive entity the government was anxious to expose to public view.[6] The sentimental exchange between Pamela and Mr. R. draped an effective curtain behind which the unseen agent of the law collected intelligence about outlaws. In the private exchange, the agent of this epistolary plot hid behind a fictional mask; in public testimony, where he hid behind his anonymity, Turner was referred to "by initial only, or even as 'the person whose name is not to be mentioned.'"[7] Meanwhile, "Richardson" and his "Pamela" helped the government write duplicitous correspondence that disguised the government's own machinations.

The sentimental and the feminine clearly served as a vehicle for the subversive. The rebels themselves appropriated the fiction of women's letters, thus providing a "proper" dress to their dangerous alliances. In 1796, as evidence of treasonous conspiracy, one state trial presented a series of letters concerning wedding plans and dressmaking projects. This letter from John Hurford Stone to Horne Tooke, dated 15 January 1794, appeared as state evidence in the trial of William Jackson: "The little commission which you gave me to the milliner, I have properly executed; it was to have been sent to the ladies last spring, but the untowardness of events at that time hindered completion, and I could not find anyone to whom I could properly entrust it, the fashion being a little changed."[8] This overtly feminine discussion, claimed the prosecution, was, in truth, a veiled message about gun-running and plans for armed insurrection.[9] In this case, the fiction of female correspondence was a very thin cover, for the feminine routinely served to cloak extra-legal activities and agitation. After the banning of popular "friendly" societies in 1798, for instance, some groups continued meeting under the cover of "benevolent" or "charitable" societies, organized under the aegis of women.[10] Governmental interference, working through open or covert agents, could move quickly to perform the translation from the language of women to the language of spies, and to bring conspiracy into public view.

These examples suggest a few significant characteristics of correspondence as it thrived in the public imagination. First, discovery of the truth of letters (as evidence) depended upon an underhanded, even illicit interception of letters: documented truth required deceit, or at least manipulation. Conversely, an exchange traveling openly might be suspect and require de-coding: Stone's sartorial comments to Tooke cannot be taken at face value, but must be translated by the state's attorneys. Second, in order to shore up the notion of a nation embattled, the letters of Jacobinical conspirators would have to have been invented even if they had not been intercepted. Samuel Turner and other government agents were encouraged to produce epistolary intrigue that could provide hard evidence. These spy fictions were needed to justify government interference in private life. Hence the third point: the treasonous conspirator (e.g. John Hurford Stone or William Jackson) would then occupy a role similar to the sentimental heroine's. Both served as the object of one invasion (rape or surveillance) and the symbol of another invasion (against "domestic" terrain). The Home Office and the English home produced these fictions of self-defense. And in both stories, the political or erotic passions of the individual could be exposed and exorcised to maintain a social, moral and political order.

Yet, as we move along this detour, we begin to detect the formation of a new fiction of letters. Circumscribing the correspondence between private lovers, "friends" or conspirators is the secret correspondence between "Richardson" and the Home Office, between the editor/interceptor of letters and the interests of Great Britain. Represented through this correspondence, women, spies and rebels all end up writing and working for governmental security.

LETTERS BEYOND DISPUTE

In June 1798, a packet of letters "written by Persons in Paris," and addressed to Dr. Joseph Priestley in America, was seized by the British Navy, placed "on record in the public registry," and subsequently published by various editors in America and England.[11] These letters provoked a remarkable and strangely paradoxical series of commentaries on the politics and propriety of correspondence. Deemed "authentic" and "beyond dispute" by their publishers, the group of letters revealed "every feature and lineament of the true Jacobin character."[12] In other words, it offered indisputable evidence about something thoroughly suspect and, to the anti-Jacobin point of view, thoroughly unauthorized. What did it mean to place a correspondence both "beyond dispute" and under suspicion? If, like the letters of the United Irishmen or the London Corresponding Society, these subversive letters originally circulated on the periphery of the law, they now served as agents of that law. Any "dispute" was behind them; the "beyond" of their new status signalled an unassailable belief in their ability to provide truth. Perhaps, in order to present a fiction "beyond dispute," a structure wherein readers recognize and repudiate the "true Jacobin character," the editor demanded from the letters' readers a willing suspension of disbelief and disputation. If so, perhaps by contesting the interception and publication of these letters (rather than the letters themselves), we may re-enter the realm of dispute and reactivate the politics of epistolary fiction in the 1790s. Political forces in this period were busy writing all letters into one all-encompassing fiction: a spy novel.

After the initial publication of the intercepted material, Priestley himself wrote a letter to William Cobbett, who had taken responsibility for the American printing. Priestley, the well-known radical and dissenting minister, wrote to counter the fears of "many people in this country [the United States], who seem alarmed at the publication of an intercepted letter, address[e]d to me..." and to "satisfy" them that the letters themselves required no alarm.[13] Indeed, Priestly clearly wanted to divert public anxiety away from his correspondence and toward the editor who had publicized and sensationalized its contents. Cobbett retaliated by printing Priestley's letter and his own rebuttal in pamphlet form, and selling the pamphlet on both sides of the Atlantic. "I pledge myself," writes the pseudonymous Peter Porcupine, "to prove that *whatever suspicions or alarms the Intercept[e]d Letters were, in themselves, calculated to excite*, it [*sic*] ought by no means to be diminished by the 'satisfaction' which the Doctor has vainly attempted to give."[14] While Priestly aims to shut down the "alarm" generated by the intercepted letters, Cobbett vows to ring an undying alarm. He promises to *prove* the suspicious nature of the "Intercept[e]d Letters," to *authenticate* the dangerous fiction of Jacobinical politics.

The difference in their forms of reference indicates the two men's alarming differences. For Priestley, a "letter" remains a personal affair, an exchange between and for "friends"; only its *publication* arouses worry or suspicion. Cobbett, on the other hand, makes the "friendship" and the "Letter" larger than life; they become public concerns, "calculated" by the very form of presentation to "excite" alarm. At the same time, according to Cobbett's odd logic, his act of publishing contravenes any doubt or suspicion about Priestley's letters. Publication means veracity: "The authenticity of the Intercept[e]d Letters was too well established [in the initial printing] to be shaken by any denial of [Priestley's]: no equivocation, no subterfuge [by the correspondents] would ... have answered the least purpose."[15] The original correspondent's word has no bearing. Only the "authentic history,"[16] a story about subversives written by the courts and the editor, can close off subterfuge and deceit.

I will turn to the "authentic history" in a moment. But first, we see here a reprise of the conflicting epistolary fictions which surrounded the Traitorous Correspondence Bill. In that context, one fiction exploited the letter's democratic potential, its ability to transcend social barriers and foster open communication. The other fiction wrote the letter into the close confines of conspiracy, where it bred secrecy and deceit. Where radicals and reformers (naively) read the sentimental fiction of openness, the ministry and conservative reaction read the fiction of spies and political intrigue.[17] Yet, when Cobbett and Priestley revive the dispute, we see that interception generates a chiasmic reconfiguration of the politics of these fictions. The reactionary publisher wants to broadcast the radicals' letters, even as he requires the fiction of a hidden conspiracy; the radical minister wants to restrict the circle of readers, even as he argues for openness in public discourse. For Cobbett, the public and the nation become the realm of the authentic. Priestley meanwhile maintains the validity of the individual and private. Each intercepts the fiction of the other. The movement of the letters is, in fact, open to dispute, double-crossing itself at every turn. Or is it?

From the journalist's perspective, Priestley has no right to limit the direction of his own letters:

This nation, whom he has so laboured to injure and defame, seized on a certain traitorous correspondence, which was *eminently calculated to expose* the impious principles and destructive projects of their [the nation's?] internal and external enemies. Interest, duty, even self-preservation called on them to publish this correspondence to the world.[18]

"Traitorous" is an ambiguous qualifier; and "them" is an ambiguous publisher. Letters, in the hands of the "authorities," turn traitor to the original correspondents, exposing their principles and projects. But Cobbett's justification exposes his own principles and projects. In his formulation, the publishing industry ("them") represents the nation's interest.[19]

Extrapolating from this, Cobbett constructs a new correspondence between government and nation, replacing that between individuals:

even allowing the publishers to be, as [Priestley] hints, the *British Government*: Yet, what reason has he to complain? The British Government is the guardian of the interest and honour of the British Nation, and is, whatever he and his traitorous correspondent may say to the contrary, *the organ by which the people express their sentiments on every national concern* – what has [Priestley] done to *merit their commiseration* or mercy?[20]

Legitimate correspondence is redefined as the institutional interception of illegitimate sentiments. In fact, the British government and the publisher assume the same identity: they co-author a didactic epistolary fiction aimed at correction and discipline, a reactionary spy novel. An institutional "they" will point out the dangers of an unfortunate or vicious correspondence, directing the readers' allegiance toward this faceless author/publisher (the fictitious Peter Porcupine), and away from the actual letter-writer or receiver. Epistolary sympathy and sentiment are rerouted by publication to arrive at national (not individual) concerns.

Cobbett does not limit himself to one individual nation: British and American interests merge in his remarks. Nor is he the "Nation's" only co-author. Another editor of the "Intercept[e]d Letters" also overrides the notion of personal correspondence in pursuit of a more widespread exchange:

These letters relate almost exclusively to public matters; and their contents must be deemed interesting to every man who has a stake in the welfare of his country, or of any other civilized nation. Of the situation of the writers, and of the means of their information, *little need be said*...

The papers themselves abound with matter of the most serious reflection. Volumes of commentary might be written on such a text... Nor is it to us alone that these instructive letters are addressed. The picture which these letters exhibit... are calculated (if anything yet can do it) to *rouse the apathy* of those surrounding governments whose ruin is fast approaching.[21]

At the expense of individual interests, and disregarding the concerns of any individual government, correspondence will perform a sort of political seduction, "instructing" and "rousing" the dormant passions of all Europe. In fact, this new correspondence will lead astray the very heart of these letters, which were originally filled with other (i.e. revolutionary) European passions, not at all dormant. An unidentified logic has "calculated" the letters' emotional effect on governments, not individuals.

A similar conversion from suspect "letters" to transcendent *Letters* marks the 1798 English publication of another confidential corre-

spondence, between the French minister Talleyrand and certain
"Envoys of the United States." First published in the United States,
then copied in England, Talleyrand's conspiratorial rhetoric fur-
nishes an occasion for patriotic fervor in both countries. The English
publisher quotes with approval his American counterpart's rousing
preface:

> never lose, nor for a moment mislay this Paper – meditate on it throughout
> the day, and let it be the last thing that revisits your mind when you awake
> from your nightly slumbers. Guard it as you would the apple of your eye –
> preserve it amongst the hallowed gifts of your parents, and when you die,
> leave it as the first, most valuable, and most precious legacy to your
> children … So shall they distinguish their friends from their foes.[22]

Traitorous or dangerous correspondence is transformed by publication into a sacred talisman, a reliable scripture, a divining-rod for
recognizing good and evil, friend and foe

But note these editors' paradoxical imperatives: the very letters
which must be imagined as vehicles of Jacobinical terror are
simultaneously "calculated" as instruments of government security.
If we read them as "alarming," we gain reassurance – the very
"satisfaction" which Cobbett steals from Priestley. Still another
paradox marks the interception. The editors insist upon the
transparency of the letters, their unobstructed legibility: "little need
be said," writes one, "because the letters themselves speak sufficiently
to those points"; and "nothing need be said, beyond what is publicly
known or what these letters will supply."[23] And yet the editor
maintains, "Volumes of commentary might be written on such a
text."[24] The prefaces themselves mediate and obstruct the public's
response. The 1798 second edition of *Original Letters Recently Written by
Persons in Paris to Dr. Priestley in America, Taken on Board a Neutral Vessel*,
contains ten pages of introduction; an average of thirteen lines of
footnoted commentary accompany each of the thirty-five pages of
actual correspondence. Casting suspicion willy-nilly, these notes
effectively distance the public from the letters themselves.

If, by one account, the message of these letters is transparent and
destined for every "civilised nation," by another interpretation the
message is inherently mysterious, spoken within a closed society. So
tight is that society, that such letters

> would never have been address[e]d to one, whose sentiments the writer was
> not well assured were in perfect unison with those he expressed, whose

secresy he could not depend on, and, in short, whose treasonable disposition he was not thoroughly convinced was very equal to his own.[25]

Priestley protests that he is "not answerable" for what another sends him in the mail; that a barrier separates the reader from the writer of letters. But Cobbett counters with the verdict common to epistolary romance: the recipient, he claims, is always already asking for it. These *Letters* speak a code of seduction and conspiracy shared by all correspondents, Cobbett tells us; he then weaves a circle round them thrice: "[Once intimate]... traitors speak and write to each other in the true traitor stile; and in that stile it is that [his friend] writes to Priestley."[26] The danger, of course, is that the general reader of the published letter – the new addressee – will fall into this dangerous and seductive circle of intimacy. Cobbett, too, steals a trick from Samuel Richardson to justify our reading of this volatile material. Only the editor's intervention legitimates our reading: in this new correspondence between publisher and public, the public, at least, will not be "answerable."

Yet the demon nature which haunts the publication of traitorous correspondence seems ever ready to escape from within the editorial circle. What if the reader understands too well the code of conspiracy? What happens when publishers make available such a contaminating exchange? Consider the double-edge of this editor's footnote to the intercepted letters:

It must be here observed, that the unceasing industry with which the English press is loaded with libels on every established government... under the form of novels, voyages, letters, and anecdotes, is one of those signs of the times... which must deserve the attention of those who wish well to morality and public order.[27]

Like special interest groups which publicize (in order to censor) "immoral" or "obscene" art, these forces of public order in the 1790s seem bent on intercepting (in order to regulate) the circulation of "libellous" material.

"PERSONS IN PARIS"

Priestley has a point when he hints that interception itself is more alarming than any letters ("many people – seem alarmed at the publication of an intercepted letter"). The new fiction that he perceives leaves no room for partiality or individual interests, no shading of differences, no recognition that friends might disagree or that perspectives may vary. Once intercepted by the law and the nation, the plurality inherent in correspondence enters a discourse "beyond dispute." The undisputable truth of letters resides not in individual expression, but in public, institutional control.

I, too, may be exercising editorial control as I gloss the dispute over these intercepted letters while deflecting attention from the individuals represented by the letters. One justification is my desire to emphasize that the functions of interception and publication actually "authorize" such correspondence. The letters then "represent" according to institutional structures. The actual letter-writers become the afterthought, of whom "little need be said" beyond what is "public knowledge." These "Persons in Paris," like the intercepted letters, exist primarily to articulate a political structure, precisely the realm of "public" knowledge. A second justification, then, is my desire to present these individuals as subjects raised – like the dead Julie or the dead Clarissa – "beyond dispute." When letters become *Letters*, potential agents of conflict become convenient posterboard fictions, characters in the political imagination. In short, the function of interception and publication replaces the sentimental subject with what Louis Althusser would call the "subject in law," inscribed in an ideologically "authentic history."[28]

Consider the figure of John Hurford Stone, the primary correspondent of these published letters, around whom the publishers construct their indisputable fiction. A friend of Dr. Priestley's and a former member of his Hackney congregation, Stone appears in the commentary as a notorious character: his letters depict not a man, but "every feature and lineament of the true Jacobin character."[29] The truth of the letter writes itself as caricature. Elsewhere, Stone's story is conceived as a legal record; the courtroom gives birth to public knowledge of him. In fact, it is hard to find Stone represented anywhere but in these letters and in court records. Just as the correspondence is placed "on record in the public registry," so is the correspondent. The editor of Stone's *Original Letters*, for example, reports this crucial evidence:

Mr. J. H. Stone is the brother of the person [William Stone], acquitted about two years ago on a charge of carrying on a treasonous correspondence with France, in conjunction with one Jackson, who was convicted at Dublin, on a similar accusation. Mr. [J. H.] Stone has been settled at Paris ever since the Revolution.[30]

(John Hurford Stone was accused in absentia as a traitor at the time of his brother's trial; William Stone's acquittal and John's exile effectively derailed any attempt to prosecute the latter.) Stone's public image as a conspirator survives despite the conclusion of the trial. The mere fact of corresponding carries suspicion beyond formal acquittal: for Cobbett and others, it remained indisputably incriminating evidence.

In fact, Stone's letters to Priestley contain little more than a rather optimistic account of recent events in France, a brief mention of Stone's trip to Switzerland, and queries about Priestley's own activities.[31] Still, Stone's notorious correspondence precedes him. The letters intercepted in 1798 are contaminated by and rewritten as the letters previously admitted as evidence in the treason trials of his brother and Jackson, in 1796. In his remarks, Cobbett "decodes" those earlier, "seemingly innocent" letters about millinery and fashion, unveiling the "double meaning" "mysteriously concealed" under their "symbols and allegories."[32] Evidently, he intends the reading public to interpret the letters to Priestley using the same tools of suspicion. With the editor's assistance, the single truth will be "brought to light."[33]

This illuminated correspondence, cast "beyond dispute," moves not outside and against, but rather around and above the law. It describes a higher law, an ideology of the public will. Cobbett characteristically drags the evidence out of the courtroom (and the arguments of law) and into "public" view, which he imagines to be above argument. He reproduces the "printed report of that trial" of William Stone which took place "on the 29th of January, 1796... before Lord Kenyon, in Westminster Hall." He then remarks that "a deceived Jury brought in a verdict Not Guilty," presumably under pressure from influential politicians such as Sheridan and Lauderdale. Cobbett concludes with the "public" account: "*It was said*, that, though John H. Stone was clearly proved to be a traitor, his brother might not be one."[34] One can dispute the findings of the court, which, after all, may bend to partisan interests. But all correspondents, suggests Cobbett, are subject to a final accounting, beyond dispute. He warns Priestley:

We know very well, that the letters are not sufficient to hang you. But, because such a defense would save your neck before a judge... do you imagine that it will save your reputation before the tribunal of the public?[35]

Despite his denunciation of Jacobinical principles, Cobbett seems to embrace the French practice of mob justice, a tribunal above and beyond the law. Similarly, the editor of *Jacobinism Displayed*, another pamphlet featuring the correspondence of John Hurford Stone, rants against the danger of corresponding and reading societies. Then, in nearly the same breath, he establishes his own network of readers. Like a chain-letter, his conclusion asks "*every one* that reads the above to *hand it to his neighbour*, being convinced that *any man* with his eyes open, cannot countenance the Jacobins."[36] The exchange mediated by these editors escapes the taint of conspiracy by imagining an unassailable public consensus.

Unlike John Hurford Stone, relatively unknown in England before his brother's trial and the public discussion of his seized letters, Priestley was no stranger to the public tribunal. In fact, the *Letters to Burke* which he published in 1791 deliberately courted public debate. They transformed the private feud between two antithetical thinkers into "a clash between the Catholic and the Protestant mentality, not a personal or temporary difference."[37] Yet despite the broad implications of the material, this group of letters, guided by Priestley himself into the hands of the public, does not presuppose a broad consensus among its readers. Nor does it suggest a conspiracy between the nominal correspondents. If anything, by relying primarily upon the writer's personal authority and experience, the letters anticipate a variety of individual responses within the public forum.[38] Indeed, Priestley challenges Burke on exactly this notion of public exchange; Burke deplores, while Priestley applauds, a contentious public correspondence:

I rather wonder, however, at this conduct in *you*, when I find you lamenting... that "it has been our misfortune, and not, as these gentlemen think it," (meaning, no doubt myself as well as others) "the glory, of this age, that every thing is to be *discussed*." For certainly, such a publication as this of yours, you could not but think, must lead to much discussion.[39]

The epistolary conventions behind Priestley's *Letters to Burke* ask for a dispute. They imagine their reader within a structure open to individual prejudices: "What appears to be *profound and extensive wisdom* to one man... appear[s] the extreme of *folly* to another; and unfortunately (owing perhaps to the differences of our educations, and early habits) this is precisely the difference between you and me."[40] Although Priestley appeals to "common principles" between himself and his opponent, his letters aim to establish tolerance for difference of opinion and belief (in this case, religious beliefs). This is a correspondence of dissent, not catholicism.

By the same token, Priestley assumes a direct line to the public, unmediated by institutional interference. The letter serves as his arena for debate, and he prepares to meet the public on that ground. In other words, if individuals wish to respond, they can express their disagreement or approval in writing. But Priestley evidently mis-judged the totalizing force of a public tribunal. In a series of riots, begun on 14 July 1791, a Birmingham mob burnt to the ground the minister's meeting house, his home and his laboratory. The violence left no room for debate: Priestley was forced from his home, and subsequently forced from England.[41]

Years later, Dr. Priestley's *Letter to a Friend in England* (1796), celebrating the virtues of the United States and their government, was published in the manufacturing towns of northern England. Priestley's strategy invokes the sentimental: the style is familiar and discursive; the reader is expected to respond as a "friend." In 1798, Cobbett the editor has no patience with the familiar and partial. In his discussion of the "Intercept[e]d Letters," he intercepts this letter too, and reads it for us: "every sentence, and every member of a sentence, is a falsehood."[42] Priestley's fondness for the individual perspective vanishes in Cobbett's universalizing light of truth. The code of sentimentality, partiality and dissent is cracked. What the mechanism of interception shows us is the transformation of a correspondence which claims authority on the basis of individual perspectives and differences, unconscious of intervention, into a correspondence which claims authority on the basis of ideological truth and public knowledge, constructed by intervention. More legitimate than the law, the public mandate for a new spy fiction replaces sentimental fiction.

THE LADY VANISHES

How does this new correspondence, this appropriation of spy fiction by the "proper" authorities, imagine the woman letter-writer, traditionally excluded from the intrigue of international politics? On the extreme margins of the "Intercept[e]d Letters," we discover some clues. In a brief postscript to one of Stone's letters, we hear a woman's voice addressing Dr. Priestley:

Pray are you continuing your speculations on the great events? are you in the press?...is there any thing here we can send you?

P.S. If pot or pearl ash could be sent, and a credit of nine or twelve months be given [to me]...I shall then be in full cash to answer it.

[At] the first opportunity, the Fr. translation of my Swiss Travels – for I have no English copy in my possession – [I will send you] ...I flatter myself you will approve of the spirit in which it is written.

With the warmest wishes for your happiness, and for all who are dear to you, believe me ever,

My dear Sir,

Your most affectionate –

My mother and sister are well, and I have two charming little nephews – the eldest is already an excellent republican.[43]

The name is suppressed, and the editor's terse comment stifles our queries: "Of the lady [letter-writer], nothing need be said, beyond what is publicly known, or what these letters will supply."[44]

Today, public knowledge of this woman is almost non-existent: the interception of her writing has meant virtual erasure from even scholarly discussion. Her note supplies a few traces, in its surprising mix of affection, business, domestic detail and political engagement. Stone's own letter offers her more direct publicity: "Of the nature of their [the Swiss] past governments, and the abuses which they contain, you will have a pretty just idea, if 2 vol. in octavo, of a *View of Switzerland*, written by Miss H. M. Williams, and now publishing in London, shall happen to fall into your hands."[45] Indeed, a footnote to these particular lines in Stone's letter indicates just how notorious this woman of public, political letters could be. The editor immediately works to marginalize – and magnify – her significance:

This passage [by Stone] affords a curious commentary on the work here mentioned [Williams' volumes on the Swiss], which [work] in principle and sentiment, can only be illustrated by the conduct of the female Patriots [in Paris]; who, after the massacre of the 10th of August, stripped and mutilated the carcasses of Swiss troops[46]

A violated body politic, represented by the mutilated Swiss guard, is the only "work" produced by women in politics, imagined as Jacobinical Bacchantes. The editor's "illustration" of Williams' writing is so shocking and outlandish that it forces us to avert our eyes from the actual "work" in question – or beyond question. In the process, the woman of letters, Helen Maria Williams, disappears from view.

In her day, Williams was, in fact, a notorious woman of letters: a more frequent visitor to the public tribunal than her companion, John Hurford Stone. Her eight volumes of *Letters from France*, written and published serially between 1791 and 1796, were read as flagrantly partisan, political letters. These letters, in fact, chart the transformation of correspondence from the familiar and sentimental to the public and political. For Williams' letters figure her as both epistolary heroine and conspirator, both Pamela and "the true Jacobin." Unlike Priestley, who refused to acknowledge the equation between the private and the political, or Stone, who became the victim of it, Williams successfully manipulated the fictions of correspondence, turning the structures of containment and publicity against each other.

The next chapter will attempt to understand the woman of letters, speaking on the margins. Through her acute awareness of the position of the woman in epistolary fiction, Helen Maria Williams manages to set the sentimental and the spy novel against each other, and create a new and unsettling history in letters.

CHAPTER 3

Helen Maria Williams and the letters of history

Some of the observations [I have] subjoined, trivial perhaps in themselves, may derive value from their connexion with the mighty event of the revolution, in the same manner as an obscure individual may be remembered who carves his name upon an immortal monument which mocks the destruction of time.

(Helen Maria Williams, *The Political and Confidential Correspondence of Lewis XVI*, vol. I, p. xxv)

Introducing a study of Helen Maria Williams' *Letters from France*, I find it hard to ignore the echo of a comment made about her, an editorial aside heard in the preface not to her own published letters, but to those of her companion, John Hurford Stone: "Of the lady, nothing need be said, beyond what is publicly known, or what these [Stone's] letters will supply."[1] Williams' epistolary account of the French Revolution and European politics appears to us now as obscure carvings upon the record of history, time-worn graffiti. Williams herself seems worthy of mention only because of her proximity to such "immortals" as Manon de Roland, Jacques-Pierre Brissot, General Dumouriez, Thomas Paine, William Wordsworth, William Godwin and Mary Wollstonecraft. But at the moment of the editor's dismissive comment in 1798, a "knowing" public would have read part or much of Williams' eight volumes of foreign correspondence, published serially in England between 1791 and 1796. Her *Letters*, especially the first two volumes, provided some of the first eye-witness accounts of events in France; they were widely excerpted, quoted, applauded and attacked in the British press. In *The English Novel in the Magazines, 1740–1815*, Robert D. Mayo calls Williams "the overwhelming favorite among writers of popular history and biography...[T]hanks to the labors of piratical miscellany editors, [she] became perhaps the best-known contemporary author to magazine writers of her generation."[2] After the publication of volume III, for instance, literary maven Hester Thrale Piozzi complained, "The entire neighbourhood borrows Helen's latest publication from me, such that I have hardly had time to read it myself."[3]

Even before 1790, Williams had gained a fair reputation in literary circles as a popular poet and sentimental novelist. Her early *Poems Moral, Elegant and Pathetic* (1783?), *Ode on the Peace* (1783), and *Peru: a Poem in Six Cantos* (1786) had been successful enough to encourage publication of a two-volume *Collected Poems* in 1786 (which was republished in 1791). Her sonnet "To Twilight" was reportedly a favorite of the young Wordsworth, who penned his first published poem, a sonnet, under Williams' influence: "On Seeing Miss Helen Maria Williams Weep" (1787).[4] In 1790 her first novel appeared, *Julia*, a highly moral revision of Rousseau's *Julie, ou la Nouvelle Héloïse*. By 1793, however, after the outbreak of war between France and England, her *Letters from France*, written in support of republican principles, had accorded her a far greater renown – a renown which alienated her former friends and admirers. A wide audience and the Revolution itself brought increasing notoriety to this foreign correspondent; and this notoriety, along with the politics of correspondence, labelled her a fallen woman.

So public, in fact, was Williams' political position, that she served as an admonition to other women writers. Letitia Hawkins, a former friend of Helen Williams, advertised her *Letters on the Female Mind* (1793) as a rebuke to the disreputable letter-writer: "I cannot but expect some atonement from you [Williams]. A candid renunciation of your political principles, a confession... I can assure you, that you will find in London such a degree of caution, that many of your former connections will be shy of entering with you on your favourite topic – French Liberty."[5] "Every female politician," snipes Hawkins, "[must be] a hearsay politician."[6] The Reverend Richard Polwhele, repudiating the women radicals of the time, singled out Williams as "an intemperate advocate of Gallic licentiousness"; Horace Walpole labelled her a "scribbling trollope"; and the *Gentleman's Magazine* complained, "She has debased her sex, her heart, her feelings," by supporting the Revolution. Notoriety, as the editor's earlier comment suggests, paradoxically erased Helen Maria Williams from polite society and serious discussion. Since the turbulent 1790s, few public mentions of Williams or her magnum opus have appeared. "What is she now?" asks a critic, William Beloe, in 1817. "If she lives (and whether she does or not, few know and nobody cares), she is a wanderer – an exile, unnoticed and unknown."[7] In her place we have the fictions of reactionary politics: "public knowledge" about "scribbling trollopes."

For me to say that "nothing need be said" about the letter-writer and that the *Letters* speak for themselves would, then, seem a self-defeating thesis. Yet I want to focus on the form of Williams' *Letters*, rather than their author, in order to show that we cannot easily locate or identify the woman within them. Reading through the eight volumes, we discover that the *Letters from France* do speak increasingly *about* (if not for) themselves: they draw attention away from the female letter-writer and toward the idea of correspondence. In fact, I will argue that Williams moves herself to a position which negates the role of the conventional epistolary heroine by scrutinizing instead the machinery which governs epistolary fictions. As the *Letters* negotiate the shifting structures of "public knowledge" in both France and England, we watch the sentimental "I" – the "proper" rhetorical stance of the woman in letters – first placed under suspicion, then threatened and finally excommunicated. In this way, the *Letters* mimic in their narrative structure the fate of their author. As Williams' individual "I" retreats to the margins of these letters, however, the letter-writer gains an enabling distance. From a perspective located on the edge of her own letters, she reads for us what may be called the *lettre de cachet*: the "hidden" correspondence between authorizing institutions and epistolary fictions.

Having emigrated to Paris from London in the early years of the Revolution, Helen Maria Williams felt the constraints of both exile and proximity. Repudiated in England for her republicanism, she was mistrusted in France for her English blood. Neither her close relationship with John Hurford Stone (a married man, living in the Williams' household), nor her friendship with leading Girondins (rivals to the Jacobins) was calculated to keep her free from suspicion. In 1793, Williams, her sisters and her mother were imprisoned in the Luxembourg Palace in a general round-up of British subjects; later they were held under house arrest. During a particularly dangerous period (late 1794), Williams fled with Stone to Switzerland, where she remained several months until Robespierre's power began to wane. (This trip provided the material for her *Tour of Switzerland* (1798).) Whether or not Williams acted as a spy for either the British or for the Girondins is debatable: she was accused of spying for both. But her *Letters from France* prove she had learned to spy upon the letter/s of the law/s that bound her: letters of sentimental convention as well as letters of legal, political and official correspondence. In the *Letters from France*, she studies the movements of letters and reports upon the conditions of their transmission and reception. How letters travel – between France and England, between lovers and prisoners, between women and the crowd – becomes more significant than what they contain. The letter-writer becomes increasingly conscious of how letters, both familiar and public, "act" as evidence in political dramas. The letters discussed and contained within Williams' *Letters* form the historical "incommensurates," to use Jerome McGann's term, which set up those obstacles that establish our own awareness of historical distance.[8] Her technique forces us to recognize what few of her contemporaries want us to recognize: that correspondence is never simply a transparent medium; rather, it promises blockage, limits and distance. In short, Helen Maria Williams asks us to read the envelope of contingency that surrounds any letter.

We should also note that Williams does not merely write about the equation between letters and women, or women and revolution; her own position is overdetermined by these equations. "Intemperate" and "licentious," she embodied events in France for her contemporary audience. More recent historians of the French Revolution have criticized her rendition of history as the product of "various and incompatible ideals…firing with a restless and muddled enthusiasm." Her "poetic brand of revolutionary sympathy…stress[es] its emotional more than its rational basis," thereby generating a "horror and elation intensifying each other."[9] In other words, her "feminine" account in letters reproduces too closely the turbulence of the Revolution itself.

Williams recognizes the paradox of her letters: read as "properly" feminine and sentimental on the one hand, they are simultaneously passionately partisan and disruptive on the other. Contemporary readers would view the ideological paradox of the sentimental woman and seditious correspondent as unnatural and scandalous. Indeed, Letitia Hawkins seems unwilling to countenance Williams' introduction of politics into a form that she herself allies with "intuition," and "the female character." Hawkins prefers to employ letters as a disciplinary tool. She writes her *Letters on the Female Mind* with "particular reference to [Williams'] *Letters from France*":

The study... which I place in the climax of unfitness [for women] is that of *politics*, and so strongly does it appear to me barred against the admission of females, that I am astonished that they ever ventured to approach it... You will grant it a path impenetrable to [a woman].[10]

By Hawkins' curiously sexualized logic, Williams cannot both write letters and write about politics: the "Female Mind" cannot both be penetrated and penetrate.[11]

This "Female Mind," which epistolary fictions such as *Pamela*, *Clarissa* and *Julie, ou la Nouvelle Héloïse* create in order to expose and control, finally has no proper place in the *Letters from France*. Williams' "Female Mind" remains an "exile, unnoticed and unknown" by design. If, as Jean Rousset claims, epistolary fiction sees letters as elements of a "cardiogramme," or as registers for the movements of the heart; if, as Janet Altman suggests, epistolarity provides "instruments" which monitor the ebb and flow of (a woman's) passions; then Williams' strategy ultimately protects the inner life of the (female) individual from such meticulous probing.[12] Despite their initial dependence on sentimental and romantic fictions, her letters eventually serve as registers for political rather than emotional turbulence. They become the "instruments" probing the inner workings of power structures. In so doing, they dismantle the correlation between the woman writer and a volatile "content."

For a helpful analogy of this approach to letters, we can look at the treatment of painted letters by Dutch artists in the late seventeenth century. Svetlana Alpers, in her book *The Art of Describing*, has considered these letters in the works of Ter Borch, Metsu and especially Vermeer, all of whom painted versions of the letter-reader/writer genre during the 1650s and 1660s.[13] Alpers stresses the non-narrative quality of the letters portrayed: their content is usually hidden from view. Instead, the artist plays with the letter as an object of visual attention, a representational surface with "a vacuum at the center."[14] Careful to fix the letter in a temporal and spatial frame, these paintings can, therefore, suggest much about the social relations which determine the letter's presence (see, for instance, Vermeer's *Mistress and Maid* or Ter Borch's *Curiosity*). But the inner world, "the essential content" of the letter and the correspondents, remains inviolate. In Vermeer's *Woman Reading a Letter* (or, *Woman in Blue*), for instance, the woman's sense of autonomy centers on her relationship to the letter, which, in turn, is shadowed by a map of the New World. The painting thus places the epistolary moment within a "worldly"

Figure 5 Jan Vermeer, *Woman Reading a Letter*, or *Woman in Blue*.

frame which seems compatible with the woman's self-possession (see figure 5). Conversely, Greuze's treatment of the "woman and letter" theme, appearing a century later, has the letter signal the woman's loss of composure. In *The Kiss*, a woman teeters at the window between public and private realms, the mediating letter suggesting her accessibility to both lover and viewer (see fig. 3).[15] The sexuality legible in the latter version participates in the eighteenth century's sentimental fiction of epistolarity, which invites the reader/voyeur to speculate upon the private world of the female letter-writer, thereby obliterating the woman's self-possession. In a sense, Williams seeks to restore to the woman with the letter that autonomy which epistolary fictions of the eighteenth century had shattered; she wants to reposition her relationship to the letter within the context of a new world. Williams' *Letters from France* interest me because of their step-by-step demonstration of that restoration.

REVOLUTIONARY RHETORIC: SPECTACLES AND THE *LETTRE DE CACHET*

There must be spectacles in the great cities, and novels for a corrupted populace. I have seen the habits of my age, and I have published these letters. (Jean-Jacques Rousseau, First Preface to *Julie, ou la Nouvelle Héloïse*)

In Williams' first two volumes, the characteristic "looseness" and instability of epistolary narrative, as well as the letter's fiction of spontaneity and familiarity, seem well suited to present the rapidly changing nature of events in France. Even more valuable in these early letters is their sense of immediacy, the simulation of a "here and now" in which the reader can imaginatively participate. For Helen Maria Williams, the letter form initially provides an open stage, and the Revolution a dizzying spectacle. Her most memorable descriptions in these volumes focus on large public events, featuring the crowds on the Champs de Mars, the congregation in Notre Dame de Paris, the revelers around the tree of Liberty, the mob at the Bastille, the mass of theater-goers and paraders. The first volumes of her *Letters* aspire to replay these dramatic moments for her British audience. Nevertheless, once she recognizes herself as performer, rather than spectator, and once she perceives the paradoxes and limitations of the spectacle around her, the letter-writer begins to play the fictions of immediacy and spectatorship against each other. In short, a second reading of the letters as public theater points to the imprisoning *lettre de cachet*.

The *lettre de cachet* skulks throughout Williams' *Letters*, providing a dark leitmotif as well as a cautionary lesson. For the French *lettre close* or *lettre de cachet* represents the antithesis of the open letter Williams sets out to write. Predicated on the *ancien régime*'s absolute authority, the *lettre de cachet* had the power to render invisible and silent any individual who opposed the sovereign or the nobility. A warrant signed by the monarch and countersigned by a minister of state, sealed to ensure confidentiality, the *lettre de cachet* could imprison anyone "without trial, without means of redress or release" at the whim of any minister of the crown.[16] Nor could the prisoner read the letter which accused him: the power of the letter rested in its inaccessibility. As "one of the most notorious scandals of the [*ancien*] regime," this emblem of secrecy and sequestration had a symbolic status which far exceeded its actual role in France.[17]

Williams concludes her first volume (originally titled, *Letters Written in France in the Summer of 1790 to a Friend in England*) with a sentimental narrative underwritten by the *lettre de cachet*. The "Memoir de Monsieur du F." relays the story of Williams' friend, the Comte du Fossé, betrayed by such a letter but later liberated by the Revolution. This sentimental memoir about the *lettre de cachet* serves as the final episode of Williams' *Letters Written...to a Friend* and reverses the assumptions of her title: this French friend's letters replace her own letters to a friend. At the same time, the memoir asks us to question the relationship between one fiction of the letter (the familiar memoir) and the other (the *lettre de cachet*). As the popular familiar letter leads to its threatening opposite, Williams throws suspicion upon the very structures which authorize her own voice. By analyzing the contradictions written into her use of letters in the early volumes, we can more readily appreciate the innovative epistolary history Williams produces in her later writing.

In July 1790, when she arrived in Paris to celebrate the first birthday of the French Republic, Helen Maria Williams was twenty-eight years old and unmarried. Her *Letters Written...to a Friend* were published after her return to England later that year.[18] In many ways, this volume fulfills the conventions for familiar letters in the late eighteenth century. A young woman, parted from a "dear Friend," has an implicit duty to write, and write regularly: "I shall send you once a week the details which I promised when we parted..." (1:1:2). Moreover, the promised "details" concern themselves more with the writer's emotional and/or sensory response to a scene or event than to any detailed illustration of the scene itself. "I shall send you...the details which I promised...though I am well aware how very imperfectly I shall be able to describe the images which press upon my mind." Her language, punctuated by apostrophes, exclamations and rhetorical questions, is often sentimental and excessive. She wonders, for instance, at "the images of universal joy which

[call] tears into my eyes, and [make] my heart throb with sympathy"
(1 : 1 : 217). In sum, she aims to animate her readers with feeling,
rather than persuade them with facts and information. The spectacles
of revolutionary France consequently make a spectacle of sentiment.

In the streets of Paris, Williams could witness the propagandistic
value of staging the Revolution as public theater and as sentimental
drama. In its fascination with festival and spectacle, the new
revolutionary community developed a mass politics based on the
public expression of genuine feeling and on the ritual rehearsal of a
"mythic present."[19] In a republic which imagined itself in terms of
Rousseauian "transparency," "heart-to-heart politics were meant to
take place in public."[20] Yet Williams need not have taken her cue
from the revolutionary spectacles which surrounded her. Rousseau's
opening remark in *Julie, ou la Nouvelle Héloïse*, which serves as
epigraph to this section, indicates another model: epistolary fiction.
Although Rousseau's "uncorrupted" letter seems to suggest a
rejection, in fact it creates another version of the public spectacle.[21]
The familiar letter of epistolary novels, or the "memoir" letter, has,
as we shall see, its own mechanisms for staging transparent emotion
and immediacy. In Williams' *Letters*, these two theaters, the epistolary
and the political, contravert and redefine each other.

It should not surprise us then that the first of the *Letters from France*
offers a grand sentimental and political display. Williams describes
her entry to Paris with a rush of enthusiasm: destiny has placed her
in the midst of an exciting event.

I arrived at Paris, by a very rapid journey, the day before the [festival of]
Federation; and when I am disposed to murmur at the evils of my destiny,
I shall henceforth put this piece of good fortune into the opposite scale... Had
the packet which conveyed me from Brighton to Dieppe sailed a few hours
later; had the wind been contrary; in short, had I not reached Paris at the
moment I did reach it, I should have missed the most sublime spectacle
which, perhaps, was ever represented on the face of the earth. (1: 1 : 1–2)

Helen Maria Williams enters France as the privileged observer of a
unique event. The value of her letters depends upon her claim to this
temporal and spatial immediacy which the letters then transfer to her
reader. The extreme she describes (evil/fortune), the superlatives she
uses ("most sublime... ever"), and the frantic stages of her journey
all encourage the reader to see Helen Maria Williams as a significant
individual, for whom an extraordinary spectacle is about to be
performed.

The "most sublime spectacle" is, of course, the Fête de Fédération, the celebration of the first anniversary of the storming of the Bastille. But this term, "spectacle," soon grows to encompass the entire experience of the French Revolution. Contrary to Williams' early expectations, this "sublime" event refuses to remain within the limits of a staged representation. Williams' attention to the carefully orchestrated Fête repeats the revolutionaries' impulse to offer every representation of an event as, itself, an event.[22] In the unprecedented conflation of event and spectacle, of history and symbolic practice, the Revolution spilled off the stage and into actuality, invading the privileged vantage point of the outside observer. Wordsworth, for instance, admitted that he entered Paris in 1791 "careless as a flower / Glassed in a greenhouse," only to realize later that he "had abruptly passed / Into a theatre of which the stage / Was busy with an action far advanced."[23] The English spectator was pulled from greenhouse to theater to center-stage: safe boundaries collapsed and those standing safely in the audience were drawn into the conflict.

An Englishwoman in France, Helen Maria Williams becomes part of the spectacle. She herself is "staged" in these early letters: once by the genre itself, once again by her political position. After all, the letters do place her in the right place at the right moment in history. That position is dangerous: Williams invites the censorious scrutiny of her British audience as well as the suspicions of the French government. The challenge her letters face, then, is to represent for her readers the spectacular events which determine her life, while removing her from the dangerous spotlight of notoriety.

At first this may seem a simple task. The conventions of sentimental fiction appear to control Williams' voice in the first volume and to guarantee a certain innocence and propriety to her correspondence. Her use of the familiar letter follows the example of the memoir-letter or *lettre de confiance* of the epistolary novel. These letters pretend to have no effect on the plot of the novel, nor on the events they relate.[24] Thus, at first glance, the formal expectations of the memoir-letter create a role for the letter-writer congenial to Williams' position in France. This role presents a writer who remains passive, receptive and ineffectual, at one remove from the conflict. Williams plays her role dutifully, actively constructing herself as the epistolary heroine, an Evelina overwhelmed by her introduction to the big city.[25] But the conventions of that very pose also dictate that she will not long remain outside the events she witnesses.

Indeed, in a variety of ways, the sentimental fiction of the letter makes a spectacle of the letter-writer. Even as it frames events, such as the Fête de Fédération, or Williams' later tour of Orléans, the conventional letter dramatizes the narrator for the reader. While relying on the unusually "sensitive" eye of its "passive" narrator, the memoir-letter composes and endorses this individual viewpoint. It then surrenders that sensitive individual to public scrutiny. We find Williams, for example, giving herself the privileged position of a spectator, at the very moment that she resigns that privilege to her reader: "I assure you, the things I hear and see, from the window at which I am writing, are sufficient to confuse a stronger head than mine. You shall judge" (1:2:18). Here, as elsewhere, the letter-writer sits center-stage as the object of our gaze: "When I recollect... [these] real sufferings, ... my mind is overwhelmed with its own sensation – the paper is blotted by my tears – and I can hold my pen no longer" (1:1:135). In fact, the memoir-letter encourages resignation. The form produces and foregrounds the letter-writer's vulnerability, her lack of self-determination, and her ineffectual role in events. Vivienne Mylne explains that, in memoirs, the letter-writer usually appears to write "under the pressure of immediate events and cannot see their outcome."[26] The form thus seems to foster the victimization of the ingenuous letter-writer. Williams' readers in England would respond appropriately to these early volumes, lamenting the "perilous position" of their heroine, worrying lest "this admirable young girl lose her life by violence among these cruel creatures."[27] Williams' later experience will show, however, that readers themselves are not the least cruel of these creatures.

Also built into the memoir form is the writer's desire to re-present, and thereby, to mediate: usually between the action depicted and the reader, but also between individuals, social classes and separate nations. To do so, the writer will stage a spectacle in her letters, thereby containing and refining an otherwise inchoate experience or story (e.g. the Revolution). Thus Williams' stagings of the Fête, of the mass in Notre Dame, and finally, of the "Memoir" which concludes the volume, offer discrete, packaged moments calculated to entertain and *move* her British audience, as she has been moved. This mediating role deflects attention from Williams' own political agenda, focusing instead upon public festivals or the sufferings of friends. Her "Memoir of Mons. F." insists upon this deflection:

If however my love of the French revolution requires an apology, you shall receive one in a very short time, for I am going to [my friend] Mons. du F.'s chateau, and will send you thence the story of his misfortunes. They were the infliction of tyranny; and you will rejoice with me that tyranny is no more. (1:1:108–9)

I am glad that you think a friend's having been persecuted, imprisoned, maimed and almost murdered, under the ancient government of France, is a good excuse for having a revolution. What, indeed, but friendship could have led my attention away from the annals of the imagination to the records of politics; from the poetry to the prose of human life? (1:1:195)

In the familiar letter, politics are understood as the continuation of a sentimental drama, or melodrama, to which Williams, and the reader she imagines, can be similarly sympathetic observers: "My love for the French revolution is the natural result of... sympathy and therefore, my political creed is entirely an affair of the heart" (1:1:66).[28]

By centering attention on the feminine heart, however, the memoir-letter actually works against the fiction of a "frame" separate or distant from political content. The sentimental representation (via friendship and love) allows the reader to fuse the written "scene" with its emotional scene-writer, until both are viewed as composed, non-threatening spectacles. The revolution is represented by and as the woman's sensitive heart.[29] Williams takes this role to its extreme when she casts herself (and her political position) in the collective and diffuse role of "the people."

At one point in the *Letters from France*, the author participates in a play, "La Fédération, ou La Famille Patriotique." Williams agrees to take a non-speaking part, "le beau rôle de la statue." She plays Liberty, who stands "guarding the consecrated banners of the nation," while other actors heap decorations, scarves, hats and words upon her (1:2:203–4). Such "living allegories" featuring young, unmarried women were common spectacles in the new republic. The practice weighted a convenient sentimental tradition with new ideological force. For "behind the appearance of a living vignette," reports Lynn Hunt, "was the desire for a transparent representation, one that would be so close to nature that it would evoke none of the fanatical strivings after false images" – a Rousseauian ideal.[30] At the same time, this practice focused the public eye upon a new political representative. In Liberty, "the people had made... their own queen for a day."[31] The figure of female Liberty replaced statues or portraits of the king in the iconography of the new nation.[32] Liberty, Williams explains, is France's all-purpose ingenue heroine: "Upon the whole, Liberty appears in France adorned with the freshness of youth, and is loved with the ardour of passion"; whereas in England, "she is seen in her matronly state... beheld with sober veneration" (1:1:71). Clearly, Williams wants us to read her into this allegorical position, where she can bring the two separate symbolic structures into correspondence. The scene accentuates Williams rhetorical stance in these early letters, a mediating or representative pose which dramatizes surrender of personality to the public will at the same time that it asserts the "transparency" of that will. "I joined," she admits, "the universal voice, and repeated with my heart and soul, 'Vive la nation!'" (1:1:21).

Not surprisingly, overt partisanship plays no role in these "familiar" letters. In order to raise the letters "beyond dispute," all feeling and desire must be general and universal ("you will rejoice with me"). In these early volumes, Williams only rarely refers to her meetings with the influential Girondins and Jacobins she knew so well; she avoids mentioning the society of radical intellectuals she regularly assembled in her salon.[33] Instead, she allies herself with the more prosaic "people" of Paris. This identification with the "people" reinforces Williams' democratic aspirations for France, and for England.

It also heightens the dynamic of the familiar letter already at work, a dynamic which reads the woman as always already representative, as allegory. The woman and the crowd move together through these early letters, but the "prose of their human lives" is circumscribed by "staged" events, or spectacles. Although both figures occupy center-stage, they do not control or govern the political machinery. Lynn Hunt, writing about the public festivals of early republican France, explains that "the people's enthusiasm" was "regularized" by "official ceremonies." "In this fashion, the popular contribution was at once recognized and partially defused."[34] The drama of both the memoir-letter and the public spectacle cooperate to upstage and thereby reform troublesome energies, channeling "the ardour of passion" for liberty into ideological practice.

Consider the central episode of the second volume of letters, an ingenious and self-conscious staging by a woman writer aware of her own representational value. Here Williams pushes the correlation between English and French "sympathies" to the limit, in a scene which epitomizes the victim/mediator status of the woman, and reinforces her identification with the revolutionary mob. It also indicates the fragile limits of that identification, and of the structures which support it. From the window of an apartment in the Palais de Bourbon, Williams, her sisters, and several French gentlemen look down upon a festival procession of Parisian "citizens." The people in the street perform an impromptu show for their elevated audience: "indulging themselves in all the enthusiasm of simple and affectionate joy, [they] danced, they sung hymns to liberty, they filled the air with cries of 'Vive la nation!'" (1:2: 144). The scene reproduces the very position Williams attempts to maintain in her letters: perched above and at a safe distance from the movements of the Parisian mob, the reporter can contain the mob in a "simple," joyful scene. But the spectator does not remain safe or distant. The crowd immediately responds to the division which creates the power relationship, and turns upon those who stand above them in the Palais de Bourbon, the edifice of monarchy. The supervisory spectators become part of the spectacle:

The people do not always reason logically ... they could associate no ideas of patriotism with the Palais de Bourbon, and accused us of aristocracy as they approached. (1:2:145)

With the threat of violence, the politics of spectating are made explicit. But the danger subsides when the women are offered as an alternative spectacle. In a moment of identification, the structures of power are ignored and the show continues.

But they [the people] did not remain long in this error. They soon perceived that we were entirely disposed to sympathize in their festivity, and also that part of the company were Englishwomen: while the gentlemen from our windows repeatedly called out in as loud voices as they could, "Vive la nation!" the people answered by crying, "Vivent les Anglaises!" (1:2:145–6)

The spotlight travels from the crowd in the street to the women on the balcony, finally fusing the two as representatives of popular revolution. The Parisian mob and the English women become "safe" substitutes for each other. This scene crystallizes the strategy of Williams' own rhetoric. Here we see the story of Williams' letters reduced to a set piece.

The reconciliation of French and English interests exacts the high price of ideology: the dangerous mob stands mollified and "corrected," repeating formulaic slogans; the women in the scene lose the ability to speak for themselves, silenced by their passive, representational function. Both woman and crowd appear in these early letters as reactive, rather than active forces; impressionable and enthusiastic, mobile yet ultimately governable under the aegis of the "nation." The threatened violence remains in the air, however, as an echo of forces not always so easily reconciled.

It may seem odd that Helen Maria Williams would actively choose this silenced and mediating role, that she would deliberately stage herself as an allegorical figure at the service of ideology. Her choice mimics, and at the same time exaggerates, the allegorical and dramatic function of a virtuous "Julie" or "Clarissa." Indeed, Rousseau himself, in the Second Preface to *Julie, ou la Nouvelle Héloïse*, declares that female letter-writers are at the disposal of their (implicitly male) readers: "Neither to betray myself or to lie, [I maintain that] they are what you force them to be. If they once [really] existed, they exist no longer."[35] What the publication of epistolary novels had encouraged, Williams' *Letters* reconstruct in a more explicitly political context. The governing structure – the published letter, the spectacle or the Palais de Bourbon – will always determine the identity of the writing subject.

Still, Williams herself wrote the script here, not Rousseau or Richardson, and not Robespierre. In other words, we might ask ourselves why she would make the spectacle of the woman so obvious? If the familiar letter already writes the female letter-writer into a convenient fiction of vulnerability, places her "naturally" as the object of our gaze, why redouble that effect by mounting spectacles within spectacles? If the letter alone will do the job, why does Williams repeatedly make a spectacle of herself? Deliberate or not, the effect "make[s] visible, by playful repetition, what was supposed to remain invisible": that is, the fictions which "authorize" these "transparent" letters, those ideological structures which would write her before she writes them.[36] Williams mimics these structures; and "To play with mimesis," writes Luce Irigaray,

is ... for a woman, to try to recover the place of her exploitation by discourse, without allowing herself simply to be reduced to it. It means to resubmit herself – inasmuch as she is on the side of "perceptible," of "matter" – to "ideas," in particular to ideas about herself, that are elaborated in/by masculine logic.[37]

By calling attention to the "ideas" which write the woman of letters as spectacle, Williams hints that she, the woman composing these letters, does not *matter* as much as the spectacle itself. Once we look around the composed spectacle, once we see the contours of the stage, things do not look quite so natural or transparent. In that second look, we notice that the epistolary spectacle *is* a political spectacle. And Williams, conflating sentimental convention with radical ideology, is pulling "proper" theater into the streets.

For the innocent frame of the familiar, or memoir-letter is on the verge of collapse in the 1790s. Letitia Hawkins' anxiety about her countrywoman's *Letters* only repeats, in a different register, the debate we have seen over "friendly correspondence" amongst the radical societies in England.[38] A "proper" genre is in the process of revealing its impropriety. The familiar letter invites, even expects, self-dramatization, but Williams dramatizes that dramatization until any proper "self" disintegrates. Bruce Redford, in his study of eighteenth-century familiar letters, suggests that the best of such letters "achieve, in Northrop Frye's words, a 'centripetal structure of meaning'," which pulls the reader's gaze toward the fictive "I" of the letter. "This autonomous 'I' inhabits a microcosm…[that] 'replaces, or makes something else' of the outside world."[39] Frye associates this centripetal and isolating movement with a court society: "The centripetal gaze…seems to have something about it of the court gazing upon its sovereign, the court-room gazing upon the orator, or the audience gazing upon the actor." This focused gaze, moreover, presupposes a high level of "decorum."[40] Redford implies that the familiar letter-writer achieves the representational value of a monarch or an orator – embodying and articulating the society she describes.

But consider the implications for someone in Williams' position. It would be difficult, if not foolhardy, to sustain this courtly microcosm within a revolutionary setting, where values and decorum redefine themselves daily and where both monarchs and orators risk death. The centrifugal force of the political changes reported by Williams defy Redford's calm assertion that the familiar letter "freezes" and "miniaturizes," that it "creates its own context, its own coherent world."[41] To place herself at the focal center of the Revolution would be to enter a vortex. Yet this is what Williams does.

Because of the turbulence and violence at the center of radical politics, this over-identification between the female letter-writer and the spectacle she presents actually threatens to alienate Williams from the reading public she wants to woo. For in the "proper" sentimental tradition which privileges (feminine) immediacy and transparency there lurks a countervailing "impropriety": the female letter-writer stands and speaks *too closely* to the matter at hand. Recent feminist film theory argues that when women are the spectators, "the female look demands a becoming," collapsing the barrier between subject and object.[42] In the revolutionary setting, a "proper" audience might not find this collapse at all "becoming." "While you observe from a distance," Williams teases. "I am placed near...the scene" (1:3:2). The boast of the foreign correspondent echoes the dilemma of the sentimental heroine. According to *Clarissa*'s Belford, this "immediacy" of mind and body, as opposed to sterile detachment, makes the heroine someone worth reading – and violating:

How much more lively and affecting, for that reason, must her style be, her mind tortured by the pangs of uncertainty...than the dry, narrative, unanimated style of a person relating...dangers surmounted.[43]

Luce Irigaray paints the danger of Williams' role when she suggests,

Nearness... is not foreign to woman, a nearness so close that any identification of one or the other, and therefore any form of property [or propriety?] is impossible. Woman enjoys a closeness with the other that is so near she cannot possess it any more than she can possess herself.[44]

Although Irigaray proposes this over-identification as an essential function "enjoyed" by women in patriarchal culture we can locate it as a historical product of sentimental rhetoric and, in Williams' case, of the gendering of the epistolary genre. Irigaray herself invokes the form and function of the letter to elaborate her remark:

Once there was the enveloping body and the enveloped body... The subject [woman] who offers or permits desire transports and so envelops, or incorporates the other. It is moreover dangerous if there is no third term [to set limits].[45]

Irigaray recalls a pre-oedipal and prelapsarian fantasy which labels the outer form of the letter, the envelope, as distinctly female, even maternal – echoing Belford's and Richardson's characterization of the letter as the "Womb of Fate."[46] Consequently, even as it "sets limits" on its contents by placing them on a set stage, the letter's "lack of a proper place" (like the wandering womb of hysteria) signals something out of control.[47] The requisite third term, a penetrating reader, alone will legitimate feminine "transport." But we do not require the physiological metaphors to see that the heroine's fusion with popular revolution risks impropriety and challenges patriarchal structure. Despite her ahistorical fantasizing, Irigaray nonetheless reminds us of the fiction that reads the woman of letters as always too familiar with – too near to – what is foreign and "other."

Earlier I suggested that this spectacular machinery, which we might otherwise call the letter of the [ideological] law, produces a sort of prison. Like the invisible *lettre de cachet*, it identifies and contains opposition. I also claimed that the elaborate staging at work in the early *Letters from France* effectively shines the light on these otherwise invisible prison walls. But the light itself does not effect a jailbreak. Having shown us the spectacle of the letter-writer, Williams moves to turn the spectacle inside out. To remove herself from the prison, then, Williams leaves the stage at the end of volume I. With the "Memoir de Mons. du F." which concludes that volume, she not only inserts someone else (an aristocratic man) into the fiction of letters, she also inserts a story about her own letters. The staged scene at the Palais de Bourbon caught in a single tableau the dynamic of these letters and illuminated the surrounding structures. But this "Memoir," a narrative about the *lettre de cachet*, situates correspondence itself as the object of our gaze. The "Memoir" within Williams' memoir-letters brings down the walls of both the familiar epistle and the letter of law.

Upon first view, the "Memoir" testifies to the sentimental and familiar (as opposed to the political and "prosaic") content of Williams' own correspondence. It tells the story of Monsieur and Madame du Fossé, "friends with whom I wept in the day of their adversity, and with whom in their prosperity I have hastened to rejoice" (1:1:72). The tale serves as powerful sentimental propaganda for the young French Republic.[48] All the conventions of epistolary romance are here: separated lovers, tyrannic father, confinement and abandoment, followed by the eventual reconciliation and social reinstatement of the loving couple, now legitimately married. Although the narrative is not explicitly told through letters, it does revolve around letters, the effect being that we read an epistolary romance at one remove. But here is Williams' innovation: as editor of their letters *and* writer of her own, she can now dictate the movements of letters between Monsieur d: F., h:s wife, and the Baron du F. (his father), controlling the reader's gaze as well as the lovers'. She decides which letters will be open to our view, and which will be *cachées*.

When she directs our attention to the letters of the "Memoir," Williams slides away the barrier which separates the "annals of the imagination" from the "records of politics." To do this, she removes the mediating figure of the woman so that the distance between spectators and actors in the political drama collapses. Distinctions blur between the inside and the outside of correspondence. Rather than parading the letter-writer, she focuses on the figure of the letter-reader:

You, my dear friend…who understand the value at which tidings from those we love is computed in the arithmetic of the heart; who have heard with an almost uncontroulable [*sic*] emotion the postman's rap at the door; have trembling seen the well-known hand which excited sensations that almost deprived you of the power to break the seal which seemed the talisman of your happiness; you can judge the feelings of Monsieur du F. when he received…an answer from his wife. (1: 1 : 163)

Williams inverts the spectacle of the familiar letter first by drawing the imaginary reader of her letters into the circle of light, identifying the reader with the "Memoir's" hero, another letter-reader. The physical effect of this letter on the reader is crucial; like Williams' trembling imaginary reader, Monsieur du F. "pressed the letter to his heart, bathed it with his tears…and read it till every word was imprinted on his memory" (1: 1 : 164). The effect is immediate and nearly debilitating, and Williams' readers are invited to picture themselves in this humiliating spectacle. Yet the wife's letter, which has produced this debility, itself remains inaccessible: Williams leaves its contents and intentions unstated.

Williams' *Letters* produce their own *lettre de cachet*. For the impressionable letter-reader with whom Williams elides our feelings is not merely a sentimental victim. He is a political prisoner: entrapped by an actual *lettre de cachet* procured by his father, he is dispossessed of his inheritance. He cannot even "possess" or hold onto this moving letter, but is "forced the next day to relinquish his treasure," even as he has relinquished his lands and money (1: 1 : 164). We reread Williams' sentimental appeal to her letter-reader and find it laden with images correlating reading with economics ("the value…

computed in the arithmetic of the heart"), with confinement and with impotence. Our position as readers parallels the prisoner's. The standard "sensations" that "almost deprived you [the sentimental reader] of the power to break the seal" have been translated to Monsieur du F.'s account. Now they indicate the forces – father, postman, law, money – that have "almost deprived" Monsieur du F. of all political power.

Nor is the letter-reader's impotence far removed from the letter-writer's. Williams' "Memoir" substitutes the [male] political prisoner for the epistolary reporter whose mind is so "overwhelmed with its sensations" that she blots the paper with tears and "can hold [her] pen no longer" (1:1:135). The one letter we do read in this tale, one which "paints so naturally the situation of [the hero's] mind," paints as well the hero's impotence and victimization. From prison, Monsieur writes to his wife in England, in the feeble hope that his letter will find its intended audience:

How could I consent to separate myself from what was most dear to me in the world? No motive less powerful than that of seeking your welfare, and that of my child, could have determined me – and alas! I have not accomplished this end … What fills my mind with horror, in the solitude of my prison, is the fear you are suffering difficulties in a foreign country. Here I remain ignorant of your fate … what am I saying? I am ignorant whether the dearest objects of my affection still live! But I trust that Providence has preserved you. Adieu! (1:1:159–62)

Supposedly transcribed and translated by Helen Maria Williams, this letter traps the letter-writer under Williams' manipulation and our surveillance. "Alas!": he abdicates self-determination to Providence's all-seeing eye. The letter allows us to survey his suffering, but it causes no change in his situation, nor in the situation of his correspondent. Rather, the letter dramatizes and heightens his suffering.

At the same time, the letter rewrites Williams' anxiety about her own dispossessed status, her distance from the English audience, and the effectiveness of her epistles. The translation travels in two directions: the victim of the *lettre de cachet* is read in sentimental terms and the sentimental correspondent is recast as political prisoner. Monsieur du F. typifies the *ancien* victim of letters: self-sacrificing, impotent, isolated and ignorant of the world beyond his view. Even when he is restored to property, family and freedom, he remains ineffective and passive. The Revolution and "Providence" (his father's well-timed death) release him, but he contributes to the movements of neither. Monsieur du F. remains a representative and circumscribed character, signifying the restoration of "social pleasures," family fidelity and benign patriarchy to France. (Du Fossé's earlier sojourn in England and his appreciation of England's constitutional monarchy are not incidental concerns in this "restoration.") An entire village fêtes Monsieur's return, which takes place, fortuitously, on 15 July 1789. The "Memoir" molds the young aristocrat's story into political allegory.

But it is an allegory about letters, as well; one which demonstrates a move away from the *ancien* structures of epistolary fiction and romance. As the hero/victim of this fiction about letters, Monsieur du F. articulates the political position of the naive correspondent, the ingenue:

Such is the history of Mons. du F. Has it not the air of romance? and are you not glad that the denouement is happy? – Does not the old baron die in exactly the right place? at the very page one would choose? ... justice was henceforth to shed a clear and steady light, one without one dark shade of relief from *lettres de cachet*. (1:1:192–4)

In this "Memoir," Williams abandons the governing fiction of "spontaneous" and "natural" letter-writing. She brings into focus the limits of the memoir letter, the vulnerability of its correspondents, its political implications for both readers and writers. These, she implies, are elements of an *ancien régime*. The structuring principle of epistolary "romance," she shows us, stands off-stage, in the "dark iniquity of the *lettre de cachet*." The introduction of this quintessentially political letter alters the reader's contextual framework, shifting it from the conventions of sentimental fiction (transparency, immediacy, vulnerability) to the hidden structures of law and government.

At the same time, the *lettre de cachet* shifts our attention away from the woman who writes letters. We realize that, like Monsieur du F., we do not have to possess or penetrate the letter in order to understand and feel its effects. Its effectiveness, in the new context Williams provides, becomes a function of its impenetrability. By the end of the "Memoir," Williams' attention to correspondence suggests a distance between the letter-writer and the confinement once dictated by epistolary form. She asks us to read a different letter, one which we cannot immediately identify as a "feminine" form. Leaving the sentimental letter in the romance of the past, she asks us to read a letter written by and for the law, the nation, the "people."

Indeed, living in France at present appears to me like living in a region of romance. Events the most astonishing and marvellous are here the occurrences of the day. (1:2:4–5)

I will call the letters of volume II "love letters" because they demonstrate Williams' desire to produce a prosperous union between England and France. Moreover, they reveal her desire to locate herself, a single woman, in a less ambiguous social role. In this series of letters, written when Williams returned to France in 1792, the letter-writer attempts to articulate the structures of her two homes: "familiar" England and "revolutionary" France. She begins by comparing the National Assembly to the House of Commons, and proceeds to compare manufacturing in England and in France (1:2:32–4); English and French philosophy (1:2:60–1); the preparation of girls for marriage, in both countries (1:2:63–4); theater and holiday customs in Paris and in London (1:2:74–84); and French palaces and English country homes (1:2:85–6). The list goes on and on, comparing the regulating structures and systems of one country with the other's, until Williams is left, finally, trying to correlate the Constitutions, educational systems and languages of the two. Ultimately, she wants to translate the French Revolution into English terms, in order to locate herself and her writing in a definite and acceptable position. Despite this wish, the dynamics of correspondence impede the romance and the process of translation. Williams' second volume of letters ends up submitting to the structures which undermine not just countries and political systems, but individual desire as well.

If we follow Williams' line of vision, her *Letters* will function as a medium for reconciling people – and nations – otherwise divided by circumstantial difference. She abandons the strategies of spectacle and containment used in volume I, exploiting instead the letter's ability to move and allow for change. She points out bridges (the Pont Neuf and "a magnificent bridge in Orléans") but letters prove more effective conduits than these structures. When a river rises and "assumes a very different character," when it "overflows its banks" and ruins bridges, "a courier is dispatched to give news of its approach." With the news, the courier gallops faster than the river, "and by this means, the people are prepared for its reception" (1:2:17). Williams believes that the foreign correspondent, like the courier, prepares her British audience for an oncoming flood, which "spreads itself over the adjacent country, and not only fills the streets in the lower parts of the town...but even the houses" (1:2:16–17). The torrent may overwhelm the structures, but, through the agency of letters, it may be "prepared for" and accommodated.[49]

Williams bases this belief in accommodation on a fiction of love letters, wherein letters channel the passions and bring about the union of young lovers. With a rather naive faith in direct communication, Williams tries to construct a political romance: if obtrusive barriers could be overcome, France and England would understand each other and be united. Once again, a story included near the end of this volume provides a narrative for this romantic belief. The story itself serves as a sort of bridge, standing mid-way between a "novel writer's...heightened colour" and "real-life incidents" where "nothing is so affecting as simplicity, and nothing so forcible as truth" (1:2:156). Williams accentuates the mediated and mediating quality of this love story. It arrives in her text, having been "sent in a letter from a friend...in Toulouse." Williams situates us in the realm of translation: between French and English, romance and truth, Toulouse and Paris, then and now. This is a romantic realm, only vaguely bound to time and place, "where you will meet with a little romance; but perhaps you will wonder that you meet with no more" (1:2:157).

The love letters we read about in this love story, however, call into question the unifying promise of such correspondence. The drama of the tale centers on letters as symbols of a faithful love, but those symbols fail. Madeleine's lover, Auguste, has moved to Paris, on the insistence of his father. Once there, the Revolution erupts, "the French nation [shakes] off its fetters," and Auguste is called to serve in the army of the Republic. Meanwhile, back in the province, Madeleine waits in a convent for news from her lover. For her, the Revolution simply figures as part of the romantic plot of her life:

Madeleine was a firm friend to the revolution, which she was told had made every Frenchman free...It appeared to Madeline, that, putting all political considerations, points upon which she had not much meditated, out of the question, obtaining liberty of choice in marriage was alone worth the trouble of a revolution. (1:2:174–5)

Williams gently mocks Madeleine's political naiveté, which she immediately juxtaposes with the heroine's romantic faith in letters:

The Count de – [Auguste's father], who was informed of the correspondence of the two lovers...contrived to have Auguste's letters intercepted at the convent. In vain Madeleine enquired with all the anxiety of tenderness for letters. In vain she counted the hours till the return of the post-days. Post after post arrived, and brought no tidings of Auguste. Three months passed in the cruel torments of anxiety and suspense, and were at length succeeded by despair. Madeleine believed she was forgotten. (1:2:175)

Madeleine's romantic faith, which equates love with letters, and revolution with marriage, has distorted her view of her own situation. She doubts Auguste's devotion, but ignores the material and political obstructions which might hinder him: the count, army, convent, inheritance and law. Williams shows us a heroine blinded by the romance of letters. Madeleine "felt like Eloisa" and quotes from the epistolary romance of "Eloisa and Abelard"; she echoes the plaints of the young woman in the *Portuguese Letters*: "'Why should I continue to lament that inconstant lover who thinks of me no more?...Oh yes! he knows I have no other refuge, no other recourse than taking the veil'" (1:2:178). Indeed, Madeleine would readily renounce the world and confine herself forever in the "holy sisterhood of the convent" – and the "holy sisterhood" of epistolary romance.

The world and the Revolution, however, intervene. Her lover returns, "with some of the municipal officers of the town, wearing their national scarves." The officers inform Madeleine that the National Assembly has passed a decree which forbids her to take religious vows. Auguste then reports that the legal will of his dead uncle has freed him from dependence upon his tyrant-father. "Political considerations" and the law save Madeleine from "her eternal renunciation of the world." The Revolution removes the old barriers and inscribes the young couple in a new social order: they beome happily married and "devout patriots." According to this tale, the changes enacted by the Revolution, rather than any individual effort or love letter, overcome the institutional obstacles which separated the lovers. The effects of revolution expose the fiction of the love letter as an obsolete religion, another structure to be overcome.

In fact, this love story unearths a fundamental crisis of epistolary faith. What if the means of correspondence, upon which Williams has based her writing, falls subject to the dictates of changing laws, unstable authority and warfare? How can she guarantee that her distant friends in England will ever receive her letters? What if the bridge so carefully constructed is borne away by the rising flood of the Revolution? The accommodating and reconciling fiction of the love letter struggles with the doubt and division churning beneath the surface of volume II. Williams directs our view to her own doubts and confusions, which subvert superficial understanding and challenge faith in transcendence.

We see this internal division and crisis of faith in the border figures which hold the letter-writer's attention. In this second volume, Williams returns often to gaze at the characters in the marketplace, figures beyond *l'ordre du jour*, as she calls them: harlequins, mountebanks, fortune-tellers, deaf-mutes, elderly men, impoverished women. These figures speak in riddling phrases; they defy Williams' attempts at translation even as they mock simplistic definitions. The writer delivers these puzzling remarks with no editorial comment; they pop out of nowhere and interrupt her narrative. "Je suis moitié marié [I am half-married]," declares a Parisian harlequin, in a jest against all comic resolutions (1:2:83). An old man speaks in paradoxes: "La révolution...me ruine, me tue, mais elle me fait vivre [The revolution...destroys me, kills me, but it/she makes me live]" (1:2:31). Despite her faith in translation, Williams often balks when she encounters these perplexing *bons mots* and double entendres. She alternates between giving a full translation in the text, a translation by footnote, or no translation at all. Some messages from Paris apparently are not transmitted as easily as she – or a character such as Madeleine – may have believed.

Not only the romance of correspondence, but the heroine as well begins to discover inner contradictions. Of all the hybrids and outcasts in France, none haunts the letter-writer more persistently than Jeanne d'Arc, whose silent statue stands "wherever I travel in France." The narrator/heroine fancies that the Maid of Orleans "looks at me with an air of reproach," but she does not classify that reproach for the reader. More than any other anomaly she faces, this warrior-maiden challenges Helen Maria Williams' attempts to ignore the political contingencies of her own situation, and to write a bridge of union between England and France. Unlike the statue of Liberty, who adapts to the demands of the state, the statue of Jeanne d'Arc represents a troubling paradox for the Englishwoman in revolutionary France. Jeanne d'Arc was a political activist, a woman who fought battles and escaped the confining role of a maiden. For Williams, she incorporates a contradiction, possessing "the heroic qualities of the other sex... [and] the soft attractions of her own" (1:2:54). Canonized for her rescue of the French nation, she was burned by the British as a witch. The unexplained reproach she poses to Williams, therefore, also serves as a warning: could Williams dare to be a Jeanne d'Arc?

She may actually have had no choice. Despite her efforts to unify French republicanism with Britain's constitutional monarchy, Williams' *Letters from France* were judged controversial at best, divisive at worst. The public reception of her *Letters* and the escalating war rhetoric in England in 1792 undercut Williams' strategy of deference and accommodation. "Wherever I travel in France," Jeanne d'Arc's image recalls the violent divisiveness of warfare – especially between England and France. War provides the extreme representation of the inner conflicts and linguistic confusions which emerge in this volume and which derail the overriding romance of letters.

Instead of inscribing her within a new social order, Williams' letters actually accentuate her own marginal status. She opens the second volume with an epistolary poem (to her friend Dr. Moore), which places her outside of familiar society, and ultimately, outside of propriety:

> How oft remembrance, while the bosom bleeds,
> My pensive fancy to your dwelling leads;
> Where, round your cheerful hearth, I weeping trace
> The social circle, and my vacant place! (1:2:13)

Her letters, like this poem, cannot return her to the "hearth" of social acceptance. Removed from the domestic center, she can only trace, like a wandering spirit, the outline of the social circle. She can only describe her own marginality. Once again we find that the voices from the borders – the vagabonds and the motley performers – combine with that of the displaced woman to disturb any sense of composure. Enigmatic and untranslatable, such voices subvert the "simplicity" and "honesty" of these letters. Unacknowledged or rejected by society, they betray the assumptions of love letters.

In the two early volumes of letters, Williams seems to employ epistolary conventions according to a romantic plan: to accommodate the new order within the old and to bring separated peoples together without violence. The politics of the Revolution would be converted into the established formulae of fiction, just as the new republic would be assimilated by a constitutional monarchy, like England's. History, however, invades the romance and interrupts the easy translation. By the end of 1792, France had entered into war with Austria. In a "second revolution," the Parisian mob attacked the Tuileries, a National Convention was convened and the monarchy formally abolished. Internal divisions in France became explicit when the Girondins and Jacobins definitively split. The first colors of the Terror were visible that fall, in the September massacres at Paris and the army's ignoble assassinations at Lille.[50] For Helen Maria Williams, the romance had ended. How could she reconcile England and France, if France was dividing against itself?

The final letter to volume II shows her resignation: "I have nothing to relate but what is melancholy and painful." Disillusioned by the course of events in France, confronted by the double-edged sword of her own writing, Williams concludes this volume with weighty ambivalence. In place of the bridge of faith and accommodation, Williams sees the mocking "gates of Janus." Instead of a happy marriage, the final words of this volume give us again the goddess Liberty; this time, however, she has a suspiciously equivocal stance, bespeaking both warning and promise. Williams' comment on Liberty implicates the letter-writer as well: "Ye shall know by her fruits." Once the letters of romance and allegory turn suspect, contradiction and deception move to center-stage.

TREACHEROUS HISTORIES

In order for the circuit of the letter to end up confirming the law of the phallus, it must begin by transgressing it; the letter is a sign of high treason. (Barbara Johnson, *The Critical Difference*[51])

In none of the subsequent volumes does the letter regain its romantic faith in simplicity and honesty. Never again does Williams allegorize the political situation into sentimental romance. The next set of letters, written in the wake of the regicide, during the first years of the English–French wars, and published together in 1793, redefines the letter's function. Where volumes I and II emphasize the affective and accommodating potential of correspondence – its "proper" "feminine" roles – volumes III and IV foreground the divisive, treacherous and even fatal elements of letters. The letter's fall from innocence

reverberates throughout these volumes. Yet, where volumes I and II
tend to chafe against the limits of epistolary discourse, which both
trap a woman as a figure in a spectacle and restrict her political
efficacy, volumes III and IV break away from those constraints. In the
latter volumes, the letters move between various points of view,
transgressing discursive limits, challenging the reader to doubt and
criticize. They present the events of the Revolution not as a
determined spectacle, or even as an inevitable plot. Instead, through
a careful re-evaluation of the power of letters, Williams uses these two
volumes to involve her reader and herself in the making of history.

An initial reading of these two volumes easily confuses the reader.
The authorial voice has changed dramatically: it has, in fact,
multiplied. Volumes III and IV hold letters from at least four and
possibly five different letter-writers, together with an Advertisement
by an unknown editor (Williams herself?). Because the author of
each set of letters is not, except in one case, explicitly signaled, and
because the volumes contain no table of contents, only a second
reading of the two volumes helps to delineate its structure. But that
second look, we shall see, constitutes an essential part of our reading.
Judging primarily from stylistic changes and hints from the unidentified editor, we can speculate that the first several letters of volume III
are written by Williams (a "familiar" voice by now), but the rest are
written as dispatches from a male correspondent covering the
movements of the French army at the front. Volume IV commences
with four letters dated from Paris, perhaps written by Williams,
perhaps not. These are followed by a group of letters from another
male correspondent, analyzing the partisan politics at play within the
French government. These are the correspondents mentioned by the
editor. But left unmentioned in the Preface is a series of letters
inserted between the others: the correspondence of General Dumouriez to his colleague General Miranda. These hidden letters, slipped
in as an appendix to volume III, contain a reading lesson which upsets
the authoritative reports surrounding them. In short, the hidden
letters demand that we read history – including these two volumes of
foreign correspondence – as an epistolary intrigue.

At the beginning of the third volume, however, we seem to be in
familiar territory. These new *Letters from France* still purport to
provide on-the-spot accounts of up-to-the-minute information. In
her opening letter, Williams repeats the metaphor of the spectacle, in
order to justify her position to her audience:

While you observe from a distance the great drama which is acting, I am a spectator of the representation – I am placed near enough the scene... I shall therefore endeavour to fill up the outline of that picture which France has presented. (1:3:2)

This new collection of letters, however, shifts the focus far away from the woman, the crowds and the misfits of Paris. The author herself moves farther and farther from center-stage in these letters. Volumes III and IV concentrate on various "scenes": the theater of war and the hall of the National Convention. But the central characters of "the great drama" are no longer young lovers or harlequins; they are generals, ministers and princes. Even "Liberty," so recently female, has become a war-like man: "If the genius of Liberty – profaned Liberty! does not arise in his might, and crush those violators of freedom...!" (1:3:6).

The change is signaled in the Advertisement: the earlier volumes, with their claims to immediacy, did not require such a mediated approach to the public. Now we are informed that the author of volumes III and IV must remain anonymous, "for particular reasons," although the reader "will be at no loss to determine from what quarter they proceed."[52] Of course, Helen Maria Williams "authors" only a portion of these two volumes, with John Hurford Stone and Thomas Christie her likely accomplices.[53] But her role in assembling and editing the collection remains a mystery. How much authority could she claim? The anonymity could be explained by the increasingly harsh reception in England of Williams' earlier work. Even her friend Anna Seward castigated Williams in an open letter to the *Gentleman's Magazine* of February 1793. What Seward objected to, in fact, was Williams' obvious *presence* in her early letters, which were "too confident," "so inflated and so pretentious." Seward saw this third volume as a potential "pallinode or harbinger to smooth her [Williams'] reception."[54] More practically, the anonymity of this volume might protect Williams from legal reprisals on both sides of the Channel. As we saw earlier, England's paranoia concerning letters manifested itself that spring in the Traitorous Correspondence Bill, which especially targeted letters from France as well as the "Jacobinical" corresponding societies (such as the Society of Friends, of which Stone and Christie were founding members). But the King's Proclamation Against Seditious Writings, issued in May 1792, would threaten the letter-writers more immediately, condemning as it did "wicked and seditious writings... tending to invite tumult and disorder."[55] At the same time, the increasing hysteria of Robespierre's Committee of Public Safety could seize upon material in these two volumes which criticized the Commune and the violence in Paris. Branded as pro-Jacobin on one side and counter-revolutionary on the other, Williams had every reason to remain anonymous. Nevertheless, if anonymity was meant to protect her, why then did the preface insist that the audience "be at no loss" to recognize the origin of these letters? Surely other readers, like Seward, recognize the origin of these letters? Surely other readers, like Seward, recognized the hand of Helen Maria Williams in these *Letters from France*.

Clearly, political repercussions do not fully explain the anonymity, nor the confusing mixed narratives employed in these two volumes. The text's origins and intentions remain suspicious: it presents several collaborators, each with different intentions, agendas and manners of presentation. Despite the editor's sly assurance, it seems that the letters do proceed from somewhat unfamiliar "quarters." In Williams' characteristic fashion, the letters that subvert a straight-forward reading and demand a second look are inserted within the letters themselves. In the unmentioned and unmentionable appendix, we peek into a fourth "quarter" and read letters of deceit. These letters betray their own intention, and that of the collaboration as well. But before we read them, we need to see the structure they will undermine.

In volumes III and IV, Williams steps back even further than before to watch correspondence at work. The correspondence of politicians and analysts, military men and scholars, rather than that of lovers, draws her attention here. She lets her collaborators "fill in the outline" of a male-dominated world, while inviting her readers to discover the cracks and gaps, the treacherous fictions that emerge from that world. Most of volume III carries a history of the campaign of 1792, written, as she says, "by a person who had the *best* information on the subject that France could afford." Most of volume IV, she tells us, contains "a disquisition concerning the popular topics of the times"; that is, an analysis of French politics. The first collaborator, a military expert, reinforces the "authenticity" of his "modern history" with allusions to the *Iliad*, to Seneca and to Cicero. The second collaborator proposes to "trace the progress of... the French Revolution and to account for the erroneous views in England respecting it" (1:3:155). To do so he repudiates the accounts of journalists and travelers, preferring the abstractions of "HISTORY," an ordered "system" of "parts" and "wholes" (1:3:208–16). If we recognize that these letters play off one another, that they are, in a sense, involved in a correspondence themselves, we will realize that Williams' voice has not surrendered to the voices of "official" history. Rather, these two volumes reject the idea of any single view of events by refracting the events of 1792–3 through several lenses. The letters of the "sentimental" woman journalist thus takes part in history alongside the war reports and the political disquisition.

But the woman's letters correspond with letters of treachery and international intrigue as well. The extra letters of the appendix, the war correspondence of General Dumouriez, complicate our reading of the composed letters of Williams and her friends. They subvert any sense of "authorized history" promoted in the volume, as well as any sense of gendered discourse. Nothing epitomizes the letter's "fall" from innocence more clearly than this appended collection. What we find are letters from France's leading general, a man depicted elsewhere in the volume as a military genius and hero. Unlike the military journalist and the political historian, Dumouriez writes of war and nation in the language of friendship and enthusiasm we identify with the female letter-writer. We follow his enthusiastic reports of victories and his heart-wrenching requests for supplies for his troops. When we read his messages to his colleague Miranda, we too are welcomed into his friendship. We participate in his battles and share his hopes for success:

Here it is that we may well say, Conquer or die! Our intimate friendship will smooth all difficulties – you are my faithful second, and I hope everything from you.

Adieu, my friend, and more than ever my friend – may we always be worthy of each other! and believe that two or three good heads are sufficient to save a republic. (Du Mouriez to Miranda, 11 Feb. and 7 Mar. 1793; 1:3:273 and 278)

Not until the final pages of volume III do we realize that the leader's letters have seduced us. The man we trusted, who invoked the language of sentiment and familiarity, has used these letters to deceive his reader: Dumouriez was found guilty of treason; these letters had served as agents in his plot. By April 1793, the general had sacrificed his troops and fled to the enemy camp. Williams' readers would have known of this treachery even as they read the war correspondence.[56] It is significant, however, that the collaborators' accounts give us no mention of the deceptions wrought by Dumouriez: we must pick them out from between the lines, by placing the letters against the background of contemporary events. To see the deception, we must be aware of the historical context.

We must also be aware of the intersection of deception and sentimentality, of authority and familiarity exposed in volumes III and IV. Taken together, the general's letters fill in the blanks left empty by Williams' collaborators. We find a spy novel in the midst of the epistolary reports. Dumouriez's correspondence introduces the treachery which the 1790s imagined lurking in the form of the letter; it forces us to suspect familiarity as well as authoritative histories. Read without these appended letters, volume III seems to transfer authority from Williams' "feminine" viewpoint to the "expert" witnesses of "official" history. General Dumouriez's deception of Miranda and the French Republic, and the call upon the reader to expose that deception, encourage us to challenge the letters of both "friends" and "officials." An unannounced and intriguing correspondence is set up in these volumes, one which implicates men and women, expertise and sentiment, spectators and actors, writers and readers. As a result of this design, the formula of written history, like the rhetoric of friendship, betrays itself.

Between the misleading letters of the appendix to volume III and the scholarly "disquisition" that fills most of volume IV, the text inserts four letters addressed from Paris. Some indications in volume IV suggest that these letters belong to Williams, and Williams' editor follows this suggestion.[57] The appearance of Latin and Greek in the text, however, hint that Williams, with her limited education, could not be solely responsible. Our doubt is significant: not only authorship and ownership, but gender and individuality are in question (could one letter be the product of two collaborators?). The letter-writer extends our doubt further by discounting her/his own abilities as reporter:

Placed amidst circumstances where the great events that are passing succeed each other so rapidly, that it is almost as difficult to consider them separately, with attention, as it is impossible to calculate their effects, you impose a task on me which I am incapable of fulfilling: for so new and unexpected are they, and so little relation do they bear to the past, that it would be rash to hazard any prediction of the future, from what we now behold. (1:4:74)

This confession upends the privileged position of the individual spectator, established earlier, in volume I:

We are too near the events to consider them with coolness and impartiality; and if you listen to the reports of others, there is such a war of opinions, and indeed, so great a contradiction of facts, that it is impossible at present to trace any true or even probable history of the causes of such an inundation of distress. (1:4:82)

Here we find another caveat to reading these letters: if we look for the single "origin" or "truth" of these various reports, we miss the point. The letters of these two volumes, with their own contradictions and "war of opinions," mirror the world around them. As individual explanations of history, they are limited fictions written within a limiting discourse. Read together, they become actors within an historical context, separate characters brought together to represent the ongoing drama. Because all these rival accounts present themselves as letters, readers are invited to respond, to fill in, to re-evaluate the written stories by the light of a changing history.

Even more letters are mentioned in volumes III and IV than in the previous *Letters from France*, and each mention discloses deception or disillusionment in the realms of power. A bitter remark, early in the letters from the military journalist, establishes the context in which we receive these epistles:

Post after post now fell into the hands of the enemy, and the people were accustomed to see nothing but treason where truth had been reposed. (I:3:73)

Written from the French countryside, these words have added significance for an Englishman writing to a country where mail was searched, confiscated and brought to trial.[58]

In several episodes, suspicion turns inside out as individual citizens accuse public officials of disinformation and shifty transactions. At one point, the letter-writer is cheated of his money by the postmaster/ magistrate in the town of Clermont:

The motives of this municipal officer were so contemptible that indignation would have been misplaced: I therefore laughed at him, making some reflections on the union of his two professions as magistrate and postmaster. (1:3:177)

Postal regulation and law are identical. Both accuse and trap the individual: in this case, the letter-writer is detained and threatened with imprisonment by the scheming official. Other letters reprinted or referred to in this collection expose the oppressiveness of official discourse and its shaky victory over sentimental and individual expression.[59] For example, a Werther-like suicide note, written by the Prince de Ligny, is referred to several times, but never found. The narrator hints that the letter never existed, but that the army created the idea of it in order to boost morale among the troops. Again, the fiction of the sentimental letter serves a political agenda.

Without these inserted tales of letters and without the deceitful letters of Dumouriez, the narrative composition of volumes III and IV would simply "progress" from the details of Williams' story (the first and briefest section) to the events of world history, a movement which seems to push the woman's experience out of the picture. Just so does *Marat Assassiné* seem to overwrite the sentimental heroine with the public hero. But the hidden and the unexpected intrigue of the letter continually throws into doubt the "official" story. The unnamed but recognizable author of these volumes, like Charlotte Corday in the painting, has made the historical "moment" into a question of correspondence. Under Williams' management, the epistolary form, to borrow from Jean Rousset, "frees itself from history conceived as a series of events, of which human beings are the agents or victims."[60] By 1793, Helen Maria Williams composes her letters – and arranges others' – with an awareness that "the events" she will emphasize are the activities of letters themselves and the effect produced by means of letters.[61] This shift from linear history to self-conscious correspondence depends upon yet subverts the strategies of epistolary fiction. It also revolutionizes our concept of written history.

LETTERS IN HISTORY

We are too near the events to consider them with coolness or impartiality ... it is impossible at present to trace any true or even probable history of the causes of such an inundation of distress. (1:4:72)

In the last volumes of the *Letters From France*, Helen Maria Williams continually points to letters as the substance from which history is made. Rather than locating the truth of origins and individual motives, she tracks the restless movement of Dumouriez's treason; for instance, Williams explicitly discounts the search for "cause" or "intention." She challenges "those who are fond of looking for more causes than are necessary to explain the effects" (1:4:95). The search for clear linear progression only leads to the claim that Dumouriez's treason was "the result of great deliberation, and connected with other plans of treachery and counter-revolution." According to this interpretation, treason would begin with Dumouriez's single intention to be treasonous: the individual's own deliberations connect him to conspiracy. Williams offers an alternative explanation, based on the general's letters: "[S]ince I have seen his confidential letters... what has long appeared to me the *true cause* is now perfect conviction" (1:4:96; my emphasis).

Williams grounds her conviction in the circumstances and the effects of Dumouriez's correspondence. She insists upon the significant difference between the general's letters from the Low Countries, written to the minister of war, and his letters from Paris, written to Miranda. She reminds us that Dumouriez's open letter to the National Convention had been suppressed against his will, and that he published the letter privately in Brabant. In reconstructing the circumstances of these letters – places, times, audience and political pressures – Williams de-emphasizes their content, shifting the "true cause" away from Dumouriez's "intention." What happens *to* letters, and *through* letters, rather than *in* letters, demonstrates the political machinery at work.

Close attention to Dumouriez's letters thus turns attention outward, from the traitor to the state of France:

I mark in his correspondence the progress of his crimes... When this correspondence is published... it will appear to the world, that of this treason the detested faction of the Mountain and the Jacobins have been the original authors. (1:4:14)

Once again, originating authority is displaced. Dumouriez's crimes, traced through his letters, have been authored by a repressive government. All of a sudden, the letters no longer reveal Dumouriez's treason. Their content is insignificant. Rather, the letters stand as evidence of the constraints placed upon the individual by the established power of the state. The spotlight swerves away from the individual's thoughts to the political structure. The "private" letter turns inside out.

The letters of Williams' later volumes provide an antidote to the *lettres de cachet* which haunt the story of the French Revolution. Whereas the unseen *lettre de cachet* symbolizes the secret workings of an incontestable and imprisoning law, these new letters, the material evidence of historical change, expose the workings of the law and remove the individual from dangerous, solitary confinement. In volume VI, Williams tells the story of one old aristocrat in prison. He, who had once been renowed as a merciless employer of the *lettre de cachet*, has taken to writing other letters from his cell. His letters are sent out to the *émigrés* princes of France, now assembled in Koblentz, inviting them to join their old colleague for dinner – in prison. Amidst such curious ironies, the pattern of oppression is inverted (II:6:23).

To appreciate this reversal in the letter's function in the *Letters from France*, we should recall Williams' own circumstances in Paris in 1793, as well as the ideological status of the letter at the time. Doubts about ownership and intention in the letter may be products of epistolary form;[62] but for Williams and many of her contemporaries, these unsettling questions also rose from particular social and political conditions. Williams, for instance, complained that her letters had been taken away from her. Printed without her consent, they provided ammunition against her both in England and France:

I had written to my friends in England, a few letters about the period of the Terror, and unfortunately, someone had the imprudence to insert extracts from them in the London journals. This indiscretion compromised my status in the eyes of the Committee of Public Safety, and this awful band began to direct its attention to me.[63]

Even as her friends betrayed her private correspondence, so was her published correspondence appropriated and distorted: Robespierre's Committee of Public Safety translated entire passages from her first two volumes of *Letters*, which had appeared in British journals.

In the meantime, British newspapers came regularly to the committee of public safety, in which passages from my letters were frequently transcribed and the work mentioned as mine; and those papers were constantly translated into French for the members of the committee... Thus I passed the winter at Paris, with the knife of the guillotine suspended over me by a frail thread. (II:6:173–4)

Excerpted, transcribed, translated, destroyed or thrown into the hands of searching police, her letters were at the mercy of forces which Williams could not control.

It is not surprising that Williams' later letters turn attention away from content and intent and toward the circumstances of letter-writing. When and where were letters written? For whom? Were they delivered? Were they intercepted? Destroyed? Published? And how? These questions, which recur with greater insistence throughout the *Letters from France*, stem from Williams' own experience: for a while, the only control she had over her letters was to destroy them. On one occasion, she describes eluding her police guard in order to find and burn "enormous piles of papers, whose discovery would have been fatal for us...notes [and] letters of...correspondents and conspirators."[64]

Among these conspirators and correspondents would have been found Jean-Jacques Brissot and Manon de Roland, as well as John Hurford Stone, Williams' companion. As we have seen, Stone also was the victim of his own letters (see chap. 1). In a letter to the English radical, Horne Tooke, John Stone typifies the doublebind he, Williams and their correspondents must have encountered in writing:

The circumstances of the two countries have hitherto prevented me from giving or receiving any information respecting you, for as there have been few or no other means of communication than the post, I have had the traitorous correspondence bill too much before my eyes, to hazard your tranquility, though I have nothing to fear for my own. Paris, 25 nïvose (15 January) Second year of the Republic 1794.[65]

Circumstances, laws and the means of communication occupy the letter-writer. The double-dating (Jacobin and English) shows Stone's care to accommodate both sides. Little did he suspect ("I have nothing to fear") that this letter would find its way into the annals of *State Trials* (xxv) and into the *Anti-Jacobin Review* (9 April 1797).[66] Clearly, letter-writers could not hope to control the movements and directions of their letters.

Letters could and would be used against the writer and reader in a court of law, in France as well as England. When, with the passing of the Traitorous Correspondence Bill and the Gagging Acts, letters turned state's evidence, and when, with the various Stamp Acts, letters funded the war, a writer in Williams' position would understand that her letters no longer belonged to her, or to her intended audience: they had been appropriated by law and politics. Williams' strategy, however, turns this appropriation to her own advantage. If the letters do not belong to her, then she is off the hook: she is no longer the subject of self-dramatization, nor is she the object of the reader's scrutiny. Since the letter belongs to the state, English or French, it will dramatize the movements and motives of the State. Williams takes the letters which would have incriminated her and, by

discarding notions of personality and intention, turns letters into
evidence against the law. Her use of these letters as the substance of
her history turns them, ultimately, into agents for change.

Letters form the object of William's attention throughout her
Letters from France, as we have seen in the early volumes. In the
"Memoir de Mons. du F." and his wife, and in the tale of Madeleine
and Auguste, the letters within did point out barriers to communication and individual happiness; but they did not themselves
overcome the barriers. In both cases, the lovers waited for the
Revolution to destroy the *ancien régime* and destroy the need for
letters. After the events of 1793 and 1794, and after the explosion of
self-consciousness and political awareness in volumes III and IV,
Williams relies on letters not only to point out, but, in fact, to override
obstruction.

Letters, once thematized, are now activated as instruments of
change. Like a *deus ex machina*, the letter arrives to subvert the
certainty of death and the limits of law. Williams testifies to the life-
giving power of the letter, when she describes her return to writing
letters, after her exile in Switzerland: "After so long a suspension of
our correspondence, after a silence like that of death, and a separation
which...seemed as final as if we had been divided by the limits of
'that country from whose bourn no traveller returns,' with what
gratified pleasure did I recognize your hand-writing, with what
eagerness did I break the seal of your welcome letter" (II:5:2).
Elsewhere, a "Letter to the Constituents" arrives from the deputies
of the National Assembly, in an effort to rally "the People" to
dispense with "the usual formalities" and "the barriers" of the
established law.[67] Choosing the public letter as the most effective
means of "proclaim[ing] to the whole republic the hateful scenes of
which they have been the witnesses and victims," the deputies expose
the measures which had been used by the Terror to silence them:
"the barriers of the city were shut, all communication cut off, the
secrecy of letters violated, the hall of the convention blockaded by an
armed force, etc." (II:5:262–3). In a gesture which circumvents both
death and rigorous law, a minister of justice writes to the National
Convention an extraordinary letter granting the reprieve of an
innocent prisoner. "His letter had not been half-read before the hall
resounded, and with the cry of 'reprieve!' rushed to the scaffold...
[D]ispensing with the usual formalities...great numbers of the
deputies rushed out to stop the execution" (II:5:26).

Among the letters Williams enlists are several written from prisoners or to prisoners. Often these letters have been hidden from the authorities, and Williams details their secret movements. These messages, passed in captivity against great odds, signal both actual and symbolic deliverance. She mentions all the "little artifices" used "to cheat the watchful severity of jailers." At the prison of the Abbaye, prisoners scribbled in code on their linen, which was sent home for laundering. At other prisons, other subversions took place:

Sometimes pieces of paper carelessly torn, and sent at different periods wrapped round fruit or vegetables, when the scattered scraps were rejoined by the prisoner, communicated the tidings he was most anxious to hear. Sometimes a tender billet was found inclosed within a roasted fowl. But one of the pious frauds most successfully employed was the agency of a dog. (II: 7: 188)

This dog paid daily visits to a man in prison, then returned home to the prisoner's wife, who

caressed the dog... with the same emotion with which Werther gazed upon the ragged little boy whom he sent to see Charlotte... At length, the idea suggested itself to the woman of enclosing a billet within the dog's collar... in defiance of revolutionary edicts. (II: 7: 189)

By an almost silly permutation, the sentimental letters of Goethe's *Young Werther* lend themselves to the subterfuge of the prisoner's wife. Williams suggests that epistolary fiction has prompted this last bit of epistolary ingenuity; at the same time, she implicates epistolary fiction in actual contemporary intrigue.

Williams associates the triumph of these "letters against all odds" with liberation from the oppression of Robespierre's tyranny. But she also places them within the discussion of liberation from literary convention and from restrictive notions of communication. The letter now symbolizes expression which breaks free of restrictions. Williams' attention to the ways and means of communicating Robespierre's fall on the ninth of Thermidor epitomize her faith in marginalized, even outlawed channels of information. The news is not told us directly: instead Williams' technique allows us to receive the news from the perspective of prisoners in Paris.

Alerted by the threatening ring of the tocsin bell, the prisoners first "sought to read their fate in the countenance of their jailors." Still ignorant of the event, some prisoners "procure[d] [illicit] newspapers at an enormous price." Others, who worked as guards, "contrived to tell the prisoners in monosyllables breathed in whispers (for all intercourse between the guards and prisoners was sternly forbidden)." Elsewhere, in other prisons,

they were informed of what was passing, by women who displayed upon the roofs of houses, which overlooked at a distance the prison walls, the names of Robespierre and his associates, written in such broad characters that the prisoners, with the aid of glasses could read them plainly; and after presenting the name, the generous informer shewed by expressive gestures, that the head of him who bore that name had fallen. (II:7:179–80)

These ingenious sign systems, which overcome the restrictions placed on human interchange, encourage and extend Williams' own experiments with materials and structures of correspondence.

The transformation from authorized history to a woman's history in letters recurs throughout the later volumes of the *Letters from France*. Consider Williams' apology for including a rather long-winded letter from a male friend, a poet, who details the conditions in Paris prisons (II:6:118ff). She points out the differences between his writing and her own: his "style of compliments," she owns, "would have led me to omit the poetry [included], if it did not *belong to the history of the letter* [now in Williams' possession]. Besides, *fiction* is the privilege of poets" (II:6:118–19n. My emphasis). In other words, the history of the letter exposes the fiction of male pretensions, even as it overruns the hierarchy of genres. This man's story, fortified as it is with classical antecedents (Virgil, Sallust), with cavalier poetry and military hymns belongs, ultimately, to women's writing: "the history of the letter."

The later letters showcase women who write challenging, history-making letters. The women who spell out Robespierre's name on the roof join the likes of Charlotte Corday, Madame de Sillery and Madame de Roland in Williams' epistolary history. When Charlotte Corday appears in volume v, for example, Williams discusses her murder of Marat in four sentences; she then devotes nearly eight pages to Corday's literary background, her public statements and, finally, to the moving letters Corday wrote as her last testament (II:5:128–35). Williams carefully deflects attention away from the deceptive letter of her crime (the letter sent to Marat) and towards the letters of her frank self-justification, and her denunciation of the Terror. Similarly, the political influence of Madame de Roland, a friend Williams cites frequently, realizes itself in her letters. Some of Roland's correspondence Williams claims to have burned, their outlaw status so strong that "to have had them discovered was certain death" (1:6:266). Indeed Roland, like Williams, was renowned in Paris for her published letters, which were usually biting indictments first of the royalists, then of the Parisian Jacobins. In the extracts from her writings which Williams does preserve and include, the Girondin heroine takes credit for her husband's infamous 1792 letter to Louis XVI, which sparked the rupture between the moderate Gironde and Robespierre's faction, the Montagne: "I composed this letter myself, which was written without much meditation. He [Minister of the Interior Roland] carried it to the council to read it aloud..." (II:6:260).[68] Accordingly, Madame de Roland complains of the cowardice of the other Girondin ministers, who balked at composing a letter to the king. Because of this failure, Roland maintains, they were overcome: "I could never have believed...that judgement and firmness of character were so rare...among men" (II:6:262-3). To write a political letter, in Roland's terms, is an act of "courage" worthy of "applause." Like Jeanne d'Arc, the woman writer takes action: she replaces the passive heroines of sentimental fiction, having gained, in Williams' eyes, an independence from the men who surround her. With sly irony, Williams juxtaposes Roland's forceful message with a pair of letters from prison, both from a young husband to his wife, written the night before his execution. The resignation and impotence of his pale letters (they never reach his wife) accentuate the confident tone of the effective woman letter-writer.

Along with the re-evaluation of the role of the woman in letters, the transformation from the sentimental to the political introduces a radical version of written history. Having confronted the fiction of letters, Williams opens the epistolary text to the context of current events. The barriers to communication, the deceptions and seductions, are no longer allegories, as they were in the "Memoir de Mons. du F." Instead, the later *Letters from France* create a story which directs our attention to the actual, material structures regulating correspondence, at a period when *all* correspondence was public – and political.

Williams' work has been accused of logical inconsistencies and repetitiveness, not to mention triviality.[69] Accusations such as these demonstrate the limitations of linear reading. They also point out the difficulty in defining Williams' work as "history" or "fiction." In fact, her work is neither; but the generic lines have been drawn and

Williams' *Letters* remain in a no man's land. What frustrates the historian would bring accolades from the literary critic if Williams' account were epistolary fiction. The beauty of such fictions depends upon the discontinuities, repetitions and improprieties history deplores. Letters in the novel give a form to chance and change:

[They] enhance an organizational structure of which the dominant note is the intersection of lines, fragmentation of discourse, ruptures of tone, continual displacement of point of view. We are far from the "uniformity of tone" and of classical homogeneity. Time itself is "disarticulated"...letters jump out to provoke sudden stops, returns, leaps and progressions on many parallel planes ... It's the triumph of the broken and sinuous line.[70]

Originally, the aesthetic of displacement and heterogeneity in letter fiction developed from an attempt to represent the movement of actual letters between individuals.[71] As it developed, the temporal, tonal and causal confusion of epistolary "reality" became so stylized that it created masterpieces of artifice, such as *Julie ou la Nouvelle Héloïse* and *Dangerous Liaisons*. Helen Maria Williams, however, returns to this *fragmentation du discours* in order to counteract the "homogeneity" of political fictions and to transmit her impressions of a *temps désarticulé*. She transfers the conventions of epistolary fiction into epistolary history.

To create a heterogeneous medley of voices, and a formal disorientation in her work, Williams juxtaposes letters and stories from various areas in France: Paris, Rouen, Orléans, Toulouse, Verdun. She inserts narratives from the distant and recent past into her own eye-witness accounts. First-, second- and third-person tales, legal documents and personal letters all overlap, and in overlapping, transform each other, as if adding a new lens to our vision. The lines of demarcation, the boundaries between these voices do not erase each other. Nor does one letter or account emerge to give the definitive perspective on an event. Rather, as in a mosaic, each segment depends on the surrounding pieces to give it significance in the larger pattern.

As they move from volume I to volume VIII, the *Letters from France* grow increasingly less self-reflective and more kaleidoscopic in their composition. Williams opens the windows of the memoir-letter and incorporates the many correspondents, the heterogeneity and multivocality of an epistolary novel. By doing so, she reveals the revolutionary rhetoric implicit in correspondence. Thus the discontinuities, repetitions and fragmentations of Williams' sentimental discourse are not accidental. Used in the context of revolution, they actually participate in Williams' strategy to "translate" the French experience to her English audience. Like the internalized letters, the discontinuities of the narrative call attention to the obstructing barriers of law, government, social convention, national identity and language. As the *Letters* move beyond the initial moment of ecstasy, time, place and identity lose their clear definitions and surrender to the epistolary movement. Time, place and identity cannot rest secure in a period of revolution.

The historical context of these letters, the events and politics of the French Revolution, compete with the "vortex" of sentimental experience and draw Williams and her readers out of a narrowly defined "feminine" discourse. The tidy packages and discrete moments of sensibility give way to a less orderly, less introspective account of the Revolution: letters escape their envelopes and the individual woman, Helen Maria Williams, no longer offers herself for public scrutiny. When she arrived in this strange, new world, and added her voice to the cries of the French people chanting, "Vive la nation!", Williams stepped away from a discourse of internalized experience and toward participation in political and social history.

CHAPTER 4

Mary Wollstonecraft and the business of letters

Helen Maria Williams' *Letters from France* invert the structure of the *lettre de cachet*, the hidden letter of absolute law which had imprisoned, in the Bastille and elsewhere, innumerable helpless individuals. As she manipulates her letters – and the letters within her letters – into the stuff of history, they expose the operations and constraints of formal institutions in France and England: the prisons, the army, the revolutionary government, the law. At the same time, these letters remove the private individual, the letter-writer, from public scrutiny and from culpability.

When Mary Wollstonecraft turns to the epistolary form, in her *Letters Written During a Short Residence in Sweden, Norway and Denmark*, she too transforms the familiar letter into a public critique. The inside-out reversals of Williams' strategy, however, do not characterize Wollstonecraft's use of the letter. Instead, the *Letters from Sweden* operate on a principle of variety and fluidity; they bank on circulation. Nor do these letters wholly abandon the dynamic of the familiar and sentimental letter. In an effort to engage the reader's sympathy, Wollstonecraft's letters exploit the conventional voice and posture of the "feminine" letter-writer. A single mother, distant from and perhaps forgotten by the "friend" of her correspondence, Wollstonecraft's letter-writer tugs at our heartstrings. At the same time, however, the figure of the vulnerable sentimental heroine plays against that of the solitary wanderer and philosopher, thereby revising the rhetoric of each. For the voice in these letters also belongs to a woman at the forefront of contemporary debates in political philosophy, a woman recognized for her incisive social criticism. Wollstonecraft's juxtaposition of reverie and commentary, of "female sensibility" and "masculine understanding," allows the reader to remark the parallels between two seemingly disparate world views. What arises to unite them is Wollstonecraft's Romantic version of "imagination," a discourse which reconciles heroine and philosopher, feeling and reason, writer and reader in a productive enterprise.

This interplay between the feeling woman and the acute thinker has occupied most of the critical commentary on Wollstonecraft's *Letters from Sweden*.[1] I would like to deflect attention from this particular tension in order to investigate a wider variety of roles imagined by the letter-writer in this text. The tensions at work in the *Letters from Sweden* extend beyond the gendered categories of feeling and thought into the realms of politics, economics and community. Wollstonecraft's use of the letter invokes not simply the sentimental memoir and the philosophical essay, but also the "open letter" of political controversy, the travel letter and the letter of advertisement. Intimacy and publicity, as much as feeling and thought, form the coordinates for our reading of these letters.

Underwriting all these relationships, authorizing all this correspondence, are the business of letters and Wollstonecraft's role as enterprising writer. The epistolary voice in *Letters from Sweden* also belongs to a woman who is conducting difficult transactions with commercial and government "agents," and reporting back to their associate, her "friend."[2] And the book is the work of an unmarried woman writer in need of money to support herself and her daughter. Despite the echoes of epistolary fiction, travel literature and Rousseauian reverie, the *Letters from Sweden* remain, first and foremost, letters written within and against the demands of "business." For Wollstonecraft, imaginative correspondence is, inevitably, a function of commerce.

I would like to push this last point a bit further. Behind Wollstonecraft's journey to Scandinavia lies the practice of traitorous correspondence itself: "correspondence" here taken in its legal sense as "commercial communication."[3] The Traitorous Correspondence Bill, passed in 1793, named "anyone supplying France or Frenchmen" with vital goods, including "any form of money, provisions or clothing" as "a traitor to be punished by Death."[4] Such was the business for which Gilbert Imlay had recruited Mary Wollstonecraft as agent and possibly as his safe "cover." Together with his contacts in Scandinavia and Hamburg, Imlay was involved in blockade-running, "a business undertaken by British and American sympathizers with France [via the neutral northern ports]...which was, strictly speaking 'traiterous correspondence' with the enemy."[5] In

1794, Imlay had purchased a boat in France, filled it with a remarkably valuable cargo of French silver and plate, hired a young Norwegian captain to sail the ship to Gothenburg, and reregistered the French *Liberté* as a neutral, Norwegian ship. (The ship's new name, the *Maria and Margaretha*, converted the names of Wollstonecraft and her maid, Marguerite, into a banner of safe passage for the illicit vehicle.)[6] With the French money, possibly acquired with the aid of Thomas Christie (J. H. Stone and Helen Williams' collaborator), Imlay probably meant to purchase naval construction materials to be brought back to Le Havre, where he then resided with Wollstonecraft. But the ship and the silver disappeared outside Arendal: the ship reported sunk, the cargo hijacked. Someone had done an end-run around the blockade-runners. Imlay suspected a doubly treacherous exchange at work and sent Wollstonecraft to act as his legal representative in his suit against the ship's captain. According to the document drawn up by Imlay on this occasion, "Mary Imlay, my best friend and wife," was "to take sole management of my affairs and business" in Scandinavia.[7]

There is a considerable amount of renaming and rerouting in this story, as channels of communication and commerce, legal and extra-legal, cross and un-cross. Positioned as the switchboard through which this subterfuge must sort itself out, Wollstonecraft has every reason to imagine her identity and her own correspondence taken out of her hands and exchanged by others. The *Letters from Sweden*, however, allow her to venture into the realm of correspondence on her own terms. In Wollstonecraft's text we find more designs against Imlay's business. Like the lost *Maria and Margaretha*, the story of traitorous correspondences remains submerged in Wollstonecraft's text. The impetus for her journey and her relationship to her correspondent stand as the two frustrating ellipses of the *Letters*.[8] Wollstonecraft's trip to Scandinavia indicates how, like valuable cargo, the very idea of "correspondence" has been hijacked for use by lawyers and merchants, entrepreneurs and legislators. Wollstonecraft wants to steer correspondence back into the realm of personal relationships and social formation. The *Letters from Sweden* deliberately represent Imlay's envoy as a female letter-writer, and they redirect her travels into a journey of social progress. But Wollstonecraft also wants to profit from these transactions. She writes the *Letters from Sweden* to regain financial *Liberté* from Imlay: "now I am writing for independence," she brags to Hamilton Rowan.[9] In her epistolary run around commerce, she ends up playing the very game she wants to avoid.

Traveling between the two spheres of "home" and "business," the letter-writer claims allegiance to neither. Instead she appeals to an imagined and imaginative community, one which would free her from a domestic economy and provide a productive alternative to a capital-industrial-based society. The countries of Sweden, Norway and Denmark stand as an appropriate backdrop for this enterprise: in the eyes of the traveler, they seem poised at the threshold between feudal and industrial societies, between monarchy and democracy, between superstition and enlightenment.[10] The flaws and virtues of each system compete for the writer's attention throughout her trip. More importantly, in 1793 the northern kingdoms had announced themselves as "neutral" in the war between France and England. For Wollstonecraft's purposes, they provided an imaginary middle ground, a distant region on which to play out conflicts closer to home: Sweden's King Gustav III had been murdered in 1792 by a liberal intelligentsia; and A. P. Bernstorff, Prime Minister of Denmark-Norway, was introducing Enlightenment reforms under an otherwise despotic monarchy headed by an imbecile king.[11] The parallels to conditions in France and England must have been compelling for both Wollstonecraft and her audience.

Those parallels also remain, for the most part, unstated and submerged in the text. On the surface of the letters, we follow the restless imagination of the traveler, as it circulates through various cultural, political and economic structures. It is no coincidence that the book begins and ends in moments of flux and transition: Wollstonecraft frames her work with boat scenes (perhaps another appropriation of Imlay's material), and refers frequently to images of movement and flight. The reader's identification with her wandering thoughts therefore grounds these letters and anchors the epistolary exchange. In the course of the journey, the alliance of writer and reader eventually replaces both the sentimental and the economic demands which once bound the letter-writer to her unnamed "friend." In that very public alliance we discover the political power of the *Letters from Sweden*. By the end of the correspondence, Wollstonecraft's letter-writer clearly responds to the demands of her imagined public, not to a unique "friend," nominal "husband" or lover.[12]

That alliance introduces its own compromises, however. For

Wollstonecraft, the letter seems to offer a form which moves outside and around the limits of oppressive or destructive structures – literary structures as well as social. Stepping outside the narrow circle of home, family and "female" identity, Wollstonecraft asks her audience to join her in a sustained critique of the "commercial machinery" of a growing capitalist society. It becomes apparent, however, that the letters themselves, and especially the persona of the letter-writer, participate in the fictions produced by that very machinery. It is men's business and her own "trickiness" that allow Wollstonecraft to break her ties to home, family and romance; it is speculation that leads her to imagine her own independence; it is financial need and her knowledge of the market that encourage her to transform her private letters into these published *Letters from Sweden*.

We will look first at this transformation from the personal to the public and social letter, then examine the competing discourses Wollstonecraft invokes to revise the fiction of a woman's correspondence. Finally, we will question the assumptions behind this sometimes tricky, sometimes treacherous, revision and consider its consequences for women of public letters.

REREADING "WOMANLY" LETTERS

Responding to the intimate tone of these letters, critical assessment has tended to separate the "poetic reverie" from the political commentary of the work, treating them as unrelated aspects of a remarkably active "mind." In fact, the two are inextricable. "Reverie" fuels Wollstonecraft's critique; imagination has a political role. Yet not surprisingly, greater favor and attention have fallen upon the "personal," "sentimental" and "womanly" features of these letters – the "poetic" or "lyric" passages.[13] Readers' responses to the *Letters from Sweden* have followed the lead of Wollstonecraft's contemporary, Amelia Alderson Opie, who found that "the cold awe which the *philosopher* had excited" in Wollstonecraft's earlier writing "was lost in the tender sympathies called forth by the *woman*."[14] This dichotomy severely limits the writer's scope: she may play either philosopher *or* woman, not both. In other words, if Wollstonecraft no longer employs the radical polemics of her *Vindications*, then she must be occupied with more "womanly" concerns in these letters. I would suggest that the letter form suited Wollstonecraft's talent and her rhetorical aims better than the systematic argument of the *Vindication*. When we avoid the inclination to read the letter as an intimate, sentimental and properly "feminine" genre, we can see that Wollstonecraft is testing a new rhetorical strategy for her political philosophy. The *Letters from Sweden* do not copy or even expand upon the private correspondence between Wollstonecraft and her lover, Gilbert Imlay. Rather, they deliberately rewrite and replace the love letters, transforming Wollstonecraft's emotional dependence and personal grief into a public confrontation with social corruption. (It is significant, for example, that Wollstonecraft's contemporary audience had no idea that she wrote these letters during a period between two suicide attempts.)[15]

In the final months of working on the *Letters from Sweden*, Mary Wollstonecraft requested from her two former lovers, Imlay and Henry Fuseli, all the letters she had written them. Imlay complied immediately; Fuseli refused.[16] Comparing the text of the *Letters from Sweden* with her letters written to Imlay, we can see the significance of Wollstonecraft's reappropriation of her correspondence. The published letters actually have more in common with the journal she kept during the trip than with Wollstonecraft's personal correspondence. Nevertheless, she chooses to keep the façade of personal letters, and she does repeat several passages verbatim from her private notes to Imlay.[17] We must be cautious, moreover, in identifying the differences between the two sets of letters, since the only extant version of the love letters has been carefully edited, with obvious deletions and unknown additions, by William Godwin.[18] We might say that Godwin edits one fiction of Wollstonecraft's letters, Wollstonecraft herself edits another. Nonetheless, several important features do differentiate the *Letters from Sweden* from the set of letters written to Imlay during that trip. First, the *Letters from Sweden* contain public, or "outward-looking" passages of social commentary and natural description, whereas the letters to Imlay focus almost exclusively on the writer's anguish and on questions about the future of the love affair. In the love letters, the central characters are Wollstonecraft, Imlay and Fanny, their daughter; few others intrude into this tight family circle. By contrast, the *Letters from Sweden* include a broad cast of characters encountered during Wollstonecraft's travels.

Furthermore, in place of economic and sociological reports, the letters to Imlay keep an obsessive account of the correspondence itself: nearly every letter reckons the number of letters sent, the number of posts arrived without a response, the time interval between letters, and the emotional weight of each message. Throughout, the writer's dependence on her correspondent is made painfully clear:

continue to write (I want this support) till you are sure I am where I cannot expect a letter... Do write by every occasion! I am anxious to hear how your affairs go on; and, still more, to be convinced that you are not separating yourself from us.[19]

Once, after four mail deliveries pass with no word from her lover, Wollstonecraft cries, "This silence is a refinement on cruelty."[20] And elsewhere: "The post is again arrived; I have sent to seek for letters, only to be wounded to the soul by a negative. – My brain seems on fire."[21] But even the letters she receives distress her:

I feel I cannot endure the anguish of corresponding with you – if we are only to correspond. No; if you will seek for happiness elsewhere, my letters shall not interrupt your repose. I will be dead to you.[22]

For the abandoned woman, traveling alone, letters form a lifeline, but one which evaporates even as she writes. As her emotional pain increases, so do reports of frail health. As Imlay grows more distant, she clings all the more to her infant child. An explicit deathwish recurs throughout her letters to Imlay.[23] Wollstonecraft had tried suicide that spring and Imlay had arranged the summer trip, in part, as a sort of therapy for her extreme depression. In her letters to him, Wollstonecraft claims that only her attachment to her daughter keeps her from another suicide attempt.

The tremendous emotional value attached to the exchange of love letters disappears in the *Letters from Sweden*, despite the book's intimate tone. In the *Letters*, her epistolary obsession is conquered. The writer has no anxiety about her correspondent's reciprocation. She does not need emotional reassurance. A dignified, if modified, autonomy replaces the desperate pleas to her lover to commit himself to her and her child. The equanimity evident only in the last of her private letters pervades the whole of the published revision. Many examples exist, but I will point only to two particular passages. In these, Wollstonecraft consciously reworks the struggle for control, so evident in the love letters, into a picture of self-reliance.

Upon her arrival in Gothenburg, early in the trip, Wollstonecraft writes to Imlay that she fell on the rocks and suffered excessively:

"how I escaped with my life, I can scarcely guess. I was in a stupour for a quarter of an hour...the contusion is great and my brain confused." Followed by a long carriage ride in the rain, her accident "sufficiently deranged" her.[24] No report of this fall, nor of her subsequent periods of "derangement," survive in the *Letters from Sweden.* On the contrary, Wollstonecraft's arrival in Norway is marked by her courage and self-reliance. Forcing her will upon a weak captain and reluctant crew, she finally commandeers a boat to shore. She receives a warm welcome in a Norwegian cottage, where she accepts due respect as a "lady" and a "woman of observation" (*LWS*, pp. 13–15). Moreover, her first walk upon the rocks brings no debilitating accident. Rather, she reports: "How peaceful was the scene. I gazed around with rapture, and felt more of that spontaneous pleasure which gives credibility to our expectations of happiness, than I had for a long, long, time" (*LWS*, p. 14). This strength of character and easy relaxation in nature set the tone for the rest of Wollstonecraft's *Letters from Sweden.*

Even when she repeats disheartened remarks from her love letters, she refashions them into evidence of courage and mental strength. On her way to Norway, she initially writes to Imlay complaining of the weather and her desolation. She quotes *King Lear*: "'When the mind's free, the body's delicate'; mine has been too much hurt to regard trifles."[25] She laments the loss of her mental powers, the loss of her youth:

How am I altered by disappointment! – When going to ___ [Lisbon], ten years ago, the elasticity of my mind was sufficient to ward off weariness, and my imagination could still dip her brush in the rainbow of fancy, and sketch futurity in glowing colours. Now I am going North in search of sunbeams! – Will any ever warm this desolated heart? All nature seems to frown – or rather mourn with me. Everything is cold, cold as my expectations![26]

Both the quote from *Lear* and the "How am I altered" lament reappear at a later moment in the *Letters from Sweden* – but with their conclusion switched:

When going to Lisbon, the elasticity of my mind was sufficient to ward off weariness, and my imagination still could dip her brush in the rainbow of fancy, and sketch futurity in glowing colours. Now – but let me talk of something else – will you go with me to the Cascade? (*LWS*, p. 131).

The "Cascade" is the falls of Tonsberg, and there Wollstonecraft dips her brush to paint an image of awesome grandeur. Her confrontation with death, suggested by the falls, produces a description of sublimity which anticipates Wordsworth's experience at the Simplon Pass (1805 *Prelude*, Bk. VI, lines 556–72).

My soul rose, with renewed dignity, above its cares – grasping at immortality – it seemed as impossible to stop the current of my thoughts, as of the always varying, still the same, torrent before me – I stretched out my hand to eternity, bounding over the dark speck of life to come. (*LWS*, p. 133).

In Wollstonecraft's description, we see an explicit turn from the peevish tone of her letter to Imlay: "Now – but let me talk of something else…" And we receive an overt invitation to an imaginative adventure: "will you go with me to the Cascade?" As if conscious of her control and talent, Wollstonecraft transforms complaint into a realization of her own power. Unlike the letters to Imlay, the *Letters from Sweden* display a woman apparently in control of the epistolary exchange, aware of the world around her, and conscious of the power of her mind and pen.

The transformation of her love letters is not the only revision Wollstonecraft performs in this text. Earlier, I described the writer's autonomy in the *Letters from Sweden* as dignified, if modified. That modification is a rejection of isolated individualism, a rejection crucial to the dynamics of the *Letters*. If we compare this work with another obvious "pre-text," Rousseau's *Reveries of a Solitary Walker*, we can see that Wollstonecraft echoes, then corrects, Rousseau's "expansive" ego. She socializes his solipsistic imaginings by inscribing them within the form of a letter to a friend.

As another stage in Wollstonecraft's lifelong dialogue with the works of Rousseau, the *Letters from Sweden* replay the themes of the solitary walker: the search for the source of human happiness, the stoic rejection of material goods, the ecstatic embrace of nature, and the essential role of sentiment in understanding. "We reason deeply, when we forcibly feel," Wollstonecraft asserts in a condensation of Rousseau's "immutable rule." Rousseau himself aimed to follow only "the principles adopted by my reason, confirmed by my heart, and which carry the seal of inner assent in the silence of the passions."[27] The *Letters from Sweden* offer more than an echo of Rousseau's themes, however. Their "desultory" mode of argument, their homeless protagonist, their recurrent flights of reverie and troubled questions ("human happiness – where, oh! where does it reside?") all point directly to the influence of the *Reveries*. In fact, several passages in the *Letters* seem to emulate episodes in the *Reveries*. Like the Solitary Walker, Wollstonecraft "botanizes" during her own promenades (*LWS*, pp. 13, 37 and 40); like him, she praises Linnaeus (*LWS*, p. 40).[28] A peaceful boat ride, where she is "carried away by the current, indulging a pleasing forgetfulness" (*LWS*, p. 76), calls to mind Rousseau's aimless navigations on the Lac de Bienne.[29] In both the *Letters* and the *Reveries*, the sight of a family of cottagers touches the heart of the wanderer and forces a sigh.[30]

Yet Wollstonecraft is not content to copy. If she echoes Rousseau's Solitary Walker, she does so in order to critique his isolation and egocentrism. The touching scene of family togetherness in the *Reveries* is placed within Rousseau's justification for abandoning his own children. For the father *manqué*, the peasant family just "had something – I know not what – which touched my heart...and I felt myself sigh without knowing why."[31] Wollstonecraft, faced with a similar scene, knows precisely her connection and the source of her emotion: "My eyes followed them to the cottage, and an involuntary sigh whispered to my heart, that I envied the mother. I was returning to my babe, who may never experience a father's care or tenderness. The bosom that nurtured her, heaved with a pang...only an unhappy mother could feel" (*LWS*, p 141). Where Rousseau mystifies the scene, then runs away from the villagers, Wollstonecraft asserts her connection with them, and with her own child.

Her critique of the Solitary Walker extends beyond the standard denunciation of the irresponsible father, however. The *Letters* take the solitary's walk away from a solipsistic island and into a progressive society. Two passages from the *Letters* and *Reveries* which parallel each other also emphasize Wollstonecraft's departure from her model. In his Seventh Promenade, Rousseau ventures into a dense forest of "black pines" mixed with "prodigious beeches" and circled by craggy rocks.[32] In this "refuge ignored by the whole universe," Rousseau imagines himself "another Columbus" on a "desert island." A noise interrupts his thoughts: he stumbles through a thicket and finds a bustling, "sordid," factory. Faced with this reminder of his fellow man, the solitary falls into despair, "as if not able even in the furthest reaches of the Alps to escape the cruel hands of men intent upon tormenting me." And he complains: "In all the world, there is only Switzerland which offers this mix of savage nature and human industry."

Wollstonecraft repeats this movement from forest to factory, but her evaluation rejects Rousseau's. While praising the awesome majesty of the Norwegian pines and aspen, Wollstonecraft does not picture herself as the conqueror of savage nature. Instead, she "stop[s] enraptured" and "does homage to their venerable shadows" (*LWS*, p. 85). At the end of the same letter, Wollstonecraft observes farmers cutting away the wood, clearing the land and selling the lumber. Against Rousseau's despair, we read Wollstonecraft's approval: "The destruction, or gradual reduction, of their forests will probably meliorate the climate; and their manners will naturally improve in the same ratio as industry requires ingenuity" (*LWS*, p. 89). Evidently, the juxtaposition Rousseau deplored exists not only in Switzerland. In case we missed the target of her remarks, Wollstonecraft develops the thought:

I never, my friend, thought so deeply of the advantages obtained by human industry as since I have been in Norway. The world requires the hand of man to perfect it; and as this task naturally unfolds the faculties he exercises, it is physically impossible that he should have remained in Rousseau's golden age of stupidity. (*LWS*, p. 89; see also pp. 30–1 and 36)

This is not the first instance where Wollstonecraft ridicules Rousseau's concept of the "state of nature" and of a "natural" solitary man. The third chapter of *A Vindication of the Rights of Woman* develops her argument at length. Here, in the *Letters*, the argument is less systematic and more subversive, using Rousseau's themes and images against his own philosophy.

Ultimately, the letter form itself, inherently political and social, repudiates Rousseau's solitary views. The insertion of "my friend" into the letter-writer's thoughts overturns Rousseau's guiding premise in the *Reveries*; that is, his irrevocable rejection of human correspondence. All the bonds which had attached him to mankind having been "violently broken," Rousseau writes the *Reveries* for himself alone:

Alone for the rest of my life, since I find consolation, hope and peace only in myself, I neither need nor want to occupy myself with anything anymore but myself... I write my reveries only for myself.[33]

And in fact, Rousseau never intended this, his last work, to be published. (It was published after his death, in 1782.)

Whereas Rousseau places happiness with "nothing exterior to the self, nothing if not one's self" and with "a sentiment of existence stripped of all other affection," Wollstonecraft will not locate happiness in solitude. In the concluding movement of her argument with the *Reveries*, Wollstonecraft follows, then flees, Rousseau's example:

Human happiness... where, oh! where does it reside?... My thoughts fly from this wilderness to the polished circles of the world, till recollecting its vices and follies, I bury myself in the woods, but find it necessary to emerge again, that I might not lose sight of the wisdom and virtue which exalt my nature.

What a long time it requires to know ourselves... I cannot immediately determine whether I ought to rejoice at having turned over in this solitude a new page in the history of my own heart. (*LWS*, p. 90–1)

"The history of my own heart" – Rousseau's stated project in the *Reveries of a Solitary Walker* – does not wholly satisfy Wollstonecraft's letter-writer. Instead she brings her readers into the text. Together, "ourselves" must determine who she is and whether she "ought to rejoice." Writing, for Rousseau, describes a narcissistic universe, creating a dialogue between "I" and "myself." Wollstonecraft breaks out of his self-enclosure by emphasizing personal relationships (mother–daughter, friends and lovers) and social progress. By framing her reveries in letters, Wollstonecraft can follow the thematic traces of Rousseau's Solitary Walker while at the same time ensuring that she never walks alone.

THE WORK OF CORRESPONDENCE

For Wollstonecraft, the letter is not a private document. She uses the letter form in nearly all the works written in her final years: in *A Letter Written on the Present Character of the French Nation*, penned just prior to the *Letters from Sweden*; in *Letters on the Management of Children*, begun in 1797 and left unfinished at her death; and, in the central portion of *Maria, or The Wrongs of Woman*, in the long, confessional letter Maria writes for her daughter.[34] All these efforts testify to Wollstonecraft's faith in the educational power of the letter form; and education, in Wollstonecraft's writings, is always the vital ingredient for social change.

In comparison with her earlier writings, especially the two *Vindications* (1790 and 1792), the *Letters from Sweden* adopt a new method, but not an entirely new argument. Rather than confront and challenge her public, she woos and reforms them. The form and style of the *Letters* bear the fruit of lessons learned from the French Revolution, lessons which Wollstonecraft had presented in *An Historical and Moral View of ... the French Revolution* (1794). The *Historical and Moral View* argued that the excesses of the Terror arose, in part, because the French people were not ready for revolution. Their "excessive sensibility," unchecked by education, had demanded too much, too soon. Looking from the perspective of early 1794, Wollstonecraft prescribed a gradual model for social change in France.[35] In the *Letters from Sweden*, written eighteen months after the *Historical and Moral View*, she applies that diagnosis to her own work:

An ardent affection for the human race makes enthusiastic characters eager to produce alterations in laws and governments prematurely. To render them useful and permanent, they must be the growth of each particular soil, and the gradual fruit of the ripening understanding of the nation, matured by time, not forced by unnatural fermentation. (Appendix to *LWS*, p. 98).

The *Letters from Sweden* temper the argumentative approach of *An Historical and Moral View* and of the two *Vindications*, bending it into a progressive narrative. The developing "argument" of the *Letters* allows the individual reader and the general public to move with the author from a nearly overwhelming sensibility toward a position of strength. Presented as an entertaining travel narrative, the *Letters from Sweden* unveil their most pointed political critique at the end, after the letter-writer has successfully "cultivated" her readers' understanding.

The "erroneous influences of sensibility," which Wollstonecraft had remarked, with scorn, in the French character, lie just underneath the surface of these travel letters, threatening the writer's own understanding and ability to "observe." The first letter sounds the melancholy tone which echoes throughout the book:

Eleven days of weariness on board a vessel ... have so exhausted my spirits, to say nothing of the other causes, with which you are already sufficiently acquainted, that it is with some difficulty that I adhere to my determination of giving you my observation, as I travel through new scenes. (*LWS*, p. 7)

Similar remarks follow, reiterating a vague sense of loss. In this first case, the memory of the death of an unnamed childhood friend leads to obscure reflections on a temporary estrangement – from her child, probably; but also, obliquely, from her lover:

Fate has separated me from another, the fire of whose eyes tempered by infantile tenderness, still warms my breast ... why starts the tear, so near akin to pleasure and pain?

I cannot write any more at present. (*LWS*, p. 59)

But let me now stop; I may be a little partial, and view everything with the jaundiced eye of melancholy – for I am sad – and have cause. (*LWS*, p. 169)

Sensibility does not, however, overwhelm the writer. Having pointed to its debilitating influence, Wollstonecraft carries on. She awakens these "sensibilities" early on in the work, in order to wean us – and herself – away from that influence. Her letters will succeed, she writes, "by setting the imagination" – not the tear ducts – "to *work*" (*LWS*, p. 38, my emphasis). The letters enlist the reader in a serious enterprise that will withstand the destructive tugs of undisciplined emotion.

Cooperative imaginative "work" pulls writer and reader away from a flood of sentimentality; but this "work" also wards off the other great danger which Wollstonecraft identified in the *Historical and Moral View*: the effects of commercial speculation. In the wake of revolutionary passion, an "aristocracy of riches" was moving in to replace the "aristocracy of birth" and to oppress mankind with a new version of slavery.[36] If, at one extreme, the emotional ties of the sentimental friend, lover and mother wait to engulf the letter-writer, at the other extreme the "mean machinery" of commerce waits to break all human connection. The warm, "overflowing" diction of the sentimental passages[37] rearranges itself into the irreversible logic of business:

Men are strange machines ... A man ceases to love humanity, and then individuals, as he advances in the chase after wealth; and as one clashes with his interest, the other with his pleasures; to business, as it is termed, everything must give way; nay, it is sacrificed, and all the endearing charities of citizen, husband, father, brother become empty names. But – but what? Why to snap the chain of thought, I must say farewell. (*LWS*, p. 90)[38]

Through an act of will, the writer refuses to submit to the destructive chain. Meditating on the prospect of man transformed into machine, Wollstonecraft introduces a fractured sentence, a stuttering question, and an end to the letter. This mechanical chain of thought snaps along with the chain of human relationships. Under the pressure of "business," as well as the demands of personal sorrow, the writer must struggle to communicate.

The *Letters from Sweden* navigate between the excesses of sensibility and of commerce, the Scylla and Charybdis of contemporary society. The letters are lashed together by the public tie between the writer and her audience; they are driven by the "work" of the imagination. The letter appeals to the public through and against the conventions of isolated introspection and romance, the staples of sentimental epistolary fiction. But the letter also functions as the mechanism of a collaborative enterprise, which offers progress without the loss of human connection.

It is an ambitious, if compromised, strategy. The letter-writer herself creates a fiction which imagines a separation between the woman writer and the world of commerce. Yet for all her protests against commerce, she is, herself, engaged in the business. Just as she never gives the full story behind her sorrow, so does she never specify the "business" which brings her to Scandinavia. An odd sort of vindication results when Wollstonecraft maps the business trip onto an indictment of business and a promotion of her own public image. In light of the commercial success of the *Letters from Sweden*, we can read Godwin's description of the trip with a knowing smile: "Mary determined to make the voyage, and take the business into her own hands."[39] The dynamics of a market economy force the professional writer to "sell" her product in a consumer society: the imaginative self is commercial property.

DRAWING THE LINES OF INTIMACY

Wollstonecraft sells herself to her English audience through these *Letters*. We have explored earlier the tacit merger between the individual woman and an anonymous public, a merger mediated by the letter. We saw it represented in the letter of David's *Marat Assassiné*, and activated at certain moments in Helen Maria Williams' *Letters from France*. The rigid barriers of class, nationality or social propriety seem to collapse under the recognition that both woman and crowd stand outside "official" discourse. The voices of the politically dispossessed join in a challenge to authority. In David's painting, they unsettle the composure of the artist and his revolutionary hero, Marat. In Williams' work, they circumvent the established channels of communication. In both, the merger hints of violence. In the *Letters from Sweden*, Wollstonecraft turns this alliance against her own emotional attachments, and against the rules of domestic romance which determine a woman's destiny. But the underriding impulse is not violence as much as progress. As the public's identification with the letter-writer develops, and as the letter-writer's identification with the public grows, her distance from the nominal "you" of the *Letters* widens. A declaration of independence replaces the love letter – and the conventional plot – of sentimental fiction. Paradoxically, at the same time that it claims independence, the personal voice of the letter-writer metamorphoses into a popular, communal voice. Introspection turns to extroversion. In an effort to woo this larger, implicit audience, the *Letters* display a collective and various, rather than an individual and predictable, "self."

To understand the rhetorical strategy of the *Letters from Sweden*, we must recognize the position of Wollstonecraft's reading audience within the text itself. The implicit "you" must be delineated from the explicit "you" addressed by the letter-writer. In her Advertisement to the book, before the letters commence, Wollstonecraft overtly appeals to "the readers" – actual or armchair travelers. She makes them the final "judge" of her success as a writer and "give[s] them leave to shut the book, if they do not wish to become better acquainted with me" (*LWS*, p. 5). "The readers" are thus situated outside the particular sentimental exchange, but within the more extensive exchange of the published text.

The readers' "acquaintance" with the letter-writer is quickly distinguished from that of her addressed correspondent. The opening letter alludes to "other causes... with which *you* are already sufficiently acquainted," and which the writer refrains from discussing further (*LWS*, p. 7, my emphasis). A line has been drawn: clearly that "you" does not include "the readers," unless that "sufficiently" is ironic. What distinguishes the two audiences – the private and the public – is access to some sentimental secret, some undisclosed sorrow, now past. "You" knows it. Indeed, "you" may even be one of the causes. The readers have nothing to do with it; they can only imagine or conjecture the cause of sorrow.

In the course of the *Letters*, "you" and "your" connection with the letter-writer grow more and more identifiable. "you" is a man, her (former?) lover, an American "deeply" involved in commerce. "You" fathered the writer's child and "you" sent both mother and child on this business trip to Scandinavia. Reviews of the book at the time of publication indicate that few people knew whether or not

"you" was married to the author of these letters (*LWS*, p. 104n.). In
1796, Wollstonecraft's readers would not be aware of the details of
her personal life; they would recognize only the public persona of the
well-known "female philosopher." "You" may well be a figure for
Gilbert Imlay, Wollstonecraft's lover; but "you" could as easily
stand as a fictional character, a textual locus for intimacy and
emotional attachment. Given enough clues, contemporary readers
could construct an identity for "you" based on the conventions of
popular romance: the dissolute rake, the cruel, insensitive lover.
Wollstonecraft expects her readers to imagine "you" and define
themselves against him.

The readers do, finally, understand what "you" cannot. At one
point, Wollstonecraft refers to "the cruellest of disappointments,"
which she encountered "last spring, in returning home." She
laments,

Know you of what materials some hearts are made? I play the child and
weep at the recollection – for the grief is still fresh that stunned as well as
wounded me. (*LWS*, p. 184)

Readers, drawing from a variety of sentimental plots, can imagine
the worst. The readers do know – or think they know, better than the
insensitive businessman – of what materials some hearts are made.
The public is invited to rush to the letter-writer's defense against
"you," her lover, the man who rules over her past and her home.
Once activated, the readers' imagination is crucial to the dynamic of
these letters: "they" rescue the writer from the villain; "they"
accompany her on her flight from sorrow, from home, from the past.

With the readers' cooperation, the writer reverses the standard
epistolary plot: here the heroine liberates herself by rejecting her
correspondent and by embracing the "world" outside of the domestic
circle. The early letters do display a lingering attachment to her
lover, but it fades as the letters progress. Letter VII, for example, ends
with the promise,

With more than usual tenderness, I therefore assure you that I am yours,
wishing that...absence may not endure longer than is absolutely necessary.
(*LWS*, p. 72)

And Letter IX concludes,

I may venture to assure you that a further acquaintance with mankind only
tends to increase my respect for your judgement, and esteem for your
character. (*LWS*, p. 91)

But her distance from him already announces itself in that "further acquaintance." By the middle of the book, her loyalty wavers, her questions turn rhetorical and her "general observations" on society begin to "point home" (*LWS*, p. 104):

What is speculation [Imlay's occupation], but a species of gambling, I might have said fraud, in which address generally gains the prize?... This censure is not confined to the Danes. Adieu! (*LWS*, p. 120)

And more directly:

most men treat their mistresses as kings do their favourites; *ergo* is not man then the tyrant of creation?
    Still harping on the same subject, you will exclaim – how can I avoid it, when most of the struggles of an eventual life have been occasioned by the oppressed state of my sex... I have before mentioned that men are domestic tyrants. (*LWS*, p. 160)

By letter XXIII, Wollstonecraft withdraws from her once "respected" and "esteemed" correspondent. Speaking with the confidence gained from worldly experience and a wide new circle of acquaintances, the letter-writer turns against "you":

I mean not to be severe when I add...that men entirely devoted to commerce never acquire, or lose, all taste and greatness of mind...But you will say that I am growing bitter, perhaps, personal. Ah! shall I whisper to you – that you – yourself, are strangely altered since you have entered deeply into commerce... never allowing yourself to reflect and keeping your mind, or rather passions, in a continual state of agitation (*LWS*, p. 187)

The whispered, personal exchange only heightens the public denunciation of "you...you – yourself." Having discovered friends and allies during her travels, and through her *Letters*, the letter-writer stands firm in her censure: "Perhaps you may think us too severe; but...the more I saw...the more I was confirmed in my opinion" (*LWS*, p. 190).[40] The readers of the *Letters from Sweden* participate in that "us" and support the letter-writer's farewell to the domestic tyrant, the fictional lover.
    The switch from the internal reader (the explicit addressee) to the external reader (the unnamed public) is responsible for much of the political power of the *Letters*. This switch is a common strategy of "open letters," political critiques masked as letters to prominent individuals, which were ubiquitous in Wollstonecraft's day. In these

letters, the writer addresses king, lord or ruler as a familiar, then proceeds to attack his policies or behavior. Published privately as pamphlets, or in journals or newspapers, these open letters invite a wide audience to participate in the letter-writer's outcry. The letter-writer thus transforms a personal grievance into a community issue, and vice versa. We see traces of this practice on the editorial pages of newspapers today. William Wordsworth's "Letter to the Bishop of Llandaff" (1793), which mixes letter and jeremiad, and Edmund Burke's "Letter to a Noble Lord" (1796) give two rather refined versions of this tradition.

Women writers and members of the working classes were especially adept at this form of radical literature. Contrary to the expectations of *Familiar Letter-Writers* and other guides, they wrote letters which attempted to stir up public indignation, rather than curry the favor of the entitled addressee. Such pamphlets were stock in trade for the radical societies of both London and Paris.[41] But the trade was open to educated women as well. Manon de Roland, an influential figure in the French Gironde party and a friend of both Williams and Wollstonecraft, achieved notoriety as a frequent correspondent in the Paris journals and as the author of a "Letter to Louis XVI," presented to the French king by his disgruntled ministers in 1792. Roland's letter was distributed widely among the republican societies in Paris, and was well known in England. A more extreme, though perhaps more typical example of this genre was Olympe de Gouges's "Letter to Citizen Robespierre," published by the author in 1792. Like Roland, de Gouges created a public voice for herself in the letter form.[42] When Robespierre refused to answer a letter she had written him, de Gouges took her correspondence to the streets, insisting upon her right to be "familiar" with the tyrant. On behalf of the French People, she proclaimed:

It is I, Maximilien, who am the author of thy Prognostic, I... Olympe de Gouges... LET US PLUNGE INTO THE SEINE! Thou hast need of a bath... thy death will claim things, and as for myself, the sacrifice of a pure life will disarm the heavens.[43]

Behind the façade of familiarity, no trace of real intimacy survives in these broadsides. An alliance does form, nonetheless, between writer and public, and it points an accusing finger at the privileged man in authority.

What Michael Bell writes about the characters of epistolary novels applies equally well to the characters of public, political letters in Wollstonecraft's era. "The characters," writes Bell, "are very often, and very primarily, concerned ... to create, with a high degree of self-consciousness, their own identity ... to objectify it in the eyes of another," in this case, the reading public.[44] The letter-writer thus becomes an enduring character who survives many performances and exists beyond the confines of any set time or place: a dramatic figure that fills the needs of the community. Referring to eighteenth-century familiar letters, Bruce Redford's comments nevertheless help explain the function of the open political letter: "The finest letter-writers project an identity that 'stands in for, or memorializes, or replaces, or makes something else' of the time-bound 'I.'"[45] The letter "becomes a form of representation ... like the performance of a play."[46]

The effect of open political letters depends primarily on the public's recognition of itself in the dramatis personae of the letter-writer. That writer plays *to* its audience; it does not play *out of* an individual self. The success of Wollstonecraft's *Letters from Sweden* derives, in part, from her ability to "'make something else' of the time-bound 'I'," something which appealed to the English reading public. The *Letters* display a variety of dramatic characters which distracts any attempt to perceive the "real woman" of the text. Without a critical sensitivity to these various personae, biographical glosses on the *Letters* can obscure the artistic scheme of the work. Wollstonecraft exchanges her own tale for those of familiar dramatic figures. The effect proves just the opposite of self-revelation: the drama is not personal, it is communal and cultural.

"I found I could not avoid being continually the first person – 'the little hero of every tale,'" she apologizes in her Advertisement. But her "first person," already a de-personalizing device, gives way to an array of heroes whose stories are already well known to her readers. Wollstonecraft quotes at least six Shakespeare plays, on at least sixteen different occasions in her letters. Trudging mindlessly through a storm, Wollstonecraft speaks the language of King Lear (*LWS*, p. 131); arriving in Denmark, she plays a melancholy Hamlet (*LWS*, pp. 173, 175, and 180); separated from her child, she fears the "thick-coming fancies" of Lady Macbeth (*LWS*, pp. 109–10).[47] The final letter goes so far as to adopt the language of both the Bible and Milton: "Yet the lightning marks not their roofs, to thunder convictions on them, 'and to justify the ways of God to man'" (*LWS*,

p. 194; also pp. 23, 128, and 180). The specific circumstances of a woman traveling in Scandinavia fade as the grand figures of British literature come into focus.

"A national character is formed by its theatrical amusements," Wollstonecraft writes in 1795, and her *Letters from Sweden* use the characters of the English stage to explore the character of her countrymen.[48] She limits herself to the figures of British, Norse and Celtic legend in order to woo an audience suspicious of the neo-classical bias of gallic republicanism.[49] Moreover, she cites the great poets of the English language – Chaucer, Shakespeare, Milton, Pope and Dryden – along with the English Bible and popular English literature, rather than point to the philosophical free-thinkers who underwrote her earlier work.[50]

The procession of dramatic figures and literary voices emphasizes Wollstonecraft's "English" as opposed to "Gallic" identity. It also distinguishes the writer from the conventional woman of sentimental fiction. Although in one move she exploits sentiment to gain sympathy, in another Wollstonecraft takes on the voice of heroic men, aristocratic men, independent men drawn into political activity:

All the world is a stage, thought I; and few are those who do not play the part they have learnt by rote; and those who do not, seem marks set up to be pelted at by fortune; or rather, as sign-posts, which point out the road to others, whilst forced to stand still themselves (*LWS*, pp. 180–1)

A Romantic hero lurks in these words, spoken in a tone which anticipates Byron, while echoing Macbeth and Lear. It becomes clear that Wollstonecraft casts herself in traditionally "male" personae, standing apart, like a signpost, from the majority of her sex.

Wollstonecraft imagines the English national character as male, and her own "masculine" posture is meant paradoxically to distinguish her and elicit public identification with her. With all her dramatic versatility, the letter-writer adopts few "feminine" roles, precisely because they would not distinguish her. She is quick to separate herself from the women she encounters, telling her readers that her host named her "a woman of observation, for I asked him men's questions" (*LWS*, p. 15). Indeed, she rarely relates her conversations with women, choosing rather to describe her meetings with business men or interesting male fellow travelers. The one woman she does address as an equal is also an unconventional figure:

she apostrophizes "Unfortunate Matilda," the former Queen of Denmark and sister to England's George III. Significantly, the traveler calls attention to the Englishness of Matilda's – and her own – taste. She praises the royal gardens, built for the queen, and muses: "I felt I was following in the footsteps of Matilda, who wished to multiply around her images of her beloved country" (*LWS*, p. 166). Wollstonecraft plays up the queen's social and political influence as well as her educational reforms, so much like those of the writer. Simultaneously, she downplays the queen's sensational history of seduction, betrayal and early death – an extreme version of Wollstonecraft's own history in 1795.[51] Oblique references to Matilda's tragedy, like the vague hints of the letter-writer's sorrow, elicit readers' sympathy but focus their attention elsewhere. Wollstonecraft uses the figure of Matilda, as Helen Williams uses Joan of Arc, to substantiate her own work and to separate herself from the passive, domesticated image of the woman.

Far apart from the intrepid male heroes and Queen Matilda stand the middle-class housewives of Scandinavia and Wollstonecraft's French maid Marguerite. These women occupy a stifling environment: the former sit within a world of heavy banquets, tedious conversation and "grotesque and unwieldy" dress. Faced with this picture of the bourgeois home, Wollstonecraft almost invariably begs for fresh air and a long walk outdoors (*LWS*, pp. 21–3, 35, 102–4, and 138–9). Thus liberated from the domestic circle, the letter-writer can converse with nature or with other travelers. She has the opportunity for unencumbered "reverie" and "observation" because Marguerite remains behind, tending the baby. In the *Letters from Sweden*, Marguerite displays the stock characteristics of the silly, uneducated woman, whose timidity only accentuates the letter-writer's "adventurous spirit."[52] Marguerite trembles at thoughts of "robberies, murders, or the other evil which instantly...runs foul of a woman's imagination" (*LWS*, p. 11). Each time the maid balks or whimpers, each time she shows her vanity or irresponsibility, Wollstonecraft jumps in to assert her own superior behavior: "I did not listen to her" (*LWS*, p. 9); "our trains of thought had nothing in common" (*LWS*, p. 175); "not apprehending any danger, I played with my little girl, whom I would not leave to Marguerite's care, on account of her timidity" (*LWS*, p. 17). The letter-writer occupies a realm distinct from these circumscribed women, bound as they are by social position and fashion, or by childcare and ignorance.[53]

In the midst of her wandering and role-playing, Wollstonecraft locates herself on a stage with few limits: the privileged realm of the writer. Less an actor than an "actor-magician," the letter-writer conjures up a cast of characters and the vision of another world for her audience.[54] Small wonder that *The Tempest* is the most often-cited work in these *Letters*. More than castle or heath, more than home or city, the "magic island" of Prospero and Ariel supplies the stage upon which these letters move (*LWS*, pp. 23–4, 107, 156, 164–5). Here we watch the performance of a Romantic artist, exercising her belief in imagination's power to envision a new form of society.

When Wollstonecraft transforms the intimate *entre nous* of familiar letters into a public, English "us," she also converts the props of sentimental narrative – the sleeping babe, the abandoned woman, the all-too-sensitive heart – into a political, yet visionary, treatise. The focus shifts gradually, leading the readers from undisclosed personal sorrow to open social concern. In one remarkable passage, the flight of imagination allows a fusion of philosophical, political and maternal cares. She writes,

What, I exclaimed, is this active principle which keeps me still awake? – Why fly my thoughts *abroad* when everything around me appears *at home*? My child was sleeping with equal calmness... Some recollections, attached to the *idea of home*, mingled with reflections respecting the *state of society* I had been contemplating that evening, made a tear drop on the rosy cheek I had just kissed... What are these imperious sympathies? (*LWS*, p. 16–17; my emphasis)[55]

The female letter-writer rewrites her personal story – a sentimental memoir – into cultural drama and finally, into commentary on modern European society. The appealing "first person" advertised in her opening refuses to remain individual. It seeks out connection:

What are these imperious sympathies?... How frequently has melancholy and even mysanthropy [*sic*] taken possession of me, when the world has disgusted me, and friends have proved unkind. I have then considered myself as a particle broken off from the grand mass of mankind; – I was alone, till some involuntary sympathetic emotion, like the attraction of adhesion, made me feel that I was still part of a mighty whole, from which I could never sever myself. (*LWS*, p. 17)

The active principle of a creative imagination forces her out of herself, out of home and society even, into the "mighty whole" of an imagined community. Wollstonecraft's "business" in Scandinavia concludes with this reversal, in words that are not hers, but borrowed from her culture: "Why should I weep for myself? 'Take, o world! thy much indebted tear!'" (*LWS*, p. 194).

TRADING ON IMAGINATION

Commerce: Holds no commerce with the summer night
            Let us break off all commerce with the muse
            For commerce of thy nature with herself
            Each into commerce with his private thoughts
            From a too busy commerce with the heart
            To hold a vacant commerce day by day
            With commerce freighted, or triumphant war
            (From *A Concordance to the Poetry of William Wordsworth*, all mentions of the word "commerce")

But to commerce every thing must give way; profit and profit are the only speculations – "double – double, toil and trouble." (*Letters from Sweden*, p. 191)

If we return for a moment to that parting quotation – "'Take, o world! thy much indebted tear!'" – we see the confluence of two movements in the *Letters from Sweden*. One movement we have already traced: tearful sentimentality and personal story turn outward to embrace social concern and world history; individual "progress" opens into the progress of human civilization. The second movement involves the work of the imagination in the commercial world – imaginative "commerce," in Wordsworth's usage. When Wollstonecraft repays the world with an "indebted tear," we witness a sort of economic closure to the book. The demands of sentiment and of commerce are reconciled by the writer's gesture. But unlike the poet Wordsworth, who could take the term "commerce" and simply slide it from the marketplace into transactions of the mind and nature, Wollstonecraft must carefully underscore the break between imagination and commerce, between the business of a woman writing and a man's "business." In other words, the work of female imagination, set free from the domestic economy, must still maintain "human values – basic, central and natural" in the face of the dehumanizing, male-identified world of commerce.[56] The *Letters* pay off Wollstonecraft's debts both as sentimental "woman" and as "worldly" philosopher: they establish her as a successful professional woman of imagination. Indeed, the commercial success of this book, suggests Sylva Norman in her introduction to the *Letters*, "could well have 'made' [Wollstonecraft] as a popular writer, had she not died the following year."[57]

Wollstonecraft's role as a professional who works with and through imagination, as a productive "mind," is carefully constructed in these letters. Moreover, the letters teach us to value such work and such a mind. Promoting the economic value of the imagination becomes, for Wollstonecraft as for many of her contemporaries, a pressing political and practical concern.

The *Letters from Sweden*, with their outbursts against the destructive force of "commerce" and "business," want to prove the productive power of the female imagination. To do so, they construct an economics of the imagination to rival that of capitalism. For Wollstonecraft, this proof requires considerable delicacy. Once she steps outside the domestic sphere, the worldly woman cannot, like Rousseau in *The Solitary Wanderer* or Wordsworth in *Home at Grasmere*, simply return home. Wollstonecraft knows too well that home is rarely a safe haven for a woman who has wandered. Nevertheless, the woman writer attempts to bring together the spheres of "home" and "world." Whereas the *Vindication of the Rights of Woman* brought the demands of the marketplace into the home, asking women to be "useful" and "productive" for the commonweal, the *Letters from Sweden* carry the values of the home – emotional security, personal relationships, stability – into the marketplace. Mediating this transition is the correspondence between the female imagination and the reading public.

The contradictory nature of this enterprise weighs heavily, compromising the imaginative even as it transforms the commercial. In her earlier writings, Wollstonecraft drew a clear distinction between industry and idleness, utility and pleasure. This distinction separated two economic systems, the productive and the wasteful, manifested in society by the industrious middle classes and the indolent, effeminate nobility, respectively. (Wollstonecraft hardly takes the lower classes into account in this model.) The Preface to the *Vindication of the Rights of Woman* indicates on which side of the line Wollstonecraft situated her work in 1792:

I shall disdain to cull my phrases or polish my style; – I aim at being *useful*, and sincerity will render me unaffected ... *I shall not waste my time* rounding periods, or in *fabricating* the turgid bombast of artificial feelings ... *I shall be employed about things, not words!* – and, anxious to render my sex more respectable members of society, I shall try to avoid that flowery diction which has slided from essays into novels, and from novels into familiar letters and conversation.[58]

In this passage, the work ethic of the middle classes rings out with a no-nonsense logic which is deliberately de-feminized. At that same period, in 1792, Wollstonecraft advised another woman writer that, "An author, especially a woman, should be cautious... In short, it requires a great resolution to try rather to be useful than to please."[59] At times, the *Letters from Sweden* seem split between these two urges: to be useful *and* to please. Passages of deliberately poetic beauty juxtapose prosaic accounts of trade, land distribution and local customs. "Business" interrupts reverie, the wanderings of the imagination distract her from giving information. The age-old question of the value of art – should it be useful or beautiful? – is recast in terms of class distinctions and the work ethic.

Before the publication of the *Letters from Sweden*, Wollstonecraft had classified the products of the imagination with waste, weakness and perversity. Just prior to these *Letters*, in her *Historical and Moral View*, Wollstonecraft advocated "the cool investigation of facts" over "the imagination of the poetical historian."[60] Imagination, she asserted, is effectively counter-productive:

Ignorant people, when they appear to reflect, exercise their imagination more than their understanding; indulging reveries, instead of pursuing a train of connection; and thus grow romantic, like the croisaders [*sic*]; or like women, who are commonly idle and restless.[61]

Imagination supports ignorance, the glorification of war and femininity. It associates with perversity:

One great cause of misery in the present imperfect state of society is, that the imagination, continually tantalized, becomes the inflated wen of the mind, draining off nourishment from the vital parts.[62]

In short, nothing could be more useless to " the progress of the world's improvement" than the exercise of the imagination.

In the *Letters from Sweden*, however, the terms change. Imagination guarantees progress, and *speculation* becomes the unnatural perversion:

Speculations of various kinds have already almost doubled the price [of grain]. Such are the effects of war, that it saps the vitals even of the neutral

countries, who, obtaining a sudden influx of wealth, appear to be rendered
flourishing. (*LWS*, p. 28)

And later,

Mushroom fortunes have started up during the war; the men, indeed, seem
of the species of the fungus; and the insolent vulgarity which a sudden influx
of wealth usually produces in common minds, is here very conspicuous.
(*LWS*, pp. 186–7; see also pp. 26 and 190)

The comments of a friend reiterate commerce's characteristic
impotence:

Why, madam...you will not meet with a man who has any calf to his leg;
body and soul, muscles and heart, are equally shrivelled up by a thirst of
gain. There is nothing generous even in their youthful passions; profit is
their only stimulus, and calculations the sole employment of their faculties.
(*LWS*, p. 189)

By contrast, the letter-writer's reveries and wanderings have en-
hanced her vitality and restored her *embonpoint* (*LWS*, p. 75). Judging
from her own experience, Wollstonecraft concludes that imagination
generates and nourishes both the emotional and the intellectual
progress of civilization.

Civilization is a blessing not sufficiently estimated by those who have not
traced its *progress*; for it *not only refines* our enjoyments, *but produces a variety*
which enables us to retain the primitive delicacy of our sensations. Without
the aid of imagination, all the pleasures of the senses must sink into grossness,
unless continual novelty serve as a substitute for the imagination, which
being impossible, it was to this weariness, I suppose, that Solomon alluded
when he declared that there was nothing new under the sun! – nothing for
the common sensations excited by the senses. Yet who will deny that the
imagination and understanding have made many, very many discoveries
since those days, which only seem harbingers of others still more noble and
beneficial. (*LWS*, p. 20; my emphasis)

By an uncommon process of refinement, imaginative production
distinguishes itself from the material, sterile grossness of commercial
industry, bringing ever-new, improved and various enjoyments to
humanity. Its benefits increase exponentially, Wollstonecraft boasts;
they represent the intellectual equivalent of Adam Smith's wealth of
nations. "Infinity" and "Eternity," "Expansion" and "Improvement" result when her imaginative powers go to work (see *LWS*, pp.
23–4, 71–2, and 92). With her reveries, Wollstonecraft takes flight;

and the effects produced by those flights argue against the gross materialism, the empty performances of the mercantile society which surrounds her (see *LWS*, especially pp. 22–3, 71–2, and 84–5).

Wollstonecraft has cast her correspondent as a member of this mercantile world; she knows the terms he will use to evaluate her performance. The language of a capitalist economy colors her own evaluations of both imagination and commercial speculation. At one point, she corrects herself: a particular view seems "picturesque – or, more properly speaking, *calculated to produce* poetical images" (*LWS*, p. 85; my emphasis). Other times she turns his language against him, as when she speaks of their child. She mocks her correspondent's financial ambitions when she counters business with both a child and a witticism:

> I would not permit myself to indulge the "thick-coming fears" of fondness, whilst I was detained by business. – Yet I never saw a calf bounding in a meadow, that did not remind me of my little frolicker. A calf, you say. Yes; but a *capital* one, I own. (*LWS*, p. 110)

She produces both the human connection and the amusing imaginative leap, whereas he cannot see beyond the livestock. The double pun reveals the writer's source of power: she "owns" the potential – the capital – for both forms of production.

Imagination scores higher than speculation in terms of productive capability, variety and social improvement: it guarantees, in short, an economic success. But a price is paid: the language of the writer and of the entrepreneur have been conflated. Placed against Wollstonecraft's earlier criteria of "labor" and "industry," and against her continued critique of "the want of proportion" between speculative gain and labor (*LWS*, p. 87), the elevated imagination totters. Its clear distinction from speculation blurs. In fact, if we follow Wordsworth's use of the term, we see that financial "commerce" and imaginative "correspondence" function along the same lines. One deals with words, the other with money, but neither generates its value – or meaning – from physical labor or material. Both conduct a sort of magical production: the "tricks of trade" echo the magician's "airy stuff that dreams are made of."[63] There is no "substance," she charges, behind speculation, a "species of gambling...in which *address* generally gains the prize" – an odd criticism from the letter-writer who aspires to "win on our attention by acquiring our affection" (*LWS*, p. 5). Her "restless, active spirit" parallels his "mind ... in a continual state of agitation" (*LWS*, pp. 76 and 187). And although she rebukes men of commerce who "allow themselves to break with impunity over the bounds which secured their self-respect" (*LWS*, p. 190), she praises her own "uncommon mind" for its intrepidity and she disdains prudence:

Men with common minds seldom break through general rules. Prudence is ever the resort of weakness; and they rarely go as far as they may in any undertaking, who are determined not to go beyond it on any account. (*LWS*, p. 8)

The rhetoric of her self-presentation places Wollstonecraft in the same class as the merchants and entrepreneurs. "Though touched by his tricking wand, they have all the arts, but none of the wit, of the wing-footed god" (*LWS*, p. 190). Wollstonecraft has her store of arts and wit, but they force her to confess her affiliation to Hermes, god of commerce *and* letters.

If the speculator trades on promises and "address," the author of the *Letters* sells progress and personality. Thus we can read in the *Letters* not just an open political letter, but also an extended advertisement. Whereas other travelogues, such as Gilbert Imlay's *Topographical Description to the Western Territories of North America* (1795) served as disguised promotional tracts for real estate (Imlay himself was involved in land speculation in America), Wollstone-craft's *Letters* use the backdrop of Scandinavia to advertise an imaginative "mind" – infinitely more attractive than any real estate in Sweden, Norway or Denmark. Her spirit fills the landscape and gives value. "My very soul diffused itself in the scene," she writes; it is this "diffused" self that attracts the customer. With the sale of the *Letters from Sweden*, Wollstonecraft did, as Ralph Wardle suggests, "make capital ... of what she had hitherto sought to conceal: her own personality."[64] But it is a staged personality, readily accessible to the English public. In this instance, personality (or "mind" or "soul") becomes commodity.

The personality of the writer in 1795 was not just an economic creation; it was also the political creation of a social class. Her own Advertisement makes the case: there Wollstonecraft asks readers to grant her right to "rank amongst this privileged number" of "witty or interesting egotists" (*LWS*, p. 5). In her efforts to create a higher form of industry, Wollstonecraft elevates a new social class: the professional, creative personality. Class distinctions infiltrate most of her observations and reveries; their message is subtle, but politically significant. She gives lip-service to her earlier image of the industrious writer: "A degree of exertion, produced by some want, more or less painful, is probably the price we must all pay for knowledge," she writes; and she wonders, "How few authors or artists have arrived at eminence who have not lived by their employment?" (*LWS*, p. 105). Yet throughout the *Letters*, the writer explicitly describes her work as "superior," "noble," and "elevated"; and she consistently identifies herself with aristocratic figures: kings, princes, queens, countesses. Her "cultivation" differs remarkably from that of the farmer (see *LWS*, pp. 84–9).

Even as her use of epistolary convention and literary allusion appeals to a popular audience, Wollstonecraft sets the letter-writer apart from the working classes, deploring their "simplicity" and lack of "polish." With condescending generosity, she raises her "passionate" self above them:

These characters have more tenderness than passion the latter has a higher source; call it imagination, genius, or what you will, it is something very different. I have been laughing with these simple, worthy folk... and letting as much of my heart flow out in sympathy as they can take. (*LWS*, p. 100)

She then enlists her "strong imagination" to produce "phantoms of bliss" which whisk her away to an elite "magic circle" (*LWS*, p. 100). During these reveries, the writer imagines herself as one of a spiritual aristocracy, dividing her time "between the town and the country." Contemplation of nature and a farming community would give her mental strength; metropolitan life would "rub off the rust of thought and polish the taste" (*LWS*, p. 105). In the subtle argument of the *Letters from Sweden*, imagination gives itself class.

Seen in its historical context, this elevation of "imagination, genius, or what you will" (*LWS*, p. 100) reveals the class negotiations at work among certain groups of professional writers. By the time of the French Revolution, a number of middle-class professional writers, in France and in England, had become well established and politically influential. As early as 1787, Mary Wollstonecraft could describe herself as "the first of a new genus" – a woman who could "support [herself] in a comfortable way" by her educational and political writings.[65] In general this group allied itself with the interests of the trade and working classes against the power of the aristocracy and landed gentry: Wollstonecraft's no-nonsense rhetoric in the *Vindications* and Thomas Paine's in *Common Sense* and the *Rights of Man* are written testaments of this alliance. With the fall of the monarchy and the subsequent chaos in France and England, however, the alliance between middle-class writers and the lower classes began to crack.[66] The middle class began to fracture into many parts, each claiming social prominence: the aristocracy of rank having surrendered, an "aristocracy of wealth" and "aristocracy of genius" vied for power in a turbulent political system. The efforts of writers such as Wollstonecraft, Wordsworth and Blake to elevate the "work" of the imagination simultaneously defined their professional and political status as writers. Writing became the mechanism for both social mobility and class definition. As Mitzi Myers writes of the Romantic autobiography, and of Wollstonecraft's *Letters* in particular: "The work [of writing] itself [is] an image of what the self can achieve."[67]

The emergence of this self-nominated class – the intellectual and the imaginative, the "unacknowledged legislators" – established in English literature what Jon Klancher has called a "meritocracy of mental energy."[68] Klancher reprints an essay from Joseph Johnson's *Monthly Magazine* of 1793, which makes explicit the politics surrounding the careful creation of the "man of intellect." As a member of Johnson's intellectual circle, Wollstonecraft must have been familiar with, and probably supportive of, the ideology at work in this essay:

The pains of intellect have hitherto, in many, or in most instances, overbalanced the pleasures; may not this have arisen from the peculiar and disordered states of society, rather than from the natural tendency of cultivation and refinement? A commercial country, the sole moving spring of which is pecuniary interest, must necessarily be unfavourable to those who, intent on mental improvement, require for their pursuit abstraction and leisure, by involving them in outside difficulties. Honour, fame, and the pleasure which is found in the pursuit, rather than pecuniary gain, are supposed to constitute the recompense of literary eminence... Talents, therefore, to adopt the commercial style, are not free to find their level. Whether republics may be less inimical to the production, the encouragement, and the reward of mental excellence, has not yet, perhaps, been sufficiently ascertained by experiment.[69]

Writers such as Wollstonecraft and her friends at the *Monthly Magazine* self-consciously parlay their talents – imagination and genius – into the tokens of a new ruling class.

The woman of intellect, however, has a further problem: what right does she have to claim "eminence" in a new political system? The doubt haunts Wollstonecraft, even as she associates with the "meritocracy" of the imagination. Mary Wollstonecraft risks double censure in her work, since for women to step beyond the home is to "risk invisibility in the 'real' world of commodity production." Yet Wollstonecraft recognizes that "remaining within the politics of personal experience will not fundamentally transform this subordination."[70] Part of that dilemma is reconciled by the letter form, which circumscribes her argument with the language of accommodation and community. Moreover, the letter allows the female imagination to travel between "home" and "world"; it describes the circulation between public and private spheres. But the letter also exacerbates the problem by commodifying and circulating the woman writer. Despite her intellectual snobbism, Wollstonecraft has, in these *Letters*, "diffused her very soul," not only in the landscape, but amongst her reading public. She is invested in them.

"THE LITTLE HERO OF EVERY TALE"

Of a character so interesting to literature and the public, some information would, no doubt, prove highly acceptable to our readers... 'The highest compliment,' said Mr. [Joseph] Johnson, 'you could pay to Mrs. Wollstonecraft, would be that of saying nothing about her'.. [but] Mrs. Wollstonecraft is not too fastidious to deny that public opinion is sometimes guided, and oftener confirmed, by the private conduct of the most eminent literary characters. *Monthly Mirror*, 1 (Jan. 1796), 131–2

I have deliberately neglected the personal history of the woman who wrote the *Letters from Sweden*, preferring to explore the rhetorical tactics of the letter form and the politics of Wollstonecraft's self-presentation. Regardless of the compromises she makes, the letter-writer wants to educate her audience with the vision of a new society. The rhetorical and political strategies of the *Letters*, however, do tend to pull the reader away from the public message and toward the story of "private conduct." Wollstonecraft's efforts to bring the values of "home" into the marketplace invite the market to come into her home. In this sense, the letter form works both for and against her. Even as she carefully distinguishes this work from her private correspondence, even though she explains that the "I" of the letters is a device to gain the readers' interest, Wollstonecraft nevertheless draws attention to the personal sufferings and sorrows which the text of the *Letters* will not explain. Not surprisingly, the suggestion of intimacy – the *entre nous* of her correspondence – directs her reader toward the hidden, "private" side of the letters; it invites the reader to imagine the writer as a romantic figure. In much the same way that *Childe Harold* produced a public fiction of Lord Byron, so the *Letters from Sweden* allowed the English public to fictionalize Mary Wollstonecraft.

We can say that the *Letters from Sweden* succeeded, in that they reached a wider, more appreciative audience than Wollstonecraft's more polemical works. The irony remains that her most sustained attack upon modern commercial society should become a great commercial coup. The *Letters* brought Wollstonecraft the financial independence she desired, and they established her, once and for all, as a professional writer.[71] Yet one could argue that the female imagination was, perhaps, too marketable: from the time of publication until recent years, readers of the *Letters from Sweden* have responded to the "woman" in the letters rather than to her challenge to the "man of business."

Without a doubt, the reading public has bought Wollstonecraft's argument that the products of the imagination are much more attractive than the mechanism of commerce. Unfortunately, that argument urges reader to ignore the "worldly" issues at stake in the *Letters*, in order to concentrate on the "feminine" questions of the narrator's sensibility and secret heartache. At the center of the text, critics have concocted a sentimental romance, and ignored the ways in which these letters deliberately displace the sentimental image of the woman writer. Most analyses of this work display what Jerome McGann calls "an uncritical absorption in Romanticism's own self-representations," without examining the strategies governing those representations.[72] By amplifying the personal voice, readers since 1796 have exaggerated the "I" of the *Letters*, and neglected the dynamics of correspondence Wollstonecraft creates. They have muted the political emphasis of the *Letters from Sweden*, which falls less upon the individual letter-writer than upon the act of correspondence itself.

Early reactions to the work reflect the somewhat paradoxical nature of Wollstonecraft's enterprise. The *Monthly Review* notices that an agitated state of mind seems to interfere with "the author's cool and settled judgement."[73] The *British Critic* remarks, "She is capable of joining to a masculine understanding, the finer sensibilities of a female."[74] Other reviews reiterate this masculine/feminine split in the *Letters*, but their attention inevitably falls on the feminine side. "The lady is a political traveler," announces the reviewer for the *Monthly Mirror*, but goes on to cite extracts "only such as may be...descriptive of the character and feelings of the author."[75] The *Monthly Review* asserts that the expressions of the "writer's heart" will "never fail to touch the readers... [Readers] will seldom see reason to censure her feelings and never be inclined to withhold their sympathy."[76] In a move typical of other journal reviews, the *Monthly Mirror* dictates how the *Letters from Sweden* should be read:

We know not to what misfortunes several of the above extracts allude; but it is evident that the mind of the fair author is not in that state of enviable tranquillity which philosophy is said to bestow. The melancholy which seems to have taken strong hold of her will probably excite that interest in the mind of the reader which her letters, considered as a source of topographical, historical and political information, we fear, will fail of producing.[77]

Similarly, the *Analytic Review* chooses not to print the critiques of commerce: "for these...we must refer our readers to the volume itself."[78] Favorable reviews were printed in journals which supported and protested Wollstonecraft's politics, because politics could be ignored for the sake of a woman's feelings. Even the most antagonistic assessment, after frowning upon certain indiscretions, rewrites the *Letters* into an acceptable, popular narrative:

We cannot be charged with intrusion on her private sorrows...surely no object can be more interesting than that of an unhappy mother, wandering through foreign countries with her helpless infant, enduring all the fatigues and inconveniences of incessant travelling.[79]

These reviewers, working only from the sketchy clues provided in the text, defuse the political critique in the *Letters* by subordinating that critique to the story of a woman's emotional duress. Yet they at least acknowledge the political content and see occasional glimpses of "masculine understanding." If, like them, we knew little or nothing of Wollstonecraft's "private conduct," we would be more inclined to look around the figure of the "woman" in the text. But ever since the publication of William Godwin's *Memoirs of the Author of the Vindication of the Rights of Woman*, in 1798, with its supplementary "Letters to Imlay," the author of the *Letters from Sweden* has become an epistolary heroine. Godwin himself makes his wife into an exemplary public fiction: "There are not many individuals with whose characters the public welfare and improvement are more intimately connected."[80]

In writing her memoirs for her, editing her personal correspondence and collecting her posthumous writings, Godwin emphasizes Wollstonecraft the feeling woman over the radical thinker. In an oft-quoted description of his wife's travelogue, Godwin stresses the romantic power of the correspondence – its softened, "feminine" properties:

The narrative of this voyage is before the world, and perhaps a book of travels that so irresistably seizes on the heart never, in any other instance, found its way to the press. The occasional harshness and ruggedness of character, that diversify her Vindication...here totally disappear. If ever there was a book calculated to make a man in love with its author, this appears to me to be the book...Affection had tempered her heart to a softness almost more than human; and the gentleness of her spirit seems precisely to accord with all the romance of unbounded attachment.

Thus softened and improved, thus fraught with imagination and sensibility, with all, and more than all "that youthful poets fancy, when they love," she returned to England, and, if he had so pleased, to the arms of her lover.[81]

Subtly, Godwin shifts from discussing the book to discussing Wollstonecraft's affair with Imlay, implying that the two were coincident. His elision distorts the facts and makes of the *Letters* an epistolary romance.

As I mentioned before, Wollstonecraft composed the *Letters* not during, but after her trip, and finished them after her final break with Imlay. Though Godwin and subsequent readers would have us think that the *Letters from Sweden* replicate the private, tortured messages she actually sent to Imlay, the two sets of letters bear little correlation. She wrote the *Letters* to claim possession over her own emotional attachments and guarantee movement from personal and senti-mental to national and political economies.

Godwin's edition of the love letters effectively excises all mention of commercial business, or the political situation in northern Europe, thereby turning Wollstonecraft's subterfuge inside out. When Godwin published the "Letters to Imlay," he sent into circulation a version of Mary Wollstonecraft that became public property and which, even today, influences our reading of her other writings. We may well wonder why Godwin wished to publish the letters of his wife to her former lover, but it is clear how he wanted the public to read them: as a sentimental romance, an epistolary fiction comparable to Goethe's popular *Sorrows of Young Werther*. Mary was, he tells us, a "female Werther";[82] and her private letters

> may possibly be found to contain the finest examples of the language of sentiment and passion ever presented to the world. They bear a striking resemblance to the celebrated romance of Werther...The editor apprehends that, in the judgement of those best qualified to decide upon the comparison, these Letters will be admitted to have the superiority over the fiction of Goethe. They are the offspring of a glowing imagination, and a heart penetrated with the passions it essays to describe.[83]

Here Godwin writes a tempting advertisement for his best-selling *Memoirs...and Posthumous Works*. For all practical purposes, the English press treated the "Letters to Imlay" as if they were a novel: one review called upon the letters of Héloïse and Abelard in order to explain the illicit liaison.[84] The presumptuous *Monthly Mirror* echoed Rousseau's *Nouvelle Héloïse*, calling the letters "a splendid and deserving monument of female worth and female renown," but complaining that letters were "inferior to those of Werther" due to a "less direful conclusion."[85]

In short, both Godwin and Wollstonecraft succeeded in putting the imagination of the publishing industry "to work" she herself was the product, the character of dozens of stories.[36] Before her death and the subsequent revelations, Robert Southey cast Wollstonecraft in "The Triumph of Woman" (1795) as a strong, militant figure: "no maid of Arc, no Roland, no Lord...or Caesar" equalled her. And William Blake paid tribute to his friend with the revolutionary Oothoon and the disturbing "Mary."[87] Later, the publication of her private letters licensed innumerable versions of her life; literary accounts served either as hagiography or as admonitions to women writers and "female philosophers." Godwin followed up his *Memoirs* with the novel *St. Leon*, which stars an impossibly perfect female character, Marguerite Louise Isabeau de Damville, whose attributes bear an uncanny resemblance to those of his ex-wife. Thomas Brown, Professor of Moral Philosophy at Edinburgh, eulogized Wollstonecraft in a long poem, *The Wanderer in Norway* (1816).[88] Women novelists especially, such as Mary Hays, Charlotte Smith, Fanny Burney, Maria Edgeworth and Jane West produced novelized renditions of Mary Wollstonecraft. Favorable and unfavorable alike, all used the figure of Wollstonecraft as a moral lesson for their readers. Clearly, once the private letters went public, the writer could only play two roles – the saint or the whore – both of them sufficiently distant from any public, political engagement. Wollstonecraft became "the mother, the wife, beloved companion, the ornament of her sex … and the benevolent friend of human kind"; or else she stood as the epitome of the licentious, "philosophical wanton," drowning in her own passion.[89]

This fictionalization of Mary Wollstonecraft continues, every time we read the *Letters from Sweden* as some sort of encoded love story. We see it when critics point away from the "social comment" which constitutes so much of this work, in order to praise the "poetic quality" of Wollstonecraft's "deeply felt emotions."[90] We misread the *Letters from Sweden* if we believe that "here as nowhere else [Wollstonecraft] could forget her theories and be herself," that the *Letters* "reveal the whole woman in all her complexity."[91]

As Wollstonecraft's own letters indicate, letter-reading is a reciprocal encounter:

I find you can write the kind of letter a friend ought to write, and give an account of your movements. I hailed the sunshine, and moonlight and travelled with you … Enable me still to be your company, and I will allow you to peep over my shoulder, and see me under the shade of my green blind, thinking of you.[92]

But that reciprocity, played out between a writer and her public, has a political thrust. Once it leaves the home, once it enters the marketplace, the letter no longer delivers a private individual for scrutiny – in fact, the *Letters from Sweden* frustrate scrutiny. Instead the letter performs a social act, diffusing the self into the world, making it public property. And that worldly self demands a public reckoning.

CHAPTER 5

Jane Austen and the look of letters

Critics and apologists, novelists and biographers have feasted upon Mary Wollstonecraft's personal correspondence. Her letters have been processed into the stuff of popular romance and adorned with flourishes of melodrama and morality. By contrast, the personal correspondence of another woman writer, born half a generation after Wollstonecraft, appears sparse and unyielding. No stormy romance, no family scandal, no tortuous self-scrutiny and no political philosophy fill the letters and expose the "authentic history" of Jane Austen. Diligent and almost dutiful about her correspondence, Austen wrote letters which, ever since their publication, have required repeated apologies from her admirers. The obstacle they raise for modern readers can remind us of the differences between the role of letters in the years 1796–1817, and our own expectations of the letter.[1] And just as her personal letters force us to revise our way of reading private correspondence, so Austen's novels beg a re-evaluation of the role of the letter in the novel. The changing history of the letter asks us to look again at the forms of personal expression and communication in the changing world of the novel.

The collected letters of Jane Austen should alert us to a shift away from the eighteenth-century fiction of the letter and warn us of invisible barriers to reading. The evident lack of affective sensibility, contemplation or personal exposure in these letters contradict some of our assumptions about the familiar letter.[2] The lack of "self" in Austen's correspondence has been blamed on the over-protectiveness of the Austen family, who substantially pruned the surviving letters. But perhaps the letters themselves protect their writer. Family members insist upon the extreme privacy and idiosyncracy of the novelist's letters, as if they were written in a code impenetrable to outside view. "To strangers," writes Caroline Austen, the letters "would be no transcript of her mind – they would not feel that they knew her the better for having read them."[3] James Austen-Leigh further restricts the legibility of the letters, insisting that they contain minutiae of incidental value: "the reader must be warned not to expect too much from them."[4] But to her sister Cassandra, no doubt, Austen's language was "open and confidential" – a description which epitomizes the contradiction.[5]

Jane Austen's unyielding letters are not an isolated phenomenon. This lack of personal revelation correlates with a similar lack in the later letters of Helen Maria Williams, and with the protected "inner self" of Wollstonecraft's *Letters from Sweden*. Moreover, in Austen's use of the letter, we witness an unmistakable divorce between the letter and the female body, a marriage that had been figured in conventional epistolary novels. In these later works, the epistle no longer pretends to represent the gestures, affects, and poses of a vulnerable body. By 1796 evidently (the earliest date we have for Austen's private letters, the year of publication for Wollstonecraft's *Letters from Sweden*, and the last year of Williams' *Letters from France*), the woman in the letter was relocated and redefined.

Unlike William Godwin, whose miscalculated tribute to his wife's private life broadcast her intimate correspondence, Cassandra Austen reportedly burned and censored the most "vital" of her sister's letters, those full of "emotional interest."[6] Supposedly, fertile records of Austen's "personal attitudes to historical events and to propriety," as well as accounts of her most fervent love affairs were sacrificed in that epistolary purge.[7] The remains offer none of the sentimental riches which nurture Wollstonecraft scholarship. Perhaps Cassandra Austen edited her sister's letters in much the same manner as Wollstonecraft revised her own correspondence into the *Letters from Sweden*, excising vulnerability and promoting the image of a social "self." Or perhaps there was little to excise: maybe the lessons taught to the professional woman writer and the epistolary heroine had filtered into everyday correspondence. In other words, Jane Austen may not have written the revealing letters we seek – at least not after the 1790s.

Strangely enough, this affective lack in the private correspondence has led to a greater appreciation of Austen's novels. In a complete turnaround from Wollstonecraft criticism, readers of Austen's work are asked to amplify the "inconsequent" and otherwise inconsequential private correspondence with the bounty provided by the beloved novels. R. W. Chapman, for example, reminds us that though "the characterization [in the letters] is incidental and hardly ever deliberate, it is by the same hand as Lady Bertram and Mrs. Norris."[8] Public fiction takes precedence over private communication. Whereas masterpieces such as *Pride and Prejudice* and *Emma* can be – and often are – read today without benefit of a critical gloss, Austen scholars must intervene to teach the uninitiated how to read and find meaning in her "opaque" and "incomplete" letters.[9]

That opacity, I am suggesting, has its own significance. "You are very amiable & very clever to write such long letters, every page of yours has more lines than this, & every line more words than the average of mine. I am quite ashamed." So writes Austen to her sister Cassandra, in 1808.[10] This emphasis on the "look" of the letter strikes us as quaint, especially since, in reading typeset copies of the letters, we have little contact with what Austen and her correspondents actually saw when they exchanged notes. We find, nonetheless, darting out from so many of her letters, frequent references to the length, penmanship and general presentation of letters. We might infer that the letter-writer revealed as much in the appearance as in the content of a missive – and perhaps more. When her brother describes Austen's letters, saying, "Everything came finished from her pen," he could be referring both to the look of the letters and to the thoughts of the letter-writer which were "clear" and "well-chosen."[11] According to her niece, Jane Austen's "handwriting remains to bear testimony to its own excellence." The letters themselves are witness, therefore, to the novelist's virtues, and to the expectations of the age:

every note and letter of hers, was finished off handsomely – There was an art *then* in folding and sealing – no adhesive envelopes made all easy – some people's letters always looked loose and untidy – but *her* paper was sure to take the right folds, and *her* sealing wax to drop in the proper space.[12]

We, who are apt to delve into the psychological depths of private letters, may find it hard to read the surfaces which were so significant to Austen's contemporaries: the messages that remain unavailable in a bound volume, and on a printed page.

The letter was, not surprisingly, a very material object for Jane Austen. With the cost of a note determined by the number of sheets it covered, and with postal charges rising dramatically, correspondents set a high value on the ability to pack loads of information onto a single page and to write neatly, with a small hand. A double-letter was a rare luxury among Austen's circle: it would not necessarily find an enthusiastic recipient, since most letters were paid for at their destination.[13] Letters, therefore, were expected to *look* appealing to the reader, who would have to purchase the pleasure of consuming them before viewing their contents. They should look as if they were worth the cost of postage. It makes sense, then, that correspondents such as Jane and Cassandra Austen kept close accounts of who wrote a better-looking letter.

The ultimate value of a letter, however, was realized in circulation, as relatives and friends passed around particularly deserving correspondence. In *Emma*, for example, Frank Churchill's letters to his father are applauded as "very proper" and "handsome," "very handsome indeed," and "pretty" by a whole community of readers. Although few of these readers remember the contents, the appearance delivers a sense of satisfaction. Just as commodities such as pianos can function as signs in Austen's world, so too can signs such as words and letters function as commodities, with both their use and their exchange value unrelated to their content.[14]

Austen's personal letters provide neither the private romance nor the provocative politics we hoped to find. We should then ask ourselves what letters do provide, especially to the novelist. From reading Jane Austen's personal epistles, we begin to suspect that for her, and for her correspondents as well, letters did not offer a window to the soul or access to the body. As a record of social engagements, as a news-sheet, as a medium for caricature, and as a familial duty, the letter, in Austen's hand, took on the tone of a village newspaper, rife with gossip and local color.[15] Moreover, her letters frequently feature descriptions or reports of letters: their length, their frequency, their value. The familiar letter functions more as a mirror of the surrounding community than as a lens through which one scrutinized the writer.

To a large extent, the letters in Austen's novels are similarly reflexive rather than reflective documents. The use of letters in these novels gradually veers away from an emphasis on the indeterminacy of expressive content and toward the surface or circumstances of expression. Marilyn Butler argues that after the novels of sensibility and the radically charged novels of the 1790s, "the fashion of focussing on a protagonist's *inner life* gave place to a concern with the conditions of *external life*; [and]...to a more closely documented treatment of history and society."[16] The use of the letter in the novel registers this readjustment. In Austen's major novels, and in the novels of her successors, we find an increasing emphasis on the letter as an object of scrutiny – a *Ding an sich* rather than a frame or medium of expression. The letter was an historical and social "thing" with a life of its own, "defamiliarized" even for the contemporary individual.

The difficulties posed by Austen's private correspondence, therefore, inflect the structure and themes of her novels as well. Questions about letters, in and out of literature, cast into doubt the means and possibilities for individual expression within social constraints. They explore the dangers and the powers of private communication, and in doing so delineate the structures which contain and create our sense of privacy. We see that although Austen does explicitly abandon the form of the epistolary novel, she does not stop testing and re-evaluating the personal letter. In every one of her finished novels it is there, playing a crucial, often decisive role, as if it were a character in its own right. Austen, like Helen Maria Williams, usually provides us with a good look at these included letters. Her narrative authority depends on our learning to see and read the letters properly.

Yet these novels also display Austen's suspicions of the letter, which often appears at odds with the "proper" narrative perspective. The letter-filled third volume of *Mansfield Park* offers a case in point. The willful and selfish Mary Crawford writes letters to Fanny Price in a manner both facile and manipulative. Fanny, who is "quite unpracticed in this sort of note-writing," must, of course, respond, and this correspondence draws her into a network of relationships over which she has almost no control. Mary uses Fanny as a means to write to Edmund Bertram, Fanny's cousin; Henry Crawford uses his sister's notes to send unsolicited postscripts to Fanny. Edmund reads over Fanny's shoulder, Henry writes under Mary's hand. In this sort of cross-writing, the problem is not that the letter cannot express enough: the problem is that it says too much. For Austen, the letter is no meager register of social interaction. Rather, it is overloaded and over-read; it has too many possibilities. Consequently, it overwhelms her heroine.[17] Fanny's composure increases later, when she receives a series of letters to which she need not respond (*MP*, pp. 415–24, 433–7). At Portsmouth she is able to detach herself from the epistolary network and remove herself to a supervisory position. A newspaper report, in fact, finally frees her from relying on letters for elucidation (*MP*, p. 439). She refrains from letter-writing as from acting, and shrinks from putting her inner thoughts into words. The self-effacing, retreating motion that shuts down correspondence ultimately bestows upon Fanny a sense of self-possession. The denial of letters written à *la* Crawford establishes Fanny as monitor and final interpreter of the society of *Mansfield Park*.

Austen's juvenilia suggests her awareness that the epistolary form, according to eighteenth-century conventions, could upset strict notions of property and propriety (in fact, Mary Crawford's letters in *Mansfield Park* exploit this possibility). The fictionalized letter travelled in a promiscuous no man's land; one could never determine to whom a circulating letter belonged. In the epistolary novel, expressive license and the heroine's vulnerability were intimately linked: the woman in these letters was up for grabs. Austen's novels both exploit and rewrite this fiction by opposing the heroine (and the narrator) to the letter.[18] Thus, in Austen's later fiction, letters no longer provide the sympathetic connection which Wollstonecraft tried to forge in her *Letters from Sweden*. More often than not, letters serve as agents of rupture and distance, rather than rapprochement. As a result, Austen must develop different strategies for connecting her characters with a public audience. Unlike Wollstonecraft, women in Austen's world shun national and international circuits and circulate only in local channels. Her heroines learn not to advertise their tears and fears.

On the other hand, we can spy on the letters in these novels in ways we cannot spy on Austen's heroines. In the role Austen creates for them, letters draw attention away from the individual woman and throw light onto social convention, public image and the realm of exchange that creates them. Thus Austen's use of letters can at times protect both the novelist and her heroines. As a letter-writer, the Austen we read keeps herself guarded and proper, giving little away. As a novelist, she brings the letter under tight control, calculating and delimiting its disruptive force.[19] The narrator in Austen's major novels, like Fanny Price, becomes a supervisor and mediator of human relationships, providing an alternative (not without problems) to the transactions of epistolary editor, government and Post Office.

Rather than giving an exhaustive analysis of the letters in Jane Austen's fiction, I will examine four distinct episodes of reading and writing letters. Together, these episodes tell the story of how the letter and the woman writer exchanged roles.

LADY SUSAN AND THE JUVENILIA

This Correspondence, by a meeting between some of the Parties and a separation between the others, could not, to the great detriment of Post Office Revenue, be continued longer. Very little assistance to the State could be derived from the Epistolary Intercourse of Mrs. Vernon and her niece, for the former soon perceived by the style of Frederica's Letters, that they were written under her Mother's [Lady Susan's] inspection, and therefore deferring all particular enquiry till she could make it personally...ceased writing minutely or often.[20]

With these words, the exchange of letters in Jane Austen's *Lady Susan* is interrupted, and the fiction moves out of the mother's epistolary control and into the hands of a not quite omniscient narrator. Generally, this passage is taken to mark the budding novelist's rejection of the epistolary form and her movement toward third-person, impersonal narrative. Much of Austen's juvenilia contains parodies of epistolary conventions – both the conventions of the familiar letter-writer and those of sentimental fiction. But *Lady Susan*, despite its satire of manners, is no rollicking burlesque; and the narrator's abrupt intervention raises more complicated questions than commentators' have acknowledged about Austen's attitude toward the letter form. This narrative switch has been explained as a technical development, a progression from a "crude" and "dying form based upon outmoded manners" toward the novelist's more "mature" and "authoritative" "art", and toward a "new kind of verbal mastery."[21] Yet it is also a matter of power and control, a "tug-of-war" between the author and her eloquent protagonist.[22] *Lady Susan*'s conclusion points to still another conflict, that between the interests of the novel and the interests of the Post Office, in its "assistance to the State." Before even considering the stories which reach their conclusion here – the story of Lady Susan and the story of Austen's epistolary fiction – we should remark on the peculiarity of the narrator's interference. The well-being of the Post Office and assistance to the state are odd concerns in epistolary intrigue, but here they emerge to mark the very border or limit of the novel's correspondence. We should also note the anxiety of maternal influence uncovered here at the border: the mother's supervision and dictation of the daughter's writing brings an end to the epistolary scheme. In its stead, the female writer establishes a new voice, one that "mingles irony, impatience, and a sense of relief."[23] At the conclusion to her last epistolary work, Austen writes herself free of a (feminized) literary tradition, but she does so while extracting questions about social and political structure.

To understand these gestures, we must keep in mind the historical context of *Lady Susan*, Austen's most serious and complete experiment in epistolary form.[24] Austen probably wrote the first version of the work between 1793 and 1794, when she was eighteen or nineteen years old, and revised it again in 1805.[25] As such, it fits just between the juvenilia and the advent of her first published work. Moreover, *Lady Susan* was composed against the background of the worst years of French Terror and English paranoia. During this period, correspondence and letter-writing carried a radical taint and triggered fears of conspiracy and sedition. Lady Susan's epistolary machinations, her desire for power, and her dangerous eloquence suit the political climate of the day. She is a British version of Laclos' Madame de Merteuil, importing dangerous alliances into English country homes.[26] The novel commences as the young widow, Lady Susan, proudly admits the havoc she has wrought: "no house was ever more altered; the whole family are at war," due to her interference (*LS*, p. 245). From the Manwaring (Man-warring?) estate she moves on to overturn the home of her in-laws, pitting brother against sister, wife against husband, father against son. Lady Susan's letters, although extremely attractive and engaging, seem to have a subversive and anti-social effect.

Readers see through her plotting – yet remain charmed. Unlike Mme. de Merteuil, Lady Susan suffers a mild and even ambivalent punishment: the conclusion reports that she marries the weak-willed but wealthy Sir James and re-establishes herself at the heart of "society." The seductive and self-determining letter-writer nevertheless submits to an outside authority: the narrator confiscates her heroine's pen and halts her epistolary reign. Ego submits to superego. Why then, with Lady Susan properly "socialized" and the radical element silenced, does the narrator apologize, even in jest, to the state and the Post Office? Why must they suffer alongside Lady Susan?

The peculiar remarks in Austen's conclusion suggest that the on-going exchange of letters actually offers support to the state and Post Office. That suggestion, in turn, implies that Lady Susan's machinations and the interests of British "society" are not necessarily at odds. Indeed, Lady Susan may not be the radical agent, the vaguely French villainess many readers assume.

Between the years of *Lady Susan*'s composition and final revision, Pitt's ministry in Great Britain had elevated the Post Office into a highly political – and corrupt – bureaucracy. Howard Robinson, historian of the British Mail, declares that "never before or since has the Post Office suffered such misuse as it endured in the decades [1784–1815]," and he documents that misuse with details of political intrigue, illegal privileges and diversion of postal revenues.[27] The House of Commons initiated at least two extensive investigations into the post during this period, in an effort to stem the abuse and to increase postal revenues. In the midst of these efforts, in order to finance an unpopular war with France, Pitt promoted a series of tax reforms, among which the Stamp Tax received widespread and vocal criticism.[28] The price of a single letter increased five times between 1786 and 1812, the largest increase coming in 1805. The Post Office began to function as a vehicle of ministerial policy, with Parliament passing more postal acts between 1794 and 1813 (eight) than in the rest of the eighteenth or nineteenth centuries (five and three, respectively). These years also marked the time of greatest intrusion into private correspondence: warrants for opening letters were so easily granted that postal surveyors hardly bothered to request official authorization.

When we set *Lady Susan* in this environment, we perceive new shades and tones in the novelist's depiction of the letter. The letter seems less a "dying form" than an overpowering one, an expression of the power of form itself, of institutions and established law. We can see this force at work on several levels in the text. First, we notice that unlike the bourgeois heroines of her early juvenilia, Austen's *Lady Susan* begins and ends with an aristocrat, settled within the social order of wealth, nobility and accepted conventions of beauty. Hardly the levelling radical, Susan exhibits the façade of the ideal eighteenth-century woman. Even her enemies admire her countenance, "absolutely sweet," her voice and manners, "winningly mild" and her "uncommon union of Symmetry, Brilliancy and Grace" (*LS*, p. 251).

In her neo-classical perfection, she typifies the deceptive power of convention. Susan relies upon the forms of propriety in order to stifle rebellious individualism in others, calling upon "calm reserve," "sentiment" and "serious conversation" to "humble the Pride" of "the self-important" (*LS*, pp. 254, 258). "There is exquisite pleasure in subduing an insolent spirit," she proclaims. Her successful campaign demonstrates that individual desire can, indeed *must*, be compatible with external constraints. Lady Susan rebukes "those women ... who forget what is due to themselves and the opinion of the World" (*LS*, p. 269); her own activities are guided by "Propriety and so forth" (*LS*, p. 302).

Although the consummate letter-writer, like her creator, surrounds herself with ironies, these pronouncements do suggest a conservative force at work. Only Susan's bright wit can energize the rigid forms which define her: Lady, widow, mother, sister, lover, wife. For all her brilliance, Lady Susan remains the most static of Austen's heroines. Though it may be true, as Mary Poovey argues, that the epistolary virtuoso is "trapped in the very paradox of propriety ... she thought she could exploit," we have to agree that her letters display a self-knowledge unrivalled in Austen's fiction.[29] Of all Austen's heroines, this one undergoes no education or self-revelation. She is always "too consistently herself."[30]

The collaboration between letter-writing, conventional structures and a static status quo, as well as the equation between letters and Lady Susan's self-possession, identify another departure from Austen's previous epistolary fiction. Not only is Lady Susan not middle class, she is not young. She is a widow and a mother; as such, she has social authority. Unlike the libertine youth of Austen's epistolary burlesques, this letter-writer circumscribes a rigid order. In fact, her daughter Frederica – a character in every way suitable for conventional epistolary romance – is allowed only one timid letter in *Lady Susan* before the mother moves in to dictate her correspondence. Susan's letters dictate her daughter's life as well, setting out dogmatic programs for education and female conduct (see especially Letters 7 and 19). Guided from strict boarding school to arranged marriage, Frederica is expected to remain silent, obedient and passive. Lady Susan forbids "that Frederica's accomplishments should be more than superficial," or that she "remain in school long enough to understand anything thoroughly" (*LS*, p. 253). At home, the girl must follow "the rules I have laid down for [her] discourse" (*LS*, p. 275). In short, Lady Susan writes her own version of *Letters on the Education of Daughters*. She echoes, cynically, the theories of Hannah More,[31] and mimics those conduct books attacked by Wollstonecraft's writings. In 1795, when Austen was writing *Lady Susan*, England had been hit by a wave of treatises on women's nature and conduct, written in response to the ideological storm following the French Revolution. *Lady Susan* participates in a discussion which would eventually "intensify the paradoxes already inherent in propriety" for women.[32]

The letters of *Lady Susan* provide the voice of an older generation, echoing the mentality of the eighteenth century. Elsewhere in the fiction, Sir Reginald De Courcy imposes his will upon his son by means of a staid letter which could easily have been transposed from Lord Chesterfield's *Letters to His Son*, or from Richardson's *Familiar Letters*. Even Mrs. Vernon, Lady Susan's epistolary rival, writes in league with *her* mother, Lady de Courcy: parental power and the older generation define the course of the novel. Frederica hardly enters into the epistolary exchange: her story is contained by the letters of her mother and her aunt. Even when she does pick up the pen, she admits to following "the letter," if not "the spirit of Mama's commands" (*LS*, p. 279). Similarly, young Reginald writes only to be continually manipulated by his father, his married sister and Lady Susan.

Above all, it is Lady Susan who sets the terms for epistolary intercourse. As if she represented the very spirit of formal authority, Lady Susan wields the letter with a dictatorial, punitive force. As she deliberates over the transgressions of the younger generation, she strikes an imperious pose: "I *must* punish Frederica...I *must* punish [Reginald]...I *must* torment my Sister-in-Law for the insolent triumph of her Look and Manner...and I *must* make myself amends for the Humiliations..." (*LS*, pp. 293–4, my emphasis). Her letters never allow us to question this vengeful necessity or her own executive authority. As Patricia Spacks notes, "the bad mother" appears in *Lady Susan* "not as inescapable nightmare, but as center of consciousness."[33]

This well-decorated but nevertheless sinister power is a far cry from Austen's earlier epistolary farces. The contrast between *Lady Susan* and the insane world of "Love and Friendship" exposes the differences five years can make. In the latter work, the uproarious adventures of Laura and Sophia offer, in letter form, a sort of anti-conduct book, written by the now middle-aged Laura to provide a "useful lesson" to a young girl. Set within a supposedly pedagogic frame, the silly egoisms of the letter-writer, the sentimental excesses of the young friends and lovers, and their ludicrous transgressions against all authority and propriety offer an hilarious critique of contemporary novels of sensibility.[34] Whereas *Lady Susan* demonstrates the seductive authority of the letter, "Love and Friendship" revels in exposing its foolishness. The epistolary heroine, having assured her reader that "In my mind ... was the rendez-vous of every good quality and of every noble sentiment,"[35] proceeds to betray that claim with every word she writes. At fifty-five, Laura still fears "the determined perseverance of disagreeable lovers and the cruel persecutions of obstinate fathers" ("L&F," p. 77). Lady Susan's immutability can hardly compete.

One of the jokes running throughout "Love and Friendship" turns on the question of parental authority that later takes control of *Lady Susan*. In the early work, the young lovers' blind opposition to their parents' advice receives none of the sympathy given to Frederica's plight. Laura's "noble" paramour protests he would never "so abjectly degrade myself" as to adopt his father's judgment ("L&F," p. 83). Other heroes and heroines consistently refuse to submit to the "despotic power" of "cruel and mercenary parents" who would marry them to perfectly unobjectionable, even desirable, mates. A young girl's greatest error, according to Laura, is "a want of proper confidence in her own opinion, and a suitable contempt of her father's" ("L&F," pp. 93–4).

Within the anarchic world of parodic sentimentalism, the heroines can rationalize theft, dishonesty and sheer selfishness, but the hyperbolic tone destroys their authority. Not only family and propriety, but time, space and reason itself are violated in this topsy-turvy world, where the most memorable "lesson" warns the reader: "Run mad as often as you choose, but do not faint" ("L&F," p. 102). "Love and Friendship," along with other early works by Austen, clearly assigns youth, egocentrism, and moral and epistemological confusion to the letter form.[36] In these exaggerated presentations, the letter signals the transgression of youth against established authority. Thus, the most meager letter in these tales, saying simply, "Madam – We are married and gone," can send a duchess into a fit and rouse a posse of 300 armed men.[37] Simultaneously, Austen's parody clearly establishes the realm of common sense, virtue and tolerance *outside* the letter frame, *with* the much-maligned parents of her protagonists and *with* the author and her readers. The parody relies upon a social consensus that stands in bemused opposition to the epistolary fiction.

In *Lady Susan*, however, epistolary art is in league with social consensus and parental authority. Rather than managing the letter into a parody of anarchy, Austen begins to see it in a more threatening aspect, as a paradigm of law. In order to explain this radical revision in Austen's approach to the letter form, we should return to her remarks in the conclusion. Between 1790 and 1795, the years between "Love and Friendship" and *Lady Susan*, the letter had undergone great social and political stress. We have already mentioned the increasingly intense supervision of female propriety in the period after the French Revolution. We see now its link with the concurrent governmental supervision of personal letters. Austen's break from the rule of the letter is more courageous than a mere dissatisfaction with obsolete form. The very terms of the break suggest the ongoing vitality of the narrator's opponent, and the hidden doubts of the young author:

Whether Lady Susan was, or was not happy in her second choice [the lackluster Sir James] – I do not see how it can ever be ascertained – for who would take her assurance of it, on either side of the question?... For myself, I confess that *I* can pity only Miss Manwaring [Sir James' intended], who...was defrauded of her due by a Woman ten years older than herself. (*LS*, p. 313).

As Austen moves away from epistolary form, we will watch how the novelist wins her due from her literary mothers and from eighteenth-century representations of women.

Having wrestled with epistolary form in *Lady Susan* and in the subsequent, lost novels, *Elinor and Marianne* (1796) and *First Impressions* (1797), Austen spent over a decade – until 1810 – waiting, revising and strengthening her skills.[38] With the publication of *Sense and Sensibility* in 1811, she announced her victory over the constraints of the letter. *Sense and Sensibility* initiates a trend in Austen's writing to establish a "new privacy" in the novel.[39] With the character of Elinor Dashwood Austen creates an interiority which remains intact and independent through the mediation of a narrative *style indirect libre*.[40] Elinor is an anti-epistolary heroine: the inner world of her thoughts and feelings finds no direct expression in the novel, although her point of view controls the story. She is bound both by a promise of secrecy and a sense of integrity and self-protection. Marianne Dashwood, by contrast, insists on making explicit her innermost thoughts; she "demands that outward forms exactly project or portray inner feelings."[41] But Marianne's *style direct*, epitomized by her letters to Willoughby, exposes her to the harsh judgment of "the World." Throughout the novel, Austen manipulates the device of the letter, setting it against Elinor's interiority and using it to emphasize Marianne's vulnerability.

In *Sense and Sensibility*, the novelist deliberately maneuvers against the very structure which fascinated and challenged her in *Lady Susan*. Here the letter's effectiveness as a story-telling vehicle is exposed as impotent and unnatural; the letter becomes a relic of a romance that never was. Although *Sense and Sensibility* rewrites the epistolary *Elinor and Marianne*, it retains enough letters (twenty-one) to make the author's point: the letter no longer represents or expresses (safely) the interior freedom which her heroines seek. It threatens to kill the sentimental heroine more by its impersonality than by its emotive force. Austen wants to recontextualize the letter and place it under the light of a new realism, a realism coincident with an expanding sense of "society" and "the World." In such a society, the lesson which Marianne must learn and the novel must enact, is that a letter's content is nothing, its appearance is all.

If we look carefully at one specific scene, we can begin to understand how and why Austen de-activates the content of letters in this novel. In the central portion of *Sense and Sensibility*, Austen connects the dangerous power of the letter to Marianne's romance with Willoughby: both prove false. Before we may examine the lovers' abortive correspondence, however, the narrator gives us instruction on how to read. Halfway through the novel, upon their arrival in London, we watch the two sisters sit down to write – letters, of course:

Elinor determined to employ the interval [before dinner] in writing to her mother, and sat down for that purpose. In a few moments, Marianne did the same. "I am writing home, Marianne," said Elinor; "had not you better defer your letter a day or two?"

"I am *not* going to write my mother," replied Marianne hastily, as if wishing to avoid any further inquiry. Elinor said no more; it immediately struck her that she must then be writing to Willoughby, and the conclusion which instantly followed was, that however mysteriously they might wish to conduct the affair, they must be engaged. This conviction, though not entirely satisfactory, gave her pleasure, and she continued her letter with greater alacrity. Marianne's was finished in a very few minutes; in length it could be no more than a note: it was then folded up, sealed and directed with great rapidity. Elinor thought she could distinguish a large W. in the direction, and no sooner was it complete than Marianne, ringing the bell, requested the footman to get that letter conveyed for her to the two-penny post. This decided the matter at once.[42]

Of course, the simple opposition between the dutiful letter of the "sensible" sister and the vaguely illicit letter of the "sensitive" sister is clear. But more complex narrative oppositions cloud the picture. In this passage, we participate in the workings of Elinor's mind, we follow her eyes as they survey her sister. By contrast, we "see" Marianne's letter, but her thoughts remain inaccessible. We and Elinor are left to speculate. In fact, this scene initiates Marianne's turn from open-hearted honesty to a covert behavior which, if not deceptive, hints of dissimulation. Only a page before, Elinor had "read" her sister like an open book: she saw "the rapture of a delightful expectation which filled the whole soul and beamed in the eyes of Marianne" (*S&S*, p. 159). This letter, however, marks a break between the interior and exterior; it separates Marianne's "soul" from Elinor's "eyes." With no recourse to her sister's thoughts, Elinor must draw her conclusions from the letter itself: imagining the missive's affective content, Elinor is misled into assuming a secret engagement. Yet her close attention to the physical details of the note almost eclipses any interest in the writer herself. And the sensible sister's thought turns to a social arrangement (engagement), rather than to any unlicensed feeling. If Marianne's inner state is now unavailable, it becomes immaterial: the letter alone speaks. Marianne's letter concretizes the tradition of epistolary fiction for Jane Austen. This letter gathers all the lawlessness of "Love and Friendship" into a single piece of paper, marked with a tell-tale "W," and places it under a scrutinizing eye.

Austen emphasizes the quiddity of the letter here, stressing its everyday, practical existence: if I write home now, shouldn't you wait? In epistolary fiction, such concerns rarely emerge; yet here we see a letter written, sealed and sent off to the London two-penny post. This concentration on the pragmatics of letter-writing remains a constant in all of Austen's fiction, and signals an obstacle to the "inner life" of her characters. On the farcical side, the heroine of "Amelia Webster" consistently points out that her "paper" limits her discourse: "I have a thousand things to tell you, but my paper will only permit me to add that I am your affectionate friend"; and "I have many things to inform you of besides, but my paper reminds me of concluding."[43] Such insistent materialism deflates the mystique of correspondence.

As in Austen's own correspondence, the surface of the fictionalized letters in her early novels is significant, and significantly opaque. In *Pride and Prejudice*, for example, we witness a debate over the letter-writing skills of Messrs. Darcy and Bingley, which is actually a discussion of orthography. This debate opens the door to Elizabeth's remarks about "reading character" – remarks which point out the prejudice of superficial "first impressions."[44] This sharp focus on the scripted word also appears in *Mansfield Park*. Fanny lingers over a scribbled fragment of a note from Edmund, its negligible contents outweighed by the mere fact of its appearance:

> Never were such characters cut by any other human being, as Edmund's commonest handwriting gave! This specimen, written in haste, had not a fault, and there was a felicity in the first four words, in the arrangement of "My dear Fanny," which she could have looked at forever. (*MP*, p. 265)

Austen tells us that Fanny reads more into the form and the handwriting of a note than we, her readers, ever could; and not surprisingly, since for us all letters in the novel are selectively represented and have uniform print and format. A barrier exists: we cannot even "see" the telling script without the narrator's help.

The markings, shown to us indirectly, hardly reveal any truth or provide any real connection. If anything, these markings close off direct correspondence with and within the text. Elinor, like us, remains in the dark about her sister's liaison. (So does Marianne, but we only learn this later.) Not for Austen alone, but for her contemporaries as well, affective communication through letters gives way to a sort of hieroglyphic art, the meaning and dynamic of which is lost without a skilled translator. A similar instance of epistolary hieroglyphics occurs in Walter Scott's *The Heart of Midlothian* (1820), when Jeanie Deans refuses to write a letter for precisely these reasons:

> We must try by all means ... but writing winna do it. A letter canna look and pray and beg and beseech, as the human voice can do to the human heart. A letter's like the music that the ladies have for their spinets – naething but black scores.[45]

The letter, which once offered a flexible, "natural" or "realistic" frame for human experience, has been reduced to a stubborn, solid object. The who, what, when, where and why of correspondence only go as far as the surface – if that far.

As a physical artifact, Austen's version of the letter serves as a misleading guide to the human heart which, in the best instances, is always changing and adapting. This view clearly separates her from her admired predecessor, Samuel Richardson, and from his letter-master, Lovelace. Correspondence, Lovelace maintains (disingenuously), "[is] writing from the heart…not the heart only; the *soul* [is] in it. Nothing of the body…when friend writes to friend."[46] For the earlier novelist, the letter was not yet solidified: like the characters it represented, it was still in process, changeable and adaptive. Epistolary writing, writing "to the moment," according to Richardson, provides "the minutiae" wherein "lie often the unfoldings of a Story, as well as of the heart…an action undecided."[47] The example of Marianne's letter, among others, places Austen more in agreement with recent critics of epistolary form. John Preston, for example, claims that "the medium (the written word and the narrative letter) is its own story: it is opaque, it attests to nothing but itself…What happens to the words on the page…[to] letters rather than people."[48] When applied to Richardson's work, Preston's opinion of the letter is possibly anachronistic; perhaps the medium was not as opaque to eighteenth-century readers as we might assume. Indeed, the careful markings and pointing fingers in *Clarissa*'s letters, especially the typographical disorder of Clarissa's "mad" letters, transposed by Lovelace, suggest that Richardson's readers demanded such "markings" and read through what Jeanie Deans would call "black scores." Such historical changes in the way readers perceive and interpret the written word are to be expected, as the work of Svetlana Alpers and Robert Darnton indicates.[49] Twentieth-century critics and readers are likely to evaluate epistolary "opacity" in the light of later narrative developments – those of Jane Austen, for example.

The movement from the "personality" of the familiar letter toward an impersonal, constrained letter is already apparent in the letters of Helen Maria Williams, as we have seen. In her early novels, Austen elaborates this transformation, objectifying the letter as an emblem of empty convention, the "letter of the law" cited by Frederica in *Lady Susan*. *Sense and Sensibility*, *Pride and Prejudice*, and *Northanger Abbey* all testify to – and escape from – the formal limitations and dictations of the letter. Even Darcy's epistle, which disrupts both Elizabeth's pride and her prejudice, is less a confession (it offers little insight into the "personality" Elizabeth will learn to love) than a legal defense.[50] The changing character of the letter, from Richardson to Austen, seems less a matter of aesthetic distancing (Austen's rejection of an obsolete form) than a reaction to actual changes in the ways and means of letter-writing.

The ability of a letter to "unfold" a story was, therefore, nearly defunct. Instead, the letter in fiction had the capacity to bolster social institutions and duties – as we see when Elinor sends a prompt note home to her mother. The effort is almost *pro forma*: as Mrs. Dashwood's reply indicates, she barely attends to the content of her daughter's missives. Elsewhere, Elinor finds it necessary to exchange letters with her officious brother. She takes the occasion to ask him for information about Edward, but her brother responds that he can "make no inquiries on so prohibited a subject" (*S&S*, p. 353). As an avenue to the personal realm, correspondence fails. Once again, Elinor must gather intelligence from sources outside the letter.

The letter's tendency to defend propriety against the claims of feeling leads Elinor (and later, Colonel Brandon) to presume Marianne and Willoughby officially engaged. Lucy Steele exploits this same connection when she boldly displays to her rival Edward's letters to herself.

> Elinor saw that it *was* his hand, and she could doubt [an engagement between Lucy and Edward] no longer … a correspondence between them by letter could subsist only under a positive engagement, could be authorized by nothing else; for a few moments, she was almost overcome – her heart sank within her. (*S&S*, pp. 134–5).

In both cases, the appearance of letters "authorizes" the fiction of a social engagement which later proves null and void. Lucy's letters, like Marianne's, point to nothing substantial. Their only power lies in representing vacant social obligations at the expense of human feeling. They are a travesty of epistolary romance.

The final travesty arrives, of course, with Willoughby's letter. It is written in his hand, but dictated with horrifying composure by his fiancée. Personal feeling surrenders to social formulae: as Marianne perceives, that letter is written "by all the World, rather than by his own heart" (*S&S*, p. 189). The letter ultimately speaks its own betrayal. The only letter in *Sense and Sensibility* whose "substance" makes "amends for the defect of its style," is Lucy Steele's, announcing her marriage to Robert Ferrars: poetic justice weds vanity to vanity, and seals the match with letters.

In general, *Sense and Sensibility* uses the letter to clarify not only the break between inner meaning and outer form, between the personal and the institutional, but also between human beings. It is significant that the lovers who correspond never unite. Moreover, the letters themselves do not "connect." They travel by indirection and are subject to mass inspection. We hardly ever see a letter read by a person to whom it is nominally sent.[51] The amount of interference provoked by letters accumulates in the course of the novel. From the outset, Sir Thomas Middleton proclaims himself the embodiment of the Royal Mail, meddling with his tenants' messages: "He insisted on conveying all their letters to and from the post for them" (*S&S*, p. 30). Postal supervisors multiply: not only does Elinor watch Marianne writing (on three occasions), but Colonel Brandon also oversees the tell-tale "W" in the hands of the footman. Later, we learn that Willoughby's fiancée, Sophia, has surveyed and read Marianne's letter as well (*S&S*, p. 321). In all, Marianne's letters to Willoughby are reported as seen four times in the novel; her loss of privacy grows proportionately. Col. Brandon remarks that "as they [Marianne and Willoughby] openly correspond ... their marriage is *universally* talked of," and mentioned "by many – by some of whom you know nothing, by others with whom you are most intimate" (*S&S*, p. 173). The "whole World," it seems, knows the significance of the letters, without even reading them. And those letters that *are* read are *over*-read, the link between correspondents constantly interrupted or mediated.

Rather than a connected story, the letters in Austen's novels portray *faits accomplis*, leaving little room for question or conjecture: "this decided the matter at once," "she could doubt no longer," "it must ... confirm their separation forever," etc. Lucy's announcement of marriage is only the luckiest and most ironic of these *faits accomplis*. For with all the supervision given to letter-writing, the notes themselves have lost the power to connect events or activate the plot: the epistolary "agent" disappears. Often, the letters simply block or divert narrative progression; like Lady Susan juggling to maintain a status quo, they circulate in order to combat structural change or individual desire.

Austen verifies this sense of inertia in the novel's belated presentation of Marianne's three letters and the single reply from

Willoughby. With Elinor, we read the letters all together: Willoughby's harsh announcement followed by her sister's love letters.
Perhaps, if we had seen them at the time of writing, in the order of
writing, Marianne's sincere expressions would have encouraged our
faith in the romance. Assembled now in this collection, *post factum*, her
letters mock their own sincerity and generosity. Willoughby's letter
defuses all the rest, robbing them of any potency they may once have
had. This collection is dead in time. Having denied the validity of
past feeling, it negates the possibility for any future movement.
Austen brilliantly frames the presentation of these letters with
Marianne's final burst of emotion – a near-scream of agony – and
her acknowledgment of exposure: "I must feel – I must be wretched
– and they are welcome to enjoy the consciousness of it that can"
(*S&S*, pp. 189–90). The collection of love letters depicts the very
death of connection and story, and they threaten the death of
Marianne.[52]

Unlike her fictional predecessors, however, the letter-writing
Marianne does not die; instead, the threat of the letter is continually
revealed and overcome in the novel. Although the institutionalizing
power of letters does temporarily silence and debilitate both
Marianne and Elinor, Austen's narrative technique rescues them
both, weaning both them and her readers away from a tragic
epistolary closure. We recognize in Austen's scrutiny of the letter the
tactics of Williams' *Letters from France*. By delineating the contours of
an epistle, Williams sought to free herself from scrutiny. Austen gives
the revision one more turn: she objectifies the letter, but not at the
expense of closing off all interiority or personal feeling, as Williams
did. If we return to our initial scene of letter-writing, we notice that
even as Marianne's letter introduces dissimulation and signals her
betrayal, Elinor's silent thoughts and feelings remain unrestrained
and open to view. In that scene, through the use of free indirect
discourse, Austen produces the "unreserved participation in the
inner lives of fictional characters" which was once reserved for the
epistolary novel.[53] Elinor's letters, we notice, never enter the novel –
they disappear, uninspected. Instead, Austen's reading lesson per-
suades us to accept the intervention of the narrator, in order to
protect the interests of her heroines.

The lesson does not, however, suggest that Elinor's "sense" should
negate Marianne's "sensibility": Elinor has plenty of sensibility of
her own. Rather, *Sense and Sensibility* creates a new arena for personal

feeling in the novel: more inward, more distant from formal restrictions. For all her self-restraint, Elinor has a "mind ... inevitably at liberty; her thoughts could not be chained elsewhere; and the past and the future ... must be before her" (*S&S*, p. 105). Austen shows us Elinor's "reveries," which echo the liberating ' reveries" described by Wollstonecraft in her *Letters*. Elinor, however, is protected from self-disclosure and public censure. Austen converts Elinor's reserve into fortifying "reserves" and self-possession: we sense she would survive Edward's marriage to Lucy. Similarly, Marianne must learn to convert her indiscriminate confidences into self-confidence and composure. Indeed, Marianne's recovery attests to the newly forged integrity of her feelings: "I could never have been happy with [Willoughby]," she admits, though shakily. "I should have had no confidence, no esteem. Nothing could have done it away to my feelings" (*S&S*, p. 350).

This "new privacy" has a cost, nonetheless. Although Austen replaces the interiority of the epistolary novel with a "safer," less constraining mode of narration, she cannot replace the social connection, the personal correspondence which the letter once promised. In its hour of glory, the letter in fiction created an interpenetration of consciousness between readers and writers which has rarely, if ever, been repeated. Individual independence, on the other hand, brings with it isolation. This retreat is whispered in Marianne's words: what was once "confidence" between sisters, or lovers, has withdrawn to an insular, protective self-confidence. Similarly, Elinor's integrity – the appeal of a unique consciousness, which Austen produces – owes much to its incompatibility with the world around it. Her mind is free to wander, her feelings are granted intensity, but that license is resolutely circumscribed by her awareness of "the World," of social forms, of definite structures. The interiority of Elinor Dashwood's world maintains its place in *Sense and Sensibility*, but it cannot replace that outer world.[54]

Austen's narrative intervention presupposes the impotence of individual feeling to "realize" anything in a world of exteriors and materials.[55] This is the new "realism" she brings to the novel. Georg Lukács defines this distinction between the nineteenth-century novel and earlier works as

the elevation of interiority to the status of a completely independent world [which] is not only a psychological fact but also a decisive value judgement on reality; this self-sufficiency of the subjective self is its most desperate self-defence.[56]

In self-defense, the inner self runs from the reign of the letter. In the process, the letter becomes more solid, material, "real."

EMMA: CORRESPONDENCE IN HIGHBURY

Reading through Austen's early work, we might assume that letters had become almost antithetical to the writing of novels; we might wonder if the familiar letter could survive in the more social novel of the nineteenth century. At the end of *Sense and Sensibility*, letters "which a few days before would have made every nerve in Elinor's body thrill," are now greeted "with less emotion than mirth" (*S&S*, p. 370). *Pride and Prejudice* repeats this dismissal of the letter. "I hope you have destroyed the letter," ventures Darcy at the finale. "Think no more of the letter," Elizabeth replies, "...every unpleasant circumstance attending it ought to be forgotten" (*P&P*, p. 368). *Emma*, however, takes advantage of Austen's new "realization" of the letter. The letter still stands in opposition to any "true" inner self; it still belongs to the public, rather than to any individual reader or writer. It invites interference and unsought relationships; it still exposes the personal to supervision and social demands. But Austen emphasizes a new opposition: rather than a conflict between the personal and the public, we find a struggle between local community – a defined, familiar "society" – and abstract, impersonal public, a formal "Society."

Tony Tanner has written that Jane Austen's view of "society" is "more a matter of 'company' and 'community' (face-to-face relationships) than of the whole state system of institutions and relationships."[57] According to this distinction, where does the letter belong and what will it represent? Should it travel through a community of close acquaintances (face-to-face society), or should it direct itself to the "world," to the state and the Post Office ("society" as institution)?[58]

When Austen locates letters within the society of Highbury, the characteristics of the letter delineated in the earlier fiction become virtues. *Emma* socializes the letter: it now functions primarily to fit the individual within an inescapable, but mobile social context. At the same time, this socialization checks the "self-sufficiency of the subjective self" which, according to Georg Lukács, defines the nineteenth-century novel. Austen returns to the letter to frustrate her heroines' retreat to an isolated, independent world. In *Sense and Sensibility*, Marianne's letter to Willoughby accumulates readers as the novel progresses, and that accumulation oppresses and nearly silences her. The letters of *Emma*, on the other hand, throw out a wide net of correspondences, catching together the worlds of private and public fictions and providing a sort of safety net for the community. Only when letters leave the hands of the local, familiar "public," only when they submit to the impersonal structure of a faceless Post Office, do they block correspondence.

Notwithstanding this socializing movement, the contents of the letters in *Emma* – and there are many – are either inaccessible or superfluous. Although everybody in Highbury reads or hears or talks about Jane Fairfax's letters to her aunt, or Frank Churchill's letters to the Westons, these letters are not reprinted for the anonymous audience of the novel. Only one letter, at the very end of the novel, is open for direct perusal, and then only after the essential information it contains has already been relayed through five separate channels.[59] Moreover, Jane Austen has us read through this letter twice, watching the responses of both Emma and Knightley. Once again, Austen gives us a reading lesson, asking us to accept connection over content, and to reread and reactivate the role of letters in fiction.

Never has the substance of letters contributed less to Austen's plot than in *Emma*. Despite their final dismissal, letters in *Sense and Sensibility*, *Pride and Prejudice* and *Mansfield Park* do carry a weight of information essential to the plot. They work with the narrator to "unfold" the story line and to remove blinding assumptions.[60] These letters also function as "social" documents in the national or impersonal sense of social: they remind the isolated characters of a world beyond the well-known "3 or 4 families in a Country Village."[61]

In *Emma*, on the contrary, letters continually pervert the story-line and introduce narrative obstruction. Tanner suggests that "in essence, a letter is written and read in retirement from the social scene"; that letters are essentially impossible "where public modes of utterance necessarily restrict the more private ones."[62] If so, then *Emma* rejects such an essence. *Emma* uses letters to reintroduce private, idiosyncratic language into public utterance. But this is a very well-defined "public." Throughout the novel, letters are passed around the community of Highbury; letters are sent within letters; letters are read and reread aloud. Everyone from Mrs. Coles to Mr. Woodhouse to Miss Bates comments upon, admires and then translates the message into a distinctive idiolect. A letter in Highbury is never a singular, private utterance; it does, however, serve to generate a wealth of unique responses. Generally, a certain "buzz" around the community welcomes the arrival of any new letter. With that "buzz," the letters of *Emma*, regardless of origin, enter the language of Highbury.

We need only listen to the variety of responses to Frank Churchill's first letter to appreciate the idiosyncrasies of its audience. Even though we never see this "handsome" letter, we do hear the telling reactions of Mr. and Mrs. Weston, Mr. Woodhouse, Emma and Mr. Knightley.[63] The information carried by this letter and others consistently spins into distracting fictions (note Emma's cogitations upon Jane Fairfax's correspondence) or into diverting conversations. Miss Bates alone can process a letter into a conversational whirlpool, drawing in any and every element of her small world (*Emma*, pp. 157–62). In Austen's most "sociable" novel, letters only appear in the context of Highbury society: the dynamic of correspondence overrides the nunciatory function of letters. A question, however, recurs: can such overlapping correspondence survive the efficient mechanism of the Post Office?

David Monaghan writes of the vertical and horizontal relationships "that stretched from lowest to highest in the village" of Jane Austen's world; the "network of face-to-face contacts...which embraced all of society." Of course, this is a "society" formed by certain exclusions.[64] *Emma*'s letters help create and sustain this restricted network: they force the individual to enter into circulation. Monaghan continues: "Anything that threatened it [the social network], such as the creation of large, centralised institutions, or the growth of cities, was viewed with distaste."[65] The rise of the Royal Mail, for instance, could threaten this face-to-face social vision. Robinson reports that before 1793, the city of Manchester had its mail administered by an aged postmistress, her daughter and one carrier. As part of the expansion which followed the Postal Act of 1794, the postmistress was pensioned, new carriers were brought in and the Manchester Penny Post "gradually extended far and wide to its subordinate communities," coordinating with nearby towns and strengthening its connection to the central office in London. The reforms in Manchester were only the first in a series of "expansions" which covered all of Great Britain by the early nineteenth century. Most "outposts" soon fell into the category of "subordinate communities."[66]

The transformation is hinted in Walter Scott's *The Antiquary* (1816), written contemporaneously with *Emma*. Set in Scotland "near the end of the eighteenth century," *The Antiquary* imagines the small world of Fairport, where 10-year-old boys get lost delivering the express mail, and where local gossips gather at sorting-time in the outpost's version of a post office. The women of Fairport meet in the postmaster's back parlour "in order, from the outside of the epistles, and if they are not belied, from the inside also, to amuse themselves with gleaning information or forming conjectures about the correspondence and affairs of their neighbours."[67] The friends of Mrs. Mailsetter, with their attempts at spying and with the wondrous fictions they spin, amuse the novelist and reader in turn. But they are eventually reprimanded by the postal authorities, and their daily amusement severely curtailed later in the novel when military and business men resort to more efficient channels of communication.[68] Although Scott's gossips, "like the sibyls after consulting their leaves," concoct "information" which "[flies] through a hundred channels, and in a hundred varieties, through the world of Fairport,"[69] the narrator effectively joins the state in regulating and blocking their local "information." On the one hand, a packet addressed to the hero of the novel frustrates the women's prying with its "strong, thick paper imperviable" and its heavy seal "which defied tampering": surely a packet "from the Secretary of State's office."[70] On the other hand, the narrator gives readers access to information the gossips cannot imagine: stories of national consequence and economic transactions which nearly erase the community at Fairport.[71]

While Scott "remembered" Fairport, and Austen created Highbury, the de-personalization and de-localization of the village post was well under way throughout the British Isles.[72] Though distant from the urban centers, villages such as Fairport and Highbury would nevertheless be incorporated into the expanding system of postal lines which radiated from London.

It is Jane Fairfax, in *Emma*, who calls attention to the "wonderful" machinery of the modern post:

The post office is a wonderful establishment!... the regularity and dispatch of it!... So seldom that any negligence or blunder appears! So seldom that a letter, among the thousands that are constantly passing about the kingdom, is ever carried wrong – and not one in a million, I suppose, actually lost! (*Emma*, p. 296)

It is telling that she applauds the institution, rather than her local postmaster. For in a novel built upon personal interference, mistakes and a complicated overlapping of messages, the mechanism of the Post Office could erase all story.[73]

The Post Office enters late in volume III of the novel, after we have already become accustomed to the flow of letters in and about Highbury. The local residents seem to have constructed a post office without walls, a diffuse system between households. But a post office building does exist in Highbury, and at a dinner party at Hartfield, the guests all learn that Jane Fairfax visits it religiously – even in bad health, even in bad weather. In the course of the ensuing conversation, we get our first real glimpse at the "riddle" of Jane Fairfax. We also get a demonstration of the shifting role of the letter.

Knightley's brother alludes to the romantic history of England's postal service – perhaps to the dawn of the age of the mail coach, in the mid-1780s. The mail coach had brought excitement, optimism and an unprecedented, powerful rush to epistolary communication.[74] By *Emma*'s day, however, the excitement was waning:

Mr. John Knightley smiled... "The post office had a great charm at one point in our lives. When you have lived to my age, you will begin to think letters are never worth going through the rain for." There was a little blush, and then this answer: "I must not hope to be ever situated as you are, in the midst of every dearest connexion, and therefore I cannot expect that simply growing old should make me indifferent to letters."

"Indifferent! Oh, no! – ... Letters are no matter of indifference; they are generally a very positive curse."

"You are speaking of letters of business; mine are letters of friendship."

"I have often thought them the worse of the two," replied he, coolly. "Business, you know, may bring money, but friendship hardly ever does." (*Emma*, p. 232)

John Knightley and Jane Fairfax articulate the growing split between
the impersonal side of the Post Office (its expansion has been fueled
by business interests) and the personal services the mail provides.
Scott's post-office gossips joke about this division when the Jane
Fairfax of Fairport, young Jenny Caxton, comes asking for letters
from her beau: they chide her for acting "as if her letters were o' mair
consequence than the best merchants o' the town."[75] At least two
fictions are at work in the scene from *Emma*: for Jane, correspondence
trades in affection and sentimental "connexion"; for Knightley,
money replaces correspondence as the emblem of circulation. As the
debate progresses, Jane Fairfax's feelings grow warmer, and her
lonely situation more apparent:

You have everybody dearest to you always at hand; I probably, never shall
again; and therefore, till I have outlived all my affections, a post office, I
think, must always have the power to draw me out in worse weather than
today. (*Emma*, p. 232)

Beyond the business/friendship debate, several issues warrant
investigation here. First, although no one sees the letters which pass
from the post office to Jane Fairfax, and vice versa, her attachment to
letters is now public knowledge. In all this, Jane risks exposure to
more than the elements. With "a blush, a quivering lip, a tear in the
eye," her body registers how much she has invested in this discussion,
and how much Mr. Knightley's business wants to erase. When the
letters of friendship cede to letters of money, emotional blackmail
lurks in the shadows.[76] The subject of the post office has, indeed,
"drawn her out" of her habitual reserve. Furthermore, the morning
trips to the post office subject Jane to the warnings and expostulations
of the assembled party. Mrs. Elton, for example, insists on sending
her "man" to pick up the "sad girl's" letters, despite Jane's protests.
We see Jane Fairfax at her most vulnerable in this scene. Her
exposure is trebled: her health, her emotions and her secret
engagement to Frank Churchill are all endangered by her allegiance
to the post office. That allegiance, synecdochically, marks her
economic fragility and her socially dependent position.

This moment of heightened vulnerability recalls the fact that Jane
has been the victim of letters – or of others' responses to letters –
throughout the novel. Jane's own account of things usually disappears under the reactions to her letters. Much of her personal
history reaches us through the letters she sends to High Street, but no

letter of Jane's ever appears in the text. Rather, they are broadcast, with much garbling and emendation, by the wonderful babble of Miss Bates. Otherwise, they provide the grist for Emma's fiction mill. "An ingenious and animating suspicion" enters Emma's brain as she hears of Jane's letter; thus she begins to concoct an elaborate story about Jane, the Campbells and the Dixons (*Emma*, pp. 160, 168–9).

Not only do Jane's letters keep her tied to an oppressive engagement, they also reduce her to a cipher within the community, open to anyone's meddlesome "Jane Fairfax-ing."[77] Even when her secret is disclosed, the "morning's post...conveyed the history of Jane Fairfax" between the members of Highbury society. And Frank's final letter, while providing yet another version of Jane's story, rejects Jane's own account of herself: "I have heard from her...[but] I dare not depend [on her words]." Rather, he begs his stepmother to write about his beloved: "Let me hear from you without delay; I am impatient for a thousand particulars" (*Emma*, p. 439). Jane is practically dispossessed by letters: no one has less control over her life than she does. In fact, Mrs. Elton's busybody correspondence on "dear Jane's" behalf, and Frank Churchill's negligence in responding to her letters nearly succeed in destroying Jane Fairfax. Together, they conspire to make her a governess, out of reach of her "dearest connexions," to be traded about in intellectual and psychological enslavement. "There are places in town, offices, where inquiry would soon produce something," Jane mentions ambiguously in response to Mrs. Elton's efforts to "place" her; "Offices for the sale – not quite of human flesh – but of human intellect" (*Emma*, p. 300). The novel offers little guarantee that Jane Fairfax will ever escape such offices and emerge with her own voice. She may remain only "inquired" and "talked about" in Highbury, always circulating in others' letters, or others' versions of her letters.

The third issue to confront, then, in the dinner scene at Hartfield, is why Jane Fairfax so fiercely refuses to resign her allegiance to the post office. To her, it offers the one security and pleasure she knows. Orphaned, destined to be a governess, too talented and "elegant" to ignore her situation, Jane Fairfax lives *for* letters as much as she lives *in* them. Like her maiden aunt and grandmother, Jane shows an extreme attachment to these emblems of "connexion." As her morning walks and her own words attest, for the solitary Jane Fairfax, the post office supplies a substitute for the secure domestic circle of a John Knightley or an Emma Woodhouse. The mail guarantees her affections even as it exposes and heightens their intensity. This concern over the dissolution of close, emotional ties, or "affections" – especially in the family group – echoes throughout *Emma*, from the constant laments of Mr. Woodhouse to Emma's anxiety over the claims of young Henry Knightley. In a world which struggles to remain *en famille*, Jane Fairfax is forced to find refuge in the post office.[78]

But what sort of refuge is it? By placing her faith in the post office, an increasingly de-personalized and de-personalizing institution, Jane Fairfax displaces her doubts about Frank Churchill, yet she remains forever outside any fixed sense of community. No one, including the reader, really knows much about her "inner life"; we know only her movements within a structured system. In fact, Jane Fairfax returns to the post office in order to shield herself from potential disclosure. She diverts attention from herself with her panegyric upon the postal system, which now bears repeating:

The post office is a wonderful establishment!... So seldom that any negligence or blunder appears! So seldom that a letter, among the thousands that are constantly passing about the kingdom, is ever carried wrong... [or] actually lost! And when one considers the variety of hands, and bad hands too, that are to be deciphered, it increases the wonder. (*Emma*, p. 296)

Jane's most expressive outburst turns into an occasion for self-effacement: as she retreats into obscurity in the scene, she asks the post office to cover for her. Her effusions cast the "wonderful establishment" into an equivocal role: whereas her facial expressions (tears, blushes) bring her to public attention, the post office both protects and negates the individual body.[79]

Indeed, an extraordinary state and commercial machinery of organization and comprehension grounds Jane's faith. But it is a faith born of desperation. As Mr. Knightley drily points out, the "wonder" of the post is no miracle, merely an army of practiced clerks, well paid: "That is the key to a great deal of capacity. The public pays and must be served well" (*Emma*, p. 297). Money, which pays for the flawless deciphering and dispatch, threatens to overcome the idiosyncrasies of individual "hands," of personal orthography and style. (Another hand-writing discussion follows the debate over the post office). Jane's faith, then, rests in a faceless, far-flung, mercenary institution. She seems to have lost all direct contact with her attachments. Even when "face-to-face," she and Frank Churchill must remain distant and separated.

In this light, we review the warnings and suggestions of the dinner party and detect a concerted attempt to draw Jane Fairfax into a familiar circle. Mr. Woodhouse offers his "kind solicitude": "young ladies are very sure to be cared for," he promises. Mrs. Elton laments, "It is a sign I was not there to take care of you." Mrs. Weston suggests, "My advice, I certainly do feel tempted to give…indeed, you ought to be careful" (*Emma*, pp. 294–6). Indeed, flawed as it is, Highbury *cares* about Jane Fairfax; they want to give her a sense of belonging. Even Mr. John Knightley, for all his gruff, businessman's pragmatism, introduces a note of sympathy for Jane's situation. He hopes one day she will depend less on the post office – but not for want of attachments. Rather, "Time will lessen the interest of every attachment not within the daily circle…As an old friend, you will allow me to hope, Miss Fairfax, that ten years hence you may have as many concentrated objects as I have" (*Emma*, p. 294).

At this point I would like to return to an earlier suggestion of the contentious relationship between Austen's novels and the post office, between an awareness of local community and the structure of abstract society. Again I emphasize that Jane Fairfax appeals not to her local postmaster, but to the national postal system, "so very well-regulated." This is certainly not the method of correspondence familiar to the eighteenth-century novel. The very interferences which once threatened the epistolary heroine – intercepted letters, confiscated letters, letters over-read or written over, editorial intervention, or biassed decipherings – all disappear thanks to the wonders of the modern mail. But if human correspondence were absolutely contained and controlled by such a mechanism, the "wonder" of *Emma* would not survive. We would never glimpse even that "something…a little disguised or a little mistaken" which "belongs to any human disclosure" (*Emma*, p. 431). Indeed, the community of Highbury, with its generous allowance for personal interference, misdirected messages and multiple idiolects would also be erased. There is no room for Miss Bates' parlor in a modern post office.

The novel depends upon the individual irregularities and "blunders" which a faceless post office denies. Jane Fairfax's mention of "blunders," in fact, touches off a chain of associations within *Emma*, for "blunders" make the novel. In a word game at Hartfield, Frank

Churchill spells out the word "blunder," but as it travels around the table, it elicits different readings from each viewer, and produces multiple resonances for the reader (*Emma*, p. 348).[80] Later, Frank echoes Jane, when he reveals his neglect about sending a letter: "Imagine how, till I actually detected my own blunder, I raved at the blunders of the post." But if he had not blundered, he may never have been forced to disclose the engagement to his uncle (*Emma*, p. 443). "Blunder" is one of the crucial words of the novel, and Emma must confront it when her own fictions begin to explode: "How to understand the deceptions she had thus been practising on herself and living under! The blunders, the blindness of her own head and heart!" (*Emma*, pp. 411–12).

One of the wonders of *Emma* is the narrator's ability to explore all these "blunders," to participate in them and, at the same time, correct them. In *Emma*, there is no monolithic, coordinating point of view: according to Elizabeth Deeds Ermarth, "The apparently reliable narrator has an unsettling habit of abandoning us to uncertainty by unexpected shifts in perspective."[81] The narrator allows what the post office cannot – direct participation in another's point of view. Austen's solution performs a sort of narrative correspondence without the constraints of eighteenth-century letters. Her use of free indirect discourse constructs that illusion of psychological reality and unconscious exchange which David Lodge calls "a more intimate relationship between fictional discourse and the processes of human consciousness."[82] As long as her secret remains locked up in the post office, Jane Fairfax will not participate in this exchange; we will never understand how her mind operates.

Emma, on the other hand, Austen allows to narrate, and to "blunder"; but unlike Lady Susan, Emma will never successfully dictate. We can read Emma as Austen's warning to her own narrative intervention, and *Emma* as her reassessment of epistolary form. If, as Ermarth suggests, Austen's narrators move closer to the status of "nobody" in both *Emma* and *Persuasion*, they do not approach the faceless regularity of a state institution. Nevertheless, the narrator does move away from the defensive posture apparent in the conclusion to *Lady Susan*, and the hard-fought dismissals of the letter in her early novels.[83] *Emma* resolves her tug-of-war with epistolary form. To achieve this, Austen schools her heroine, a humorous version of her own earlier narrative personae, in the reading of letters and the writing of fiction.

Emma, who "with insufferable vanity had...believed herself in the secret of everybody's feelings, [who] with unpardonable arrogance proposed to arrange everybody's destiny" is a novelist in the making (*Emma*, pp. 412–13). Not surprisingly, Emma deplores any exchange of letters which does not center on Emma. She thus contrives to "make her escape from Jane Fairfax's letter"; she applauds herself when she "is able to escape from the letter itself." On the other hand, letters wherein "the charm of her own name [is] not wanting" support her belief in her power. Where "'Miss Woodhouse' appeared more than once," she finds an epistle "gratifying," "stimulative" even "irresistible" (pp. 162, 444). For Emma, others' letters represent unwanted connection and potential subversion: she wishes to remain independent, and in control. She shows extreme suspicion, therefore, of Robert Martin's short letter to Harriet. She fears its "bewitching flattery" will outweigh her own plan for her protégée. Above all, secret correspondence provokes her sovereign wrath. About Frank's and Jane's liaison, she roars, "What has it been but a system of hypocrisy and deceit, – espionage and treachery!" She re-imagines the two lovers in terms of the duplicitous fictions of political correspondence: "To come among us with professions of openness and simplicity; and [to form] such a league in secret to judge us all! – Here have we been...completely duped" (*Emma*, p. 399).

Like other practitioners of the art of fiction, sitting in both government and literary offices, Emma senses that epistolary form "surrenders control of the discourse" to the letter-writer, and she responds by imposing her own controlling fictions upon the characters.[84] Thus Robert Martin's proposal crystallizes her plot to unite Harriet and Mr. Elton; and the reading of Jane Fairfax's letter generates the unjust story of Jane's illicit love for the husband of her best friend. While everyone else expresses concern for Miss Fairfax's ill-advised trips to the post office, Emma sits back, elaborating the story of intrigue she has, herself, concocted (*Emma*, p. 298). She fancies herself master of the game of human secrets and social intercourse, but in fact she is not listening at all. She has not learned that no one "masters" the Highbury style of correspondence.

Emma's authorial pretensions, of course, all come to a crashing end, but she emerges from the wreckage with a more accommodating perspective. It is at this point that Austen reintroduces the letter, and completes her revision of correspondence. Now that Emma can adequately "read" a letter, so can the reader: the novel's only included letter arrives after the marriage plots have been resolved. Frank Churchill's letter rewrites the novel from another perspective: "You must all endeavor to comprehend...See me, then,...arriving on my first visit to Randalls." The plot is already known to us, only the explanations and the emphases change. Typically, Emma balks at receiving this alternate version: "she guessed what it must contain, and deprecated the necessity of reading it...She wanted no explanations, she wanted only to have her thoughts to herself" (*Emma*, pp. 436–7). As the novel has proved, however, no one can limit her thoughts to herself. Frank's letter forces Emma to yield to intrusion, just as Jane Fairfax yields to interference. That Frank's letter actually provides no new information emphasizes its function as correspondence, rather than as message. Moreover, this break in Emma's authorial point of view exemplifies the whole process of the novel, which asks the reader to negotiate between individual perspectives, languages and blunders.[85]

Thus Austen reintegrates the letter into the social novel. At the close of *Emma*, we find Emma and Knightley sharing letters, reading over each other's shoulders, commenting aloud on the page before them. The letter's role has shifted from that of a messenger which controls events to that of a social artifact, to be displayed, examined and re-examined. Knightley explains to Emma that in responding aloud to Frank's letter, "I...feel that I am near you" (*Emma*, p. 445). Their reading the letter offers an occasion for yet another revision, for greater openness and stronger connection. In short, the letter promotes correspondence between alternating fictions – Frank's, Emma's, Knightley's and all the prior chapters of the novel. And it keeps the small world of *Emma* from splintering into solipsistic "thoughts to oneself."

THE MOMENT OF THE LETTER: *PERSUASION*

Persuasion, Austen's last completed novel, is usually treated as the exception to many rules about the novelist's work. In her use of the letter in fiction, however, *Persuasion* perpetuates the conflict emergent in *Emma*: to maintain a local correspondence, separate from the intruding, homogenizing language of society. Again, Austen reserves the letter for the final moments of the story; and again, the letter forces a re-evaluation of the narrated point of view. It marks a reconciliation between distinct versions of the novel's progress, and between the long-separated lovers. At the same time, *Persuasion* announces the letter's final blaze of glory before it retires from the novel. Captain Wentworth's letter to Anne Elliot, written under the guise of a business letter, written in the crowded room of a Bath inn, under the noise of scattered conversations and concealed under the scattered papers on the desk, seems almost too precarious, too threatened to survive the crush of the world. Yet it effects a greater revolution than any letter in Austen's previous novels. "The work of an instant," it flashes forth, illuminating the very structures which are extinguishing the power of private correspondence.

The letter scene in the penultimate chapter of *Persuasion* has received much – and much deserved – critical attention.[86] In the words of B. C. Southam, "nowhere else" does Austen "seize upon a more profound 'phase of life'...nowhere else is the 'stress and passion...of every passing moment' disclosed so surely."[87] Accent falls upon the eloquent, concentrated fragility of the scene, as if this "moment" knotted up "the fine line between disaster and fortune" which threads through the novel.[88] Here at last Wentworth reveals his undiminished love for Anne Elliot and offers her "a heart even more your own than when you broke it eight years and a half ago."[89] Against the ponderous rhythm of the salon scene, against the weighted language of the salon conversations, Wentworth's letter shocks like a thunderclap. The moment of its delivery brings to the fore the "sense of temporal uncertainty," the "lack of harmonious progression" which distinguish *Persuasion* from its predecessors.[90]

With it, Austen unleashes a potential in the epistolary form which had been mocked in "Love and Friendship," stifled in *Sense and Sensibility*, and reawakened in *Emma*. The power of discomposure, of confusion; the ability to disrupt time and place; the chance to create an incomplete, inarticulate but effective language, and to communicate beyond formal constraints: the letter scene generates this unsettling energy. Normally, we associate this potential with the lyrics of the Romantic poets – Shelley's "Hymn to Mont Blanc," or Coleridge's "Dejection: An Ode," for example – rather than with the measured prose of an Austen novel. But Wentworth's letter, and the impetus behind *Persuasion* which it exposes, both aim to express this same lyric power, this same desire to explode form.

In *Persuasion*, Austen creates a silent explosion, demonstrating the social pressures which lead to the political "quietism" of later

Romantic literature.[91] However quiet, it is nonetheless a revolution: not only against the novel which Austen inherited from the late eighteenth century, but against the society which sustains the novel. In a world composed of vain names ("Elliot of Kellynch Hall") and based on empty histories, Austen tests the fundamentals of her fiction: that communication constitutes community, and that reality has room for the work of the individual imagination.[92] In the process, she reconsiders the parameters of the social novel: its dependence on progressive, logical time and on identifiable place its narrative assurance; its defined characters with defined consciousnesses; its integration of the individual with the social. Should the novel still position its hero and heroine with a name and a home? The letter plays a crucial role in this re-evaluation. In her previous novels Austen insisted upon the letter's increasing impotence in the greater "World" of public events and social relations. It represented connection, if not clear communication; it could not effect change, only reconsideration. In *Persuasion*, the letter remains impotent in the world of social forms, yet it creates a world of its own, an alternative community. With the quiet exchange of Anne Elliot and Captain Wentworth, *Persuasion* brings two displaced individuals to center-stage, then removes them altogether from the world of the novel.

Let us look first at the "moment" of the letter. Mrs. Musgrove and Mrs. Croft are at one end of the room, discussing the weddings of the Musgrove daughters and disparaging the idea of long engagements. Across the room, by the window, stand Anne Elliot and Captain Harville, deep in conversation about Captain Benwick and Harville's sister. Not far from them, Wentworth sits writing a letter, conducting a specific transaction for his friend Benwick. As our attention switches from one spot to another in the salon, we feel the mounting force of an unarticulated undercurrent. Each phrase in the air is transformed by Anne's consciousness into a message or physical signal to herself: "she felt its application to herself, felt it in a nervous thrill all over her" (*Persuasion*, p. 231). The conversations are both public and, more intensely, privatized. Momentarily, the flow of words halts: in a "hitherto perfectly quiet division of the room," Wentworth drops his pen with a slight sound. Some message is forcing its way through the noise. Anne now feels his presence "nearer than she supposed," and the pressure builds. He has, with that gesture, entered into her conversation, into her very language. The barriers between distinct subjects and subjectivities all dissolve in Anne's consciousness of the scene. Wentworth finally exits abruptly, leaving Anne even more confused and somewhat dazed. After this protracted and overladen prologue, Austen delivers the letter with a rush which dizzies the reader as much as Anne Elliot:

> She had *only time*, however, to move closer to the table ... when footsteps were heard returning; the door opened; it was himself. He begged their pardon, but he had forgotten his gloves, and *instantly* crossing the room to the writing table, and standing with his back to Mrs. Musgrove, he drew out a letter from under the scattered paper, placed it before Anne with eyes of glowing entreaty fixed on her *for a moment*, and *hastily* collecting his gloves, was again out of the room, almost before Mrs. Musgrove was aware of his being in it – *the work of an instant!*
>
> The revolution which *one instant* had made in Anne, was almost beyond expression. The letter, with a direction hardly legible, to " Miss A. E.–." was evidently the one he had been folding so hastily. While supposed to be writing only to Captain Benwick, he had been also addressing her! On the contents of that letter depended all that this world could do for her! Any thing was possible, any thing might be defied rather than suspense. (*Persuasion*, pp. 236–7, my emphasis)

The identifiable objects – the forgotten gloves, scattered papers and writing table – serve to anchor a moment which might otherwise spin off into the realm of the miraculous, somewhere beyond the here and now of the Bath salon. The brief and disarming apparition seems too good to be true, and too true to Anne's unspoken desire to be real. Before she even opens the letter, the moment itself, " the work of an instant," has the power to obliterate material surroundings, or at least to remove Anne from them and redefine " this world " for her. As Anne recognizes, the fleeting exchange stands at the edge of an explosion: the episode moves " *almost* beyond expression "; it ignores the surveying world (Mrs. Musgrove is " *almost* " totally unaware); and it defies the deliberate unfolding of a linear narrative. It " defies any thing ... rather than suspense." With the arrival of the letter comes the expansive moment of desire: nothing can wait, and everything can change.

The forced, almost cramped immediacy of the exchange hardly makes sense – which is the point. The principal characters have been wrenched out of the circumscribed reality which separated them. Wentworth's sudden departure, then startling return and re-exit almost seem more like a stutter in the story-line than a serious progression of events – as if Austen, editing the scene, included two separate "takes." Neither Anne nor Wentworth is in full command of the situation, yet the episode moves them beyond reasonable "understanding" to a new, shared comprehension. Anne's impatience matches the letter-writer's. They both need to rearrange the limits of time and space. There is no time for communicating through the proper channels, no time to send for a servant to run to the post office, no time, even, to wait and meet later. Austen literally destroys the time-lag implicit in letter-writing by having Wentworth respond immediately to Anne's words, by having him hand the letter directly to her. Even the narrator is loath to intervene the letter appears directly in the text, with only Anne's reaction as a gloss. As direct as Anne's dialogue, the letter enters the realm of the spoken, rather than the reflective; the spontaneous rather than the measured. Time and space will conspire against the lovers, as every earlier encounter (in the octagon room, in the theatre box, in the various parlors of various friends) has taught them. Any instant may bring invading troops of Musgroves or Elliots. Austen pushes her lovers to this "revolution of an instant," this rejection of the phenomenal reality and of the world which divides them. After eight and a half years of waiting for the no longer inevitable, Anne Elliot and Captain Wentworth salvage their own "spot of time."[93]

Persuasion introduces several such breaks in the "seamless quality," "the logical and natural progression" which is the hallmark of Austen's narrative style.[94] The disruptions are too well orchestrated to dismiss as "an artistic falling off," due to Austen's inability to revise completely.[95] The overturning of any objective measure of time and place recurs throughout the novel, whenever Anne Elliot feels overwhelmed by the physical presence of her long-lost love. These moments of phenomenological vertigo coincide with a loss of composure or self-possession. They expose Anne's desire.

At the first appearance of Wentworth, "a thousand feelings rushed on Anne." The "few minutes" of an otherwise uneventful meeting expand to an almost painful fullness for her: "the room seemed full – full of persons and voices – but a few minutes ended it" (*Persuasion*, pp. 59–60). In the short, sparse description Anne seems to be holding her breath, fearing that the barrier of "eight years... almost eight years since all had been given up" might collapse under the weight of these few minutes. Her sense of oblivion surfaces again as she plays the piano at Uppercross and Wentworth dances before her (*Persuasion*, pp. 71–2). It becomes even more pronounced after their conversation in the octagon room, where objective reality nearly melts away. Anne, who:

in spite of [Wentworth's] agitated voice...and in spite of all the various noises of the room, the almost ceaseless slam of the door, and the ceaseless buzz of persons walking through, had distinguished every word; was struck, gratified, confused and beginning to breathe very quick, and *feel a hundred things in a moment*...Anne saw nothing, thought nothing of the brilliancy of the room...her eyes were bright and her cheeks glowed, – but she knew nothing about it. (*Persuasion*, pp. 183–4; my emphasis)

Later, just before the delivery of the letter, when Wentworth's pen drops and he glances at her, "the two ladies continued to talk...but Anne heard nothing distinctly; it was only a buzz of sounds in her ear, her mind was in confusion...a thorough absence of mind" (*Persuasion*, pp. 231–2). With these moments of "absence," Austen leads her heroine to the moment of revelation.

Given these episodes, I find it hard to identify the sense of time (and place) in *Persuasion* as nostalgic, "autumnal," or "recollected in tranquillity."[96] The resolution of the plot fights against patience, composure and a measured progression of history. Anne Elliot does try to escape from the "revolution" of the moment of desire, when time seems to lose its bearings and rooms to lose their boundaries. She consistently searches for breathing space, for a "half-hour's solitude and reflection," or "an interval of meditation." Such retreats, Austen indicates, are not only untenable, they are evasions of the truth of Anne's love. Anne must learn to enter the disorienting flux of the revolutionary moment.

Nor should we assume that Anne is alone in her discomposure, or unusually susceptible to bouts of vertigo. Her fortitude after the accident at the Cobb should dispel any idea of a frail heroine. Since the narrative point of view is almost entirely Anne's, however, the reader is privy to those moments of overwhelming dizziness which remain invisible to Anne's family and friends.[97] Prior to his erratic behavior at the inn, Captain Wentworth's loss of self-command – first evident at the Cobb – does not clearly correspond to nor coincide with Anne's own confusion. The letter, finally, breaks through this impasse. Its very existence, we have already noted, introduces a physical immediacy and possibility hitherto frustrated in the novel. By its language, moreover, it displays Wentworth's confusion, and it intensifies the mutual dependency of the lovers. The letter creates a language and a world apart for Anne and Wentworth.

[Anne's] eyes devoured the following words:

"I can no longer listen in silence. I must speak to you by such means as are within my reach. You pierce my soul. I am half agony half hope. Tell me that I am not too late... I offer myself to you again with a heart even more your own than when you broke it eight years and a half ago. Dare not say that man forgets sooner than woman, that his love has an earlier death. I have loved none but you... You alone have brought me to Bath. For you alone I think and plan. – Have you not seen this? Can you fail to understand my wishes? – I had not waited even these ten days, could I have read your feelings, as I think you must have penetrated mine. I can hardly write. I am every instant hearing something which overpowers me. You sink your voice, but I can distinguish the tones of that voice, when they would be lost on others. – Too good, too excellent creature! You do us justice indeed. You do believe that there is true attachment and constancy among men. Believe it to be most fervent, most undeviating in F. W " (*Persuasion*, p. 237)

The starts and stops, the questions and the candid vulnerability convincingly report Wentworth's turmoil, even as they point out the weakness of this missive as a formal composition. Unlike Frank Churchill, who can "write a letter, indeed," Captain Wentworth is no master of the word game: he can "hardly write"; he is "overpowered." Beyond the explicit supplication of this letter lies Wentworth's self-denial. Having made a name for himself in the Navy, having become "somebody" in the eyes of the world, he returns finally to self-surrender in the letter: "I offer myself to you again... even more your own... For you alone I think and plan." With these words he collapses the years distance, events and social obligations which have made Anne a "nobody to father and sister," and made himself a commanding officer The letter echoes his lonely cry at the Cobb – "Is there no one to help me?" – and Anne's silent response. Anne has "pierced" his soul, she has "penetrated" his feelings.

Underlying the loss of self-sufficiency is linguistic interdependency. Just as it rejects phenomenological and social barriers (and we recall Wentworth's earlier impatience with the channels of communication in the Navy – too slow and too impersonal (*Persuasion*, p. 108)), so too does this letter override the limits of language. Wentworth's letter literally hangs on Anne's every word. His message is governed by her expressions: the full meaning of his "half"-way language requires the recipient's remembering her concurrent discussion with Captain Harville. This interdependence replaces the less vulnerable compositions of Austen's other male writers. The careful narrative provided by a Darcy, for example, might have provoked Anne's rejection of men's "history":

Men have had every advantage of us in telling their own story. Education has been theirs in so much higher a degree; the pen has been in their hands. I will not allow [men's] books to prove anything. (*Persuasion*, p. 234)

Wentworth, then, must drop the pen in order to prove his love, and to prove himself an exception to the general rule.[98] Drop it he does, twice, converting his business correspondence into a love letter dictated by a woman's argument (and thereby avenging the Jane Fairfaxes against the John Knightleys of the world). He does not even attempt his version of the story, or furnish any proof beyond mere expression. In the interpenetration of subjects and discourses, "he is open to a more equal (unscripted) relationship, in which the old patterns of dominance and deference are abandoned, deleted – dropped."[99] Significantly, the letter functions as the vehicle for this social–sexual revolution. Like Anne's consciousness, Wentworth's letter defies limits and devours the words in the air about it. As the stories of Benwick, Harville's sister, and the Musgrove daughters fade away, the letter affirms and intensifies the language, the unique understanding, shared by Anne and Wentworth. "The sharp knowing in apartness," which D. H. Lawrence criticized in Austen's novels, gives way to a knowing in togetherness.[100] With the letter, the lovers complete each other's meaning, heal each other's confusion and extract themselves from their immediate context.

"Such a letter was not soon to be recovered from": it reproduces the upheaval of the preceding moment within the realm of language, and sustains that upheaval for the rest of the novel. In Anne, it produces "an overwhelming happiness," such that she can no longer "seem like herself." So distracted, so *ecstatic* is she that she must actually leave the room: caught up in her new world, "she began not to understand a word...said" by anyone around her (*Persuasion*, p. 238). We watch as the letter removes the lovers from the society of the novel: it privatizes their language into a personal code. Previously, Anne had "acknowledged it to be very fitting, that every little social commonwealth should dictate its own matters of discourse." Now it becomes not only fitting, but necessary for emotional survival. Miss Bates' parlour has shrunk and de-materialized; the local language of Highbury distills itself into the barely articulate correspondence of *Persuasion*'s lovers. Their "spirits dance in private rapture," but the union they imagine – which the letter tentatively represents – exists in utopia, a no man's land beyond the here and now. They walk in the realm of romance:

> where the power of conversation would make the present hour a blessing indeed; and prepare it for all the immortality which the happiest recollections of their own future lives could bestow. There they exchanged again those feelings and those promises ... there they returned again into the past, *more exquisitely happy ... more tender, more tried, more fixed* in a knowledge of each other's character, truth and attachment; *more equal* to act, *more justified* in acting. And there ... heedless of every group around them, seeing neither sauntering politician, bustling housekeepers, flirting girls, nor nursery-maids and children, they could indulge in those retrospectives and acknowledgements ... which were so poignant and so ceaseless in interest. All the variations of the last week were gone through; and of yesterday and today there could scarcely be an end. (*Persuasion*, pp. 240–1; my emphasis)

The "little commonwealths" of shared interest become "something evermore about to be." The lovers experience something excessive and edenic, something inordinate and out of logical order. Political and domestic concerns bustle and hurry away from their world. In the intensity of their privacy, they are nearly silenced, or spirited away.

The implication for the two lovers is severe: like Keats' lovers in "The Eve of St. Agnes," their ecstasy does not belong in this world. Austen transfers them from home and family to an idealized community, the navy, which is as unstable and marginal as the letter itself. Intrinsically rootless, "a floating, drifting, changing population," the navy offers no more substantial security than a letter traveling between ship and shore.[101] In the end, Anne and Wentworth have none of the guarantees of Austen's other, landed couples: "his profession was all that could make her friends wish that tenderness less" between the two. For although Anne "gloried in being a sailor's wife," she must "pay the tax of quick alarm" and live with "the dread of a future war" (*Persuasion*, p. 252).

The final moment of the letter and of the novel suspends Anne Elliot and Captain Wentworth in a realization of their past, present and future which they alone can share. Even the narrator of the novel can barely penetrate their shared understanding at this point. The draft manuscript of *Persuasion*, reprinted with the finished novel, offers a pessimistic version of this impenetrability. In the earlier version, the reconciliation of lovers relies on a discourse of negation.

Anne cannot pronounce for Wentworth the words, "*he may*." She can only signal her attachment to him by denying her attachment to her cousin: "No, Sir...there is no message...There is no truth in any such report." Wentworth copies her denial: "'No truth in any such report?' he repeated, 'No truth in any part of it?'" "'None.'" A "silent but very powerful dialogue" follows, underscoring the lovers' and the narrator's inability to cut through the strictures of language (*Persuasion*, p. 263). The silent colloquy suggests that "no truth" can be spoken, at least not in the language of the novel. It leaves the lovers in the realm of the negative, and robs them of capability. This unutterable impotence, reminiscent of King Lear's tragic "nothing," may have prompted Austen's revision and her reconsideration of the letter's potential.

The letter offers itself as a last-ditch, tenuous moment of liberation and possibility, even as it crystallizes the romantic departure from the "real" world. Its power rests on the promise that men and women can and will communicate. This is the redemption Austen allows in *Persuasion*. She emphasizes the mutuality of the lovers' "persuasion": the letter sheds its ego-centrism along with its dictatorial authority. This meeting of minds, this correspondence, which the rest of the novel so forcefully resists, gives us the satisfaction of joining Anne and Wentworth, briefly, in their fragile bubble. But we are at the outer limits of narrative discourse here – without history, content or context to support us.

The letter has traveled a good distance from the self-promoting epistles of the eighteenth century, and the self-generalizing efforts of Wollstonecraft's *Letters from Sweden*. *Persuasion* relies on the letter's ability to focus on exceptions, on what or who has been left out, pushed out of the general. Like the poetry of the period, this novel leads toward the subjective and the lyrical moment. In a direct departure from Austen's earlier novels, *Persuasion* relies more on metaphor, descriptive landscape, and a unified, single point of view – what Mikhail Bakhtin would characterize as a "univocal" presentation.[102] The style is "inflected at nearly every level by the subjectivity of the heroine."[103] The letter, however lyrical it may be, nonetheless pierces through this homogenizing "univocality." It opens up a dialogue which breaks through Anne's sympathetic, if limited, point of view.

Whereas Wordsworth in "Tintern Abbey" and Coleridge in "Frost At Midnight" could exploit a unique sensibility, and subordinate to it the representation of an entire world, Austen's *Persuasion* is caught between the forms and discourses of an "outside" society – even that of the navy – and the private expression of an individual whom that society cannot "hear." The lyric poet risks the danger of extreme solipsism: thus both Wordsworth and Coleridge insert a sympathetic audience into their poems, as a touchstone with reality. The novelist, however, risks having her heroine appropriated or silenced by the rush and roar of society. Anne's story could well be obliterated by the noise of history. This pressure forces Austen into an unprecedented alliance with her heroine: nowhere else in her novels does the narrator bolster the heroine's voice and perspective so consistently and without irony. As a result, the novel strains between truly lyric, univocal moments and an increasingly disconnected medley of heterogeneous voices. The letter tries to bridge this split by rescuing Anne from her isolation and establishing the terms for a new community. But it cannot incorporate the "World" disintegrating around it. Like a lyric fragment, it remains on the border of the dominant discourse: it is always, only, true "in part."

In *Sanditon*, which Austen never completed, the "bubble" does finally burst, as incompatible languages – of advertising, Byronic romance, hypochondria and economics – clash on the shifting sands of a seaside resort. The fragment offers little hope that anyone with an ounce of sense, such as the heroine, can make any impact upon this world, or glean any meaning from its babble. The dislocation and disconnection of *Sanditon* are already afloat in *Persuasion*: the letter of reconciliation only suspends the moment at the edge of coherence. Despite the universalizing, totalitarian rhetoric of post-Waterloo England, British society was fractured, the world was in flux and words traded meaning day by day. Austen perceived this dissolution behind the victorious façade of the British empire in 1815. *Persuasion*'s letter introduces, once again, the volatility of revolution: "the loss of any sense of a true, authoritative 'centre', and the possible disappearance of any common language."[104] In the British novel of the nineteenth century, "such a letter was not soon to be recovered from."

CHAPTER 6

The letters of Frankenstein

I knew my silence disquieted them, and I well remembered the words of my father: "I know that while you are pleased with yourself you will think of us with affection, and we shall hear regularly from you. You must pardon me if I regard any interruption in your correspondence as a proof that your other duties are equally neglected."

(Victor Frankenstein, in *Frankenstein*)[1]

Correspondence: ... 1. The action or fact of corresponding, or answering to each other in fitness or mutual adaptation; congruity, harmony, agreement. 2. Relation of agreement, similarity, or analogy. 3. Concordant or sympathetic response. 4. Relation between persons or communities ... 5. Intercourse, communication (between persons). 6. Intercourse or communication by letters.

(*Oxford English Dictionary*, 1971)

In an age when letters were a primary form of social and political discourse, the outer structure of Mary Shelley's *Frankenstein* seems not altogether innovative. Shelley chose to frame her first novel with letters from an Arctic adventurer, Robert Walton, to his England-rooted sister, Margaret Saville, and this choice seems consistent with literary trends in a society anxious for connections and continuity, for human correspondence in an age of instability. In 1818, epistolary form might have appeared too conventional a device for an ambitious novelist, as Austen's work indicates. By the same token, its very anachronism could render the letter eminently appropriate for a young woman writing.[2] Letters, as Victor Frankenstein's Genevan father hints, were elements of a Rousseauian social contract; as signs of "relation between persons and communities," they were proof of civilization. In *Frankenstein*, however, Mary Shelley gives us a lesson in reading a different sort of correspondence. The conventional and

176

familiar letter fails: Victor never writes his family, Walton's missive never ends, and something monstrous escapes. The novel rips open the envelope of form, so to speak, and its letters give way to something illegitimate, without formal identity. At the same time, this novel performs what the now stagnant epistolary form once promised. *Frankenstein* invites us to maintain correspondence even as it forces us to accept deformity, to dismiss authority and to listen to the voices of destruction. Ultimately it asks us to understand what Mikhail Bakhtin has called the "dialogic discourse of the novel."[3]

Even as she extends the disruptive energies of correspondence beyond the formal structure of an epistolary novel, Shelley carries the familiar letter into unfamiliar territory. As the quote from Alphonse Frankenstein's letter to his son reveals, letter-writing has become a question traded between men – not, as in Austen's *Lady Susan*, between mothers and daughters. In *Frankenstein*, the dutiful letter enters into the discourse of law, science and rationality even more explicitly than in *Lady Susan* or *Emma*: as we shall see, it is read alongside the demands of "proof," "truth" and "evidence." But that version of the letter is, in Shelley's logic, impotent. The novelist steps outside of this exchange; in fact, she deliberately undermines any "regular" or closed economy of correspondence, law, family or truth.

For Mary Shelley, letters suggested proofs neither conventional nor, necessarily, civilized. The daughter of two philosophical radicals, Mary Wollstonecraft Shelley inherited her own disturbing legacy of letters. For her, the fiction of private correspondence had exploded almost coincidentally with her birth and her mother's death. A list of Mary Wollstonecraft's writings indicates that the mother of Mary Shelley was a prodigious letter-writer; but these letters produced mixed effects. On the one hand, the public applauded Wollstonecraft's *Letters from Sweden* (1796), as we have seen. This epistolary travelogue caused William Godwin to remark: "If ever there was a book calculated to make a man in love with its author, this appears to me the book." Soon following the publication of the *Letters*, Godwin and Wollstonecraft became lovers and devout correspondents themselves. The offspring of their communion, Mary Shelley, was born the following year. Yet Shelley knew of less prosperous letters as well. She had read her mother's *Posthumous Works*, which appeared a year after Wollstonecraft's death in childbirth. These volumes contained Wollstonecraft's intimate correspondence with Gilbert Imlay, and brought severe censure upon the professional woman of letters. The *Posthumous Works* also contained the unfinished novel, *Maria, or The Wrongs of Woman* (1798), in which the heroine strives to preserve her sanity in the form of a long letter to her daughter. Like the novel itself, the mother's letter stands incomplete, verging on incoherence. It communicates an unsettling message of betrayal and impotence. These more disturbing letters, sent from Shelley's mother, add a nether region to the "civilized" letter-writing promoted by Alphonse Frankenstein, the Swiss magistrate. It is this nether region that Mary Shelley explores in the deformed letters of *Frankenstein*.

Shelley wrote her first novel as Austen was publishing *Emma*, and the desire to make sense of communication and community propels both works. But Austen's *Persuasion*, which appeared in bookstores nearly simultaneously with *Frankenstein*, wanders closer to the borderlands where Shelley walks. If, in *Persuasion*, the letter provides a moment of hope that communion will be realized in the novel, in *Frankenstein* that fragile moment is crushed. Instead the novel reaches outside of itself for coherence – to us, its audience and to the "World."

At issue in *Frankenstein* is "the communication of life," as Shelley indicates in her introduction. Victor Frankenstein's method of "communicating life" will oppose, but finally cede to that of the woman novelist. Unlike its protagonist, and unlike the great epistolary novels which precede it (*Pamela, Clarissa, Werther, Julie* or *Evelina*), *Frankenstein* resists communicating a life *per se*, the history or "progress" of a single individual. This novel works to show the limits of that individuality and to replace the individual voice with a network of voices. In spite of its title, *Frankenstein* refuses to be solely Victor Frankenstein's story. The novel has a new task, which requires the combination and confusion of identity. Like Frankenstein's monster, the novel itself is a representation of human life which exceeds the dimensions of any one individual. "Of component parts animated" (*F*, p. 227), it communicates life through a variety of voices. These voices may threaten destruction of all formal relations, but destruction occurs only if we refuse to listen.

We see the move from individual to multiple, competing voices in the structure of *Frankenstein*. The conventional letter form dissolves in this novel. Walton keeps writing, as he moves from letters to a letter journal. But Victor Frankenstein intrudes and Walton's journal becomes Victor's confessional autobiography. When the monster subsequently invades his master's narrative, civilized and formal authority gives way to the illegitimate and the violently novel. Rival fictions of the letter, one civilized and authorized, the other subversive and outlawed, collide in the fantastic landscape of *Frankenstein*. Finally, when Walton resumes his letters, he abandons the formalities of dating and address: we read no proper valediction or closing signature as the book ends. The letter surrenders its defining role.

The voice that resonates at the end of *Frankenstein* is a novel voice, a disruptive, unsettling, bastard monster. Throughout the intricately structured narrative, a wide-ranging revision of literary form takes place. Traditionally, prepared packages of isolated experience and expression form the letters of an epistolary novel. This structure of correspondence helps define the boundaries of each character within a group of correspondents. The power to circumscribe and locate specific individuals (such as Jane Fairfax or Lucy Steele) accompanies the letter into novels such as Austen's. *Frankenstein* refuses this structure and power. When Victor and the monster enter the narrative, echoes and repetitions, parallel stories and mirror images obscure the boundaries of individualism. Communication in *Frankenstein*, verbal communication as well as the generative "communication of life" itself, is wilfully deformed; at the same time, the idea of correspondence is reformed.[4]

The conventional epistolary novel could not contain the deformity figured in the monster, or in Walton's fractured letter. Yet, at the very edge of civilization, on the brink of dissolution, both the novel and the monster beg for a response. If we examine the structures of this novel, its narratives, languages, even its geography, we will find that the function of the letter, if not its form, remains essential to the function of the novel.

THE AUTHOR, VICTOR AND NARRATIVE AUTHORITY

If we look at the structure of *Frankenstein*, questions of narrative authority immediately confront us. The text itself tangles the story line, and questions of valid authorship emerge even before the reader can articulate them.[5] Because of a triple narrative (Walton's, Victor's, the monster's) and an elaborate series of parallel personalities and events, we wonder just whose story we are hearing. Is the monster's tale a demonic projection of Frankenstein's tormented psyche? Is Frankenstein only a bizarre secret-sharer, concocted by a lonely seafarer wandering on the outer limits of sanity? Is the whole story only a drama of Mary Shelley's adolescent mind, the dream-work fabricated by a troubled girl? The text offers no clear answer.

The author anticipates our questions. She writes her introduction in order to "give a general answer to the question so very frequently asked me – how I, then a young girl, came to think of, and dilate upon so very hideous an idea." She begins to defend herself: "It is not singular..."[6] Yet she insists it is her own work: "I certainly did not owe one train of feeling to my husband."[7] Notwithstanding this assertion, Mary Shelley traces the conception of her "progeny" to one summer's exchange of ghost stories, to a group contest and to a conversation between Lord Byron and Percy Shelley, "to which I was a devoted, but nearly silent listener."[8] The responsibility for the singularity is shared. Without her husband's "incitement" *Franken-stein* "would never have taken the form in which it was presented to the world...Its several pages speak of many a walk, many a drive, and many a conversation when I was not alone."[9] If we ask to whom the story of *Frankenstein* belongs, we get a very "general answer" indeed, filled with family relationships, literary links and overheard conversations. This novel *is* the offspring of correspondence. As the stories within stories overlap, we agree that it "is not singular," at all; and its lack of singularity makes it monstrous.

We must begin to read *Frankenstein* more as a well-wrought "baggy monster" of correspondences, and less as a singular, alien phenom-enon. If we read it as an interactive combination of tales, rather than one linear narrative, we can refrain from casting the novelist into the narrow role of a "young girl" with "so very hideous an idea." *Frankenstein* is Mary Shelley's *novel*: it is no more her story than Walton's, Victor's or the monster's. Within the text, the various narrators slide from their own stories into the histories of others, and with each movement we are asked to extend our "willing suspension of disbelief." As the novel multiplies its story-tellers and listeners, it renews the problem of narrative authority. Whose story do we believe? – the novel defuses such a question. The fantastic nature of the stories preclude rational explanation or judgment, and we do not finally ask for reasonable proof. Rather, the listener must establish a sort of correspondence among the various narrators, a "relation of agreement, similarity or analogy" which will support a sort of blind faith in the tale. *Frankenstein* makes this un*reason*able, but perhaps inescapable demand.

Victor Frankenstein, scientist and story-teller, traps himself within the conflicting demands of certified authority and negotiated correspondence. To introduce his own hideous tale, he must appeal to some sort of relationship with Walton. He relies upon his listener's parallel circumstances to render the unnatural believable:

when I reflect that you are pursuing the same cause, exposing yourself to the same dangers which have rendered me what I am, I imagine that you may deduce an apt moral from my tale...Were we among the tamer scenes of nature, I might fear to encounter your unbelief perhaps your ridicule; but many things will appear possible in these wild and mysterious regions. (*F*, p. 232)

Even as he calls upon Walton's sympathetic and imaginative response, however, Frankenstein reveals that he does not fully trust this response. The scientist reinforces his narrative with a gesture toward verifiable "truth":

nor can I doubt but that my tale conveys in its series *internal evidence of the truth* of which it is composed. (*F*, p. 233; my emphasis)

Victor Frankenstein wants to establish, irrefutably, his authority in the text. He diverts his listener away from the intrinsic parallelism of the tales – "the relation of agreement, similarity or analogy" between them. Instead, he invites the reader to follow the "series" of his tale to its "internal evidence of the truth." We can follow this single narrative line, or series, but as we track the story inward to its heart, we enter the monster's narrative. There we discover no originating truth and no guarantee. A seemingly infinite series extends into more tales as the monster invokes Goethe, Milton and Plutarch. Indeed, authority for the narrative seems lost, receding further and further from sight, into the impenetrable caverns of the Alps, or "toward the very heart of non-meaning, toward the lifeless pole."[10] The scientist has no evidence; Victor's narrative line leads to no "internal" originating authority. It leads to the monster.

But to end there at "the very heart of non-meaning" requires that our reading follow Victor's criteria for authority, that we accept his "line" and repudiate the monster. Peter Brooks, for example, identifies the "truth" conveyed by *Frankenstein* as monstrosity itself, or language as "monstrous." He can read the stories within stories as an infinite regress, as the "metonymic sliding" of the monster's "miserable series of being."[11] According to this Barthesian analysis,

Frankenstein demonstrates a one-way movement in language, accompanied by inescapable contamination. It writes itself into the Dead-Letter Office:

There is no transcendent signified because the fact of monsterism is never either justified or overcome, but it is simply passed along the chain, finally come to inhabit the reader himself who, as animator of the text, is left with the contamination of monsterism… the text remains as indelible record of the monstrous, emblem of language's murderous lack of transcendent reference.[12]

But I think we ignore the *informing* structure of Mary Shelley's novel if we accept this one-way, fatal movement in language, or if we, like Victor facing the monster, shudder at our inability to "justify" or "overcome" the novel. If we fail to read the correspondences between the stories, the two- and three-way dialogue of the text itself, we fail to see the epistolary dynamic of the novel. A reader can follow the successive narratives along a temporal chain, a series of being, that leads, ultimately, to death and loss. Such a reading would only replicate Frankenstein's own fatalistic quest: "nothing can alter my destiny; listen to my history and you will perceive how irrevocably it is determined." Brooks' interpretation traps itself into a sequential determinism that the structure of the novel denies. The movement of *Frankenstein* is not one way, but back and forth between overlapping stories, one always revising or translating the others. Temporal sequence throws itself into the kaleidoscope of mirroring narratives, until the three major tales seem to stand side by side. They present themselves not as successors to one another, but as three versions of the same tale, one commenting upon and responding to the other two. It is a technique which recurs in various guises in the nineteenth-century novel: in the historical novels of Walter Scott, in the intricate plots of Dickens' masterpieces, in George Eliot's *Middlemarch* and Emily Brontë's *Wuthering Heights*.

Frankenstein is not, then, an example of fiction and subsequent repetition, with an Ancient Mariner contaminating the joys of a youthful Wedding Guest. In *Frankenstein*, the listener does not just walk away sadder and wiser: he responds, he translates, he adds his own story.[13] Mutual authority extends over a common field of references, overwhelming any one-way reading. Brooks is forced to contradict himself by describing the one-dimensional signifying chain as a "system… in which everything is mutually interrelated and interdependent."[14] He wants to stratify the connections into a temporal sequence rather than accept the multi-dimensional structure of the novel.

Readers like Brooks may have been seduced by *Frankenstein*'s "entitled" voice, that of the scientist who tells a story. His narrative method subtly copies his scientific method, a step-by-step examination designed to discover "the cause of generation and life," within "the structure of the human frame" (*F*, pp. 46–7). Just as the "internal evidence" of the story-teller points to the lost end of an infinite series, so does the "cause" sought by the scientist lead to obsessive, incessant research:

> None but those who have experienced them can conceive of the enticements of science. In other studies you go as far as others have gone before you, and there is nothing more to know; but in a scientific pursuit there is continual food for discovery and wonder...and I, who continually sought the attainment of *one object of pursuit*, and was solely wrapt up in this, improved...rapidly. (*F*, pp. 45–6)

"The more fully I entered into the science, the more exclusively I pursued it for its own sake," Victor tells Walton: we wonder if he has made a "scientific pursuit" of story-telling. In any case, the product of his research, the creature of the novel, finishes Victor's story by parodically satisfying Victor's scientific ideal: the pursuit of this "one object" never ends. During the bizarre chase scene at the Arctic, the monster will not allow Victor to cease his singular pursuit. The monster provides "continual food for discovery and wonder," continual food to nourish his creator. This ironic literalization of Frankenstein's method reveals the futility of that method. It reveals the story-teller's lack of control over his story-line as well as the scientist's lack of control over the object of his research. The "internal evidence" betrays Victor, because it always moves beyond him.

The deformed nature of the novel also moves beyond the obsession of its protagonist. Victor's narrative authority depends upon a secret he refuses to communicate, that is, the "cause of generation and life." As long as that secret remains in his possession, Victor can dictate to his listener: "[Y]ou expect to be informed of the secret with which I am acquainted; that cannot be; listen patiently to the end of my story," he warns Walton (*F*, p. 52). Victor's story has authority and significance because, he assures us, only he is "capable of bestowing animation upon lifeless matter." But the scientist's boast betrays him as a mere story-teller (one among many) creating stories, animating lifeless matter, with no verifiable authority. The creature he animates has no single origin; it is a composite being: a fiction. The patchwork monster with its visible seams and borrowed language subverts Victor's secret by exhibiting "the fictional history of its own production."[15] No wonder Victor begs Walton not to listen to the monster's voice, not to respond to an alternative story: "He is eloquent and persuasive...but trust him not...hear him not!" (*F*, pp. 198–9). Victor must insist that only one secret truth exists in life – and he alone holds it.

Call it "truth," "internal evidence," or "the cause of generation and life," the form of the novel refutes it, and the action of the novel condemns it. If we patiently follow Frankenstein's tale for "evidence" of some *prima causa*, we place our faith in a compelling but impotent authority. Though he claims the power to create life unassisted, ultimately Frankenstein creates nothing new: his method is seductive, not productive. Persuasive and adept, Victor narrates with all the markings of what Julia Kristeva calls "rhetorical discourse":

The rhetorician [as opposed to the stylist] does not invent a language; fascinated by the symbolic function of paternal discourse, he *seduces* it...he "leads it astray"...but not to the point of leaving cover.[16]

The secret, with its claims to authority and its denial of correspondence, destroys life as effectively as the monster. Frankenstein betrays his own intentions, not only as a narrator, but as a member of a family and community. What truly horrifies Victor is the possibility that his story is not singular and exclusive at all, but that it depends upon – indeed relates to – other stories. The idea of interdependence, of life communicated through physical human intercourse or through heterogeneous verbal exchange, appears monstrous and threatening to Victor Frankenstein. By withholding his own voice in order to protect his secret, Frankenstein, not the monster, brings about Justine's death. Similar betrayal awaits Victor's fiancée. In the one letter Victor does send, he still resists open communication: he brandishes his secret to ward off human connection. To his future bride he writes:

I have one secret, Elizabeth, a dreadful one; when revealed to you, it will chill your frame with horror...I will confide this tale of misery and terror to you the day after our marriage takes place, for, my sweet cousin, there must be perfect confidence between us. But until then, I conjure you, do not mention or allude to it. (*F*, p. 187)

The secret – the myth of paternal power and exclusive, vital authority – becomes Victor's weapon against his greatest fear: human intercourse. For him, intercourse is one more type of correspondence, explosive with creative potential but consequently "dreadful," "horrible," terrifying. The secret stands between his authorial status as sole parent of "a new species [that] would bless me as its creator and source" and the confession that his word, his story, has no meaning or life without human connection. The secret cuts like a knife: Elizabeth's and Justine's deaths demonstrate that as long as the mystery remains veiled and unshared, the singular story will end in death.

WALTON, LETTERS AND CORRESPONDENCE

As we have seen, the novel's narrative structure, as much as the events of the novel, upsets Victor's logic. Monstrous intrusions tangle the narrative line and challenge the terms of authority Victor seeks to establish. We are given more evidence than the scientist is willing to accept. Other story-tellers find other listeners, propose different terms and follow different methods in this novel. Robert Walton, for example, is not held bound to Victor's word forever. Walton does hear the monster's version, and his sister, the recipient of the letters, hears his version of both Frankenstein's and the monster's versions. As Mary Poovey notes, "Walton's epistolary journal literally contains and mediates the voices of the other two narrators, and so he may be said to have the last, if not the definitive, word."[17] Truly Walton's voice mediates, but it is in turn mediated by an awareness of his audience: he speaks a language to which his sister will respond; it is shaped by experiences and feelings they both have shared. His voice is guided by the connections which bind them.

Like Victor, Walton must appeal to some response from his reader in order to alleviate doubts: "Do you understand this feeling?" he asks at the outset (*F*, p. 19). He offers the possibility of shared experience to substantiate his own and Frankenstein's words: "Will you smile at the enthusiasm I express concerning this divine wanderer? You would not if you saw him" (*F*, p. 232). Unlike Victor, however, the letter-writer proffers no hope of verifying evidence. Walton simply trusts that his sister's reaction will correspond to his own. At the other end of the correspondence, Walton's sister and reader posit a sort of blind faith in the letter, believing without seeing and asking for no proof. Letters – especially printed letters which obliterate individual handwriting – always call out for this blind faith. Yet even when Walton's letters dissolve, the appeal remains. When the monster tells his tale to the blind man De Lacey and when he covers Victor's eyes to ensure he will listen, we spot the vestiges of epistolary logic in this novel. Understanding shifts from the realm of visual evidence to that of verbal sympathy. From the "blind faith" and distance required by the letter form emerges the possibility of a language that mediates difference and communicates life.

The particular correspondence between Walton and his sister exemplifies the process of communication which lies at the heart of Julia Kristeva's essay, "De L'Un L'Autre" (translated as "From One Identity to an Other").[18] Two divergent discourses, according to Kristeva, can "maintain a presence within the discourse of the other." The sister, the silent but omnipresent Other, performs a function as vital as that of the brother, the speaking or writing subject.[19] We have no idea who of this pair came first; although he seems to initiate the correspondence, she is already situated before the letter. The novel begins, "To Mrs. Saville, England": already the brother's directive unlocks the sister's presence within the text. This interlocutory relationship, maintained by Walton's words and Margaret Saville's position beyond his words, corresponds well to Kristeva's description of the symbolic and the semiotic in language.[20] As the signifying function travels from one identity to the other – the writer appealing, the reader responding – the authority of origins, identities and structures disappears. To which party does a letter belong? Kristeva's model of the novel depends upon just such an identity in flux: like letter-writing, the novel places its faith not in a definite presence, but in perpetual movement and in relative, not absolute, understanding: "Do you understand this feeling?" Novelistic discourse depends upon an audience reading and listening between, within and beyond the lines.

Walton's signature does not close his letters, nor does it close the novel; instead, the novel takes up the epistolary movement. *Franken-stein* works not to place significance in any one narrative, but to "maintain a presence" of each within the others. "The internal evidence of the truth" is always in motion in the letters that pass between parties. Fittingly, the monster substantiates his narrative with the letters of Felix and Safie. Written from one culture to another, translated from the language of the East to the language of the West, and copied again by the monster, the lovers' letters "will prove the truth of my tale" (*F*, p. 119). These criss-crossed love letters, taken from the heart of the novel, are preserved; the laboratory journal of Frankenstein's experiment is not. "That series of disgusting circumstances," as the monster dubs the scientific record, is rejected.[21] Walton likewise chooses the love letters over his friend's tale to anchor his own belief:

His [Victor's] tale is connected and told with an appearance of the simplest truth, yet I own to you that the letters of Felix and Safie, which he showed me, and the apparition of the monster seen from our ship, brought me to a greater conviction of his narrative than his asseverations, however earnest and connected. (*F*, p. 207)

Of course we, the readers, never see these love letters, just as we never really "see" the monster; we only hear of them, second- and third-hand, and thereby trust in their existence. For all we know, they may be a mere fiction. Both the novel and the narrator urge us to read not for the "simplest truth" of a rational sequence, but rather to read through correspondence, to look beyond the composition and respond with blind faith.

For Mary Shelley, the importance given to letters travels from the external frame to the inmost lesson of living language. The translation or exchange of languages in dialogue guarantees the life of the utterance – not necessarily in its original form of expression, but in its multiple possibilities. That generative possibility is stressed by Shelley in an 1823 letter to her friend, Leigh Hunt:

– & remember, if you must write [to me], the good hacnied maxim of *multum in parvo* and when your temples throb distill the essence of 3 pages into three lines & my "fictitious Adventure" will enable me to spin them out & fill up intervals not but what the 3 pages are best – but "you understand me."[22]

Given the "understanding" between friends, language can, in Shelley's logic, contract, expand and spin off into the stuff of fiction. Her novel *Frankenstein* explodes not just with the complicity of language which Victor fears, but also with the prolific power of discourse. To speak in a novel, and to speak especially in this novel, is to speak in context: every utterance establishes a new language as it refracts existing languages.

We have the neat model of Safie's and Felix's cross-cultural exchange. But we also have the monster's challenge. The reassuring love letters fall into the hands of a deformed and destructive monster, just as the epistolary novel itself surrendered to the Jacobin novel, the gothic novel and the historical novel of the late eighteenth and early nineteenth centuries. Like the "hideous progeny," the creature with no sister or lover, the bastard novel confronts us with a form which challenges the very possibility of relation, intercourse or correspondence. The creature's voice, however, insists on relating: "Listen to my tale...listen to me...Hear my tale..." (*F*, p. 98). The visible evidence of the monster – his deformed, threatening form – fades and gives way to the voices emerging from the monster's specific context.

I want to stress the novelistic traits of Shelley's monster. His narrative shifts from his story to the De Lacey's and back, disturbing any single, narrative line. His story, like his body, moves constantly, delving into one text after another just as he himself pops in and out of Victor's dwellings. He reaches into these texts and dwellings not to steal or even defile authority, but rather to search for analogues, for correspondents in language, for human intercourse. His voice intrudes and interrupts, but it also sets off echoes within and without the novel: Milton, Goethe, Plutarch, Byron, Coleridge, both Shelleys, as well as Victor himself, the De Laceys, Satan, Adam, Eve. The monster's voice asks for relationship with every listener. The voices which echo in our voices speak in the monster's: we hear our world in him. In this sense, the monster demands a level of correspondence beyond Walton's. Less secure than Walton's letters (to his closest relative), less localized (to a married sister, with a family, in a home, in England), less formalized (in an envelope, in letter form, dated, signed), the novel voice nonetheless finds an audience. The monster abandons all hope for a formal mate and turns against all structure. Yet despite his destruction of form, his challenges to authority, his rage and his violence (and, perhaps, because of them) his voice resonates through all the layers of verbal exchange in *Frankenstein*.

THE NOVELIST'S LANGUAGE AND THE LANDSCAPE OF THE NOVEL

The monster's story does not exclude the story of his maker, nor does Walton's tale displace the other two. Rather, the voices intersect, which causes them to create new utterances. We can picture the novel, therefore, as a common plane upon which many stories and many languages intersect, regardless of internal contradiction. In his essay, "Discourse in the Novel," Mikhail Bakhtin explains this distinctive "heteroglossia" of the novel:

All languages of heteroglossia, whatever the principle underlying them and making each unique, are specific points of view on the world, forms for conceptualizing the world in words, specific world views, each characterized by its own objects, meanings and values. As such they all may be juxtaposed to one another, contradict one another, and be interrelated dialogically. As such they encounter one another and coexist in the consciousness of real people – first and foremost in the creative consciousness of people who write novels.[23]

Bakhtin's characterization of novelistic discourse corresponds to the composition of *Frankenstein*. The authorial voice sounds as one among many, without intrinsic authority or precedence:

Authorial speech, the speech of narrators, inherited genres, the speech of characters are merely those fundamental compositional unities with whose help heteroglossia enters the novel; each of them permits a multiplicity of social voices and a wide variety of their links and inter-relationships.[24]

Similarly, authorial intent retreats into a proliferation of intentions. What we read is not Mary Shelley's submerged polemic against an array of repressive figures (father, mother, husband, self), but an ongoing dialogue between many voices, many languages: an encounter of all prior forms on a common plane.

The author is not to be found in the language of the narrator, not in the normal literary language to which the story opposes itself (although a given story may be closer to a given language) – but rather, the author utilizes now one language, now another, in order to avoid giving himself up wholly to either of them; he makes use of this verbal give-and-take, this dialogue of languages at every point of his work, in order that he himself might remain, as it were, neutral with regard to language, a third party in a quarrel between two people (although he might be a *biased* third party).[25]

Bakhtin's description reminds us of Mary Shelley's introduction to *Frankenstein*, where the author presents herself as a third party attendant upon the conversations between two literary figures. Lord Byron's and Percy Shelley's discussion, "to which I was a devout, but *nearly* silent listener," questioned the very purpose of novelistic discourse: "The nature of life and whether there was any probability of its ever being *discovered* and *communicated*" (my emphasis). The discovery belongs to Victor Frankenstein: "I succeeded in discovering the cause of generation and life," Victor tells Walton. And he boasts: "Nay, more, I became myself capable of bestowing animation upon lifeless matter" (*F*, p. 51). Discovery is one step, animation another, but neither guarantees the widespread communication of life. He may talk as much as he likes, but Victor, unlike Mary Shelley, entertains no conversation. The nature of Victor's discovery ironically disproves his method, as we have seen. The discourse of the novel, by contrast, does communicate a sense of life which informs the listener.

The novelist, listening to the conversation between poets, explains her own mode of literary discourse. Not by spontaneous generation "would life be given" to her creation. Rather, the remains of earlier forms "would be re-animated," perhaps in a novel: "perhaps the component parts of a creature might be manufactured, brought together, and enbued with vital warmth."[26] The novelist makes use of what Bakhtin calls the "verbal give-and-take" of the poets, but she also allows their dialogue to comment upon her novel, as well as Frankenstein's activities. The novel's component parts refract each other, become "dialogized," as we watch the poets' dialogue refract the author's intentions and her strategies refract the scientist's efforts.

So we find the author placing herself at a remove from the languages of the novel, yet implicated in them. Like Margaret Walton Saville, a "nearly silent" reader, Mary Wollstonecraft Shelley speaks through, but not in the language of the novel. The continual refraction of authorial intent frees her from a unitary and single language. It also frees her from a single literary tradition. Evidence of many literary genres exists within the text; the epistolary, the journalistic, the lyric (*F*, pp. 93–4), the sentimental and the epic are only the most explicit. A study by Lee Sterrenburg locates in *Frankenstein* the language and rhetoric of popular discourse as well: the radical–conservative debate over Godwin's Utopianism, carried on in the journals of the day; contemporary writings on the Revolution in France, especially Burke's *Reflections* and Wollstonecraft's reply; as well as the psychological confession-biography popular at the time, used by George Walker, Hannah More and William Godwin.[27] Sterrenburg reads Mary Shelley's use of contemporary political language as a move "beyond ideology," and cites her for "animating" what "had hardened into stereotype and rhetoric."[28] But the "animation" occurs not only in the use of political discourse, but in all the languages which inform the text, from the stereotypes and rhetoric of gothic fiction to those of Enlightenment philosophy to those of the Bible. Even the orientalism popular in the literature of this period enters the novel. Enunciated by Clerval and represented by Safie, the language of the East relocates our perspective on the western tradition. Her novel gives Mary Shelley the status of a "stylist," in Kristeva's terms. Unlike Frankenstein, the rhetorician, the stylist

no longer needs to seduce the father by rhetorical affectations ... [I]n place of the father, [the stylist] may assume a different discourse; neither imaginary discourse of the self, nor discourse of transcendental knowledge, but a permanent go-between from one to the other.[29]

The novel functions as Shelley's go-between, her world among worlds, her voice among voices.

The critical questions of *Frankenstein* concern not the sources or objectives of Mary Shelley's language as much as the form itself, the correspondence of the novel through which, but not in which, she speaks. By opening the letter within the context of the novel, Shelley verifies the intrinsic, ongoing dialogism of language. By involving so many languages in the refraction of her own intentions, Shelley remains free of the conventions, while refusing to cancel the voice of any one tradition. At the same time that she includes conventional forms, however, she opens them, like so many boxes for Pandora. The inherited forms which the novel employs

open up the possibility of never having to define oneself in language, the possibility of translating one's own intentions from one linguistic system to another ... of saying "I am me" in someone else's language, and in my own, "I am other."[30]

Novelistic discourse provides possibilities truly monstrous, not because they are alien to conventional discourse, but because they comprehend and yet escape such discourse. The monster, as novel, rises as "component parts animated," and masters the languages of his culture. We fear to look at the monster precisely because he does embody the component parts of his world, an unmanageable whole. The linguistic baggage of this monster (Is he speaking French or English or German? Is he reading English, German and Latin in translation?) poses a challenge to language itself, a challenge not unlike that of Moby Dick's or Mont Blanc's infinity of significance. These symbols deny our locating an end to meaning or an origin of truth. But in the face of such infinity, we are allowed to move up and down, back and forth, weaving correspondences. Bakhtin and Kristeva have given us a model of the "literary word" as "an intersection of textual surfaces rather than a point (a fixed meaning), as a dialogue among several writings...Diachrony is transformed into synchrony."[31]

The most helpful illustration of this almost topographical dynamic in language may be found in the topography of the novel itself. The landscape of *Frankenstein* offers a spatial correlative to its narrative structure. One crucial encounter will demonstrate how the novelistic form we are discussing informs even the scenery of *Frankenstein*. Let us return to the image of the common place as an alternative to the pointed object of Victor's search, and perhaps we will glimpse that "magic scene" and "immensity of prospect" that he dismisses.[32]

After Justine's trial, Victor Frankenstein removes himself from his family and journeys in the Alps. What appeals to Victor in this escape is the isolation it affords him. The sights and sounds of the lower world tumble down the mountain side and Victor wakes to find himself alone on the bare glacier, "elevated" to "the solemn silence of this glorious presence-chamber of imperial nature" (*F*, p. 91). But the lyrical language should not fool us: when Victor Frankenstein speaks of "imperial nature," we hear his imperial voice and his alone. The presence chamber and the imperial silence belong to the emperor-narrator at the moment of his achieved ascendancy. He rests, "waited on and administered to by the assemblage of grand shapes which I had contemplated" (*F*, p. 249). He continues onward and upward in a vertical line, "without a guide," for "the presence of another would destroy the solitary grandeur of the scene." As he seeks the most desolate, barren peak, Frankenstein seeks to establish his own solitary grandeur; yet every step towards isolation invites a greater intrusion from his surroundings.[33] The individual path cannot remove itself from intersecting influences, and silence threatens to invite noisy destruction:

The path, as you ascend higher, is intersected by ravines of snow, down which stones continually roll from above; one of them is particularly dangerous, as the slightest sound, such as even speaking in a loud voice, produces a concussion of air sufficient to draw destruction upon the head of the speaker. (*F*, p. 92)

There is no escape from intersection, from the voices that surround the individual. In the mind of a man such as Frankenstein, however, intersection and interdependency constitute a threat. It is the effort to escape into silence, to gain ascendancy and singularity, to stand atop the silent peak and command the elements that, perversely, renders one's own position dangerous, and renders one's own voice lethal.

So it is with pointed irony that Mary Shelley chooses to level Victor Frankenstein as he reaches the imposing heights of his "bare, perpendicular rock."[34] Once there, Victor commands the "wandering spirits" of the Alps to accept him as one more "icy and glittering" peak, to drive away from him his humanity and the "joys of life"; just at this point, however, Frankenstein's exposed, supervital self comes rushing at him with all the power and pathos of human relation. The creature confronts his maker on what Frank Randel has called "the first thoroughly humanized mountain in the book and, arguably, in the [Romantic] tradition."[35]

For an instant, Frankenstein persists in his delusion of power-in-isolation and orders silence: has he not achieved a position that allows him to dismiss the inadmissible from his presence-chamber? "Devil...how dare you approach me? And do you not fear the fierce vengeance of my arm...? Begone, vile insect! Or rather stay, that I may trample you to dust!" (*F*, p. 94). Here again, the rhetorical questions invite an inescapably unsettling answer: they expose the true impotence of the speaker. Victor Frankenstein is knocked off his imperial heights in the face of his creation. Even if he closes his eyes – or if the monster closes them – he cannot escape into silence. "Listen to my tale...hear me...listen to me Frankenstein...Hear my tale": the creature and his story beg Frankenstein to accept the relation.[36] Having reached the end point of its vertical climb, Victor's linear progress, threatened with annihilation, moves into the monster's "hut upon the mountains" and into the monster's narrative. Here the novel begins to open inwardly and outwardly in an expanding web of people and events. We can understand almost visually Julia Kristeva's words on the novel form: "If there is a model for poetic [i.e. novelistic] language, it no longer involves lines and surfaces, but rather, spaces and infinity."[37]

We can also see that Shelley has deliberately de-centered the central mountain episode, so crucial to the poetic tradition of her time, and created a novel without a central *point*. Structurally, the mountains of poetic tradition will not provide the buttresses for this gothic novel. Nor, for similar reasons, will the titans of the literary canon justify or even minister to the voice of *Frankenstein*. A new day dawns and the spirits of the mountains, those "mighty friends," have retreated. Frankenstein will never be included among the company of those "icy and glittering" peaks; instead he must listen to the excessively human voice of the monster, of the novel. Even its protagonist's poetic aspirations lead *Frankenstein* to its novel voice.

Frank Randel almost rests on the easy conclusion that Mary Shelley practiced literary one-upmanship with her male contemporaries, in a content of literary mountain-climbing between the poets and the novelist. But he looks again and observes that "the mountainous center" of the novel is balanced by other "equally generative locales."[38] Given a third glance, however, this balance starts shaking. Each "generative locale" in the topography of the novel is a potential volcano. Frankenstein's birthplace, the workshop, the De Lacey home: every hearth seems to explode or implode with monstrous inevitability. Even as we search for a thematic center (is it Mary Shelley's dream vision? Or the De Lacey episode? Or...?), the book offers no geographical or structural point of rest.

Attention to the specific character of this novel leads us back to the structural and geographical instability of the letter. Literary correspondence must be able to function with no central position, without even two fixed and balanced poles. The center removed, there yet exists an entire field of play between two mobile points, no matter how far and wide each point moves. In place of an object in focus, the novel reveals a vast, ever-expanding plane of intersections.[39] We are left, at last, with neither the comfortable home, nor the glittering peaks. Instead we face the Arctic expanse. Like nature's own *tabula rasa*, the Arctic scene offers everything and nothing – depending on our response.

Early readers of *Frankenstein* felt its challenging, unsettling effect. Percy Shelley, in his published "Remarks on *Frankenstein*," expressed awe at the novel's ability to compel the reader's sympathy and involvement, and, at the same time, to destroy all frame of reference. The simple line of connection explodes into an open field of "astonishing combinations":

We debate within ourselves in wonder as we read it, what could have been the series of thoughts...which conduced, in the author's mind, to the astonishing combinations of motives and incidents and the startling catastrophe, which compose this tale.

As Percy Shelley continues, the combinations do not remain within the author's mind, nor does the startling catastrophe remain contained within a single tale. At all points, the reader must enter the active world of the novel. Significantly, Percy describes a present, ongoing and shared experience, using "we" and the present tense. He too exploits the novel's topography:

We are led breathless with suspense and sympathy and the heaping of incident upon incident, and the working of passion out of passion. We cry, "Hold, hold, enough!" – but there is something to come; and like the victim whose history it relates, we think we can bear no more, and yet more is to be borne. Pelion is heaped on Ossa, and Ossa on Olympus. We climb Alp after Alp, until the horizon is seen blank vacant and limitless; and the head turns giddy, and the ground seems to fail under our feet.[40]

The Quarterly Review, with less admiration, found a similar, unsettling openness in this novel. While it admits the powerful demand the novel makes upon its reader, the *Review* finds itself "revolted" by "this kind of writing":

the greater the ability with which it may be executed the worse it is – it inculcates no lesson of conduct, manners or morality; it cannot mend and it will not even amuse its readers ... it fatigues the feelings without interesting the understanding; it gratuitously harasses the heart, and only adds to the store, already too great, of painful sensations.[41]

The overload of sensation and the lack of moral support accompanies, indeed *defines* the sense of "poetic language" (Kristeva's term) or "dialogism" (Bakhtin's term) found in the novel form. But it is also a vestige of the letter's ability to involve and overwhelm its reader. Because of its dialogism – explicit in the letters, implicit in the discourse – the novel continually breaks the law by allowing the outlaw to speak. When letters in the novel free themselves from the formal demands of propriety and individual identity, as they do in *Frankenstein*, they enter "the very place where social code is destroyed and renewed."[42]

Even as it unsettles, however, the novel, like the monster, forces a dialogue. It invites our responses to its tales and invites itself into our stories. The movement back and forth of letters leads to the shifting stories and the dialogized language which establish communication amidst the rupture. Along with doubt in determined answers or identities, there emerges a blind faith in ongoing correspondence. The power of this novel rides in between-ness, in the spaces that open up between speakers, as between mountain peaks; in the cracks that appear between statements, as between ice floes; in the seams that emerge between stories, as between monstrous "component parts."

Dialogism in *Frankenstein* does elicit an unsettling ambivalence. As consequence of that ambivalence, "it posits its own process between sense and nonsense, between language and rhythm, between the symbolic and the semiotic."[43] The pronounced conventions of the epistle form yield to the disruptions implicit in that form. The line of rupture is, all the same, the line of juncture, as Kristeva notes. It is the distance and difference between correspondents that allow for letters and reveal dialogue.

That difference, suspended like a question mark, allows us to respond to Mary Shelley's "hideous progeny" from age to age: "Do you understand this feeling?" With this appeal to head and heart, the unfinished letter becomes novel for each reader. The numerous adaptations from the nineteenth century onward demonstrate how this novel speaks in so many different contexts – political, ethical, aesthetic, scientific – the list is endless and cross-referential. Each culture writes its own *Frankenstein*.

Like Walton, we never reach the pole – not precisely. As letter-writers, we never quite get to the point; as readers, we may miss the point altogether. We have learned, nevertheless, from the exchange, from the verbal give and take. We have stepped into a new language between poles, a world that invites critics to look and listen yet again.

Conclusion, or the death of the letter: fiction, the Post Office and "The English Mail Coach"

This is my letter to the World
That never wrote to Me—
The simple News that Nature told—
With tender Majesty

Her Message is committed
To Hands I cannot see
For Love of Her—Sweet—countrymen—
Judge tenderly—of Me

(Emily Dickinson (1862))

"In the beginning," writes Jacques Derrida in his "Envois," "in principle, was the post, and I will never get over it. But in the end I know it, I become aware of it as of our death sentence."[1] This concluding chapter is an effort to know the post in England in the first half of the nineteenth century, when it began to imagine itself as the alpha and the omega, the beginning and the end of communication and exchange. This conclusion also tries to know how the post was imagined, particularly by writers who, a century and a half before Derrida, could not "get over it," but discovered ways to communicate in, through and around it. Thomas De Quincey's 1849 essay, "The English Mail Coach," is perhaps the most explicit example of a text, like Derrida's "Envois," obsessed with channels of communication and fascinated by the death sentence they convey, especially to a feminized correspondent. But De Quincey's is an obsession shared by many writing in a post-epistolary age: Austen, Scott, Gaskell, Dickens and others looked for ways around the letter. For by post-epistolary, I mean an age where one imagines the post where once there were letters, where one reads the movements of the mail coach, not the vagaries of epistolary sentiment, and where one begs the postman, not the lover, for correspondence. And like

197

Derrida, I am trying to place the voice of the other, specifically of women and the lower classes, within the post, in an era when fictions such as *Pamela* seem quite distant and almost unimaginable. Finally, this chapter is concerned with and concerned about possibilities for different versions of correspondence in the aftermath of Waterloo and during the period of reform – in the years, that is, which saw the rise of the modern Post Office.

THE VEXATIOUS LETTER

In the 1790s, the public was asked to imagine the letter as the tool of division – of spies, Jacobinical conspiracies and seditious corresponding societies. This image underwrote a series of laws which facilitated government intervention in personal correspondence and propelled the rise of the modern Post Office. In 1793, Charles James Fox could still object in Parliament to this interference and this "fiction" of traitorous correspondence:

Is it not a situation of the country horrible to relate... that correspondence and conversation are to be pried into with such inquisitional jealousy, as to make it dangerous for them to commit their thoughts to paper, or to converse with a stranger, but in the presence of a third person?[2]

Yet you can read that fiction of conspiracy made historical fact, and that "third person" made a welcome institution, a generation later. In a passage from *The Confessions of an English Opium Eater* (1856, rev. ed.), De Quincey reverses the terms of Fox's outrage. He gratefully abandons an undesirable letter, mistakenly addressed to him, to state supervision:

The vexatious letter in my custody... the odious responsibility thrust upon me... [hindered] the freedom of my own movements... Indignant I was that this letter should have the power of making myself an accomplice in causing anxiety, perhaps even calamity... In some way I must contrive to restore the letter [to the post office]... [The] letter would poison my very existence, like the bottle-imp, until I could transfer it to some person truly qualified.[3]

The young man of De Quincey's *Confessions* is loath to take responsibility for this troublesome letter. It has arrived from France, during the period of the Napoleonic Wars, and he is certain "this most filthy of letters" will taint him with crime and guilt. Eventually, he hands it off to a peasant woman, "more truly qualified" to handle such "filthy" material, and she "restores" the letter to the post office, where it "belongs." With the letter repudiated, the young De

Quincey turns to an alternative bottle-imp, opium, for reveries which will not hinder the freedom of his movements.

Here we have encapsulated a parable of the fate of the letter in the first half of the nineteenth century: few serious writers would touch it. Those who did were anxious to keep it unopened, or mediated and translated by proper authorities. The letter's taint of illegitimacy attached itself less to letter-writers and readers than to those who transported messages. And novelists, like De Quincey, often arranged to rid themselves of correspondence. In *Frankenstein*, the monster conveys the letters of Felix and Safie despite Victor's protests, and the novel, as a vehicle for such correspondence, shows itself a monstrous form. In a different mode, Walter Scott's *The Antiquary* (1816) places letters in the hands of illiterate beggars, foolish gossips and a boy riding a pony – "a monkey on a starved cat" – only to have the letters reclaimed later by magistrates, military personnel and the King's emissaries.[4] Caroline Lamb, who sets *Glenarvon* (1814), like *The Antiquary*, in the last years of the eighteenth century, crosses adulterous love letters with letters threatening violence and relating crimes: Irish rebels and outcasts are the couriers for both sets of correspondence. The Byronic Lord Glenarvon balks at this conflation, denouncing his mistress's plaintive letters as ' an unfeminine persecution" of himself, thereby eliding her missives with those of the volatile peasantry.[5] Once domestic and political order is restored, the need for such letters ceases. Glenarvon surrenders Lady Avondale's love letters, "those testimonies of her guilt," to a censorious third party: the family and friends of her husband.[6] At the same time he abolishes all contact with the United Irishmen and their conspiracies: he leaves Ireland to fight for the English king. The "unfeminine" letter-writer dies; the rebel Irish are suppressed. Illicit correspondence is halted by "the strong arm of power"[7] and becomes the symbol of a fallen woman and a failed past.

We could simply imagine the early nineteenth-century novel as a Dead Letter office, a depository for "vexatious" letters that should never circulate or be opened. For in the fiction of the period we find the letter abandoned, burned, buried, silenced, sent home or submitted as legal evidence. The finale to Jane Austen's *Pride and Prejudice* (1813) typifies this refutation: "I hope you have destroyed the letter," ventures Darcy at the close. "Think no more of the letter," Elizabeth replies,"...every unpleasant circumstance attending it ought to be forgotten."[8] In Scott's *Redgauntlet* (1832), the politics of such forgetting become apparent. Midway through the novel, a "third-person" narrator intervenes to shift the work from an epistolary format – an exchange of letters between two young men with antisocial and Jacobite tendencies – to the more "progressive" mode of a totalizing narrative. "A genuine correspondence," according to the narrator,

can seldom be found to contain all in which it is necessary to instruct the reader for his full comprehension of the story... [V]arious prolixities and redundancies occur in the course of an interchange of letters, which must hang as a dead weight on the progress of the narrator.[9]

In the interests of "fullness," "progress" and instruction, then, the partisan politics of the letter are discarded as dead weight.

In the years between revolution and reform in England, we find the metaphorical death or literal exhaustion of the familiar letter in literature. First recast as an antisocial, conspiratorial or illicit form of expression, the letter in fiction then becomes a mere ghost of itself, the memory of a force (the United Irishmen, the Jacobite Scots, or the corresponding societies) no longer capable of producing its own history. It becomes a helpless woman. Charles Lamb describes the burdens and restrictions which had combined to batter a distinctly female letter; having suffered much at the hands of the Post Office, a letter was "boarded up, freighted, entered at the Customs House." This "thing of delicate nature" was now "passed about... handled between... rude jests," then, after "waiting a passport here, a license there, the sanction of the magistry," would finally arrive at its destination "tired out and jaded." For Lamb and others, the letter only gave evidence of the impossibility of communicating personal feeling: "How few sentiments, my dear F–... can we set down... as quite sea-worthy." A letter, sighs Lamb, offers but "the positive testamentary disposal of a corpse."[10]

The punishing regulation and imagined death of communication between individuals, figured in a feminine letter, has severe consequences, especially for the woman writer. Is her writing implicitly dead on arrival? Unlike De Quincey, she has little recourse to the vehicle of the opium dream;[11] unlike Scott, she stands apart from the progress of a totalizing history. (In Scott's *The Heart of Midlothian*, notably, the heroine refuses to send a letter to London, preferring the arduous journey so as to plead her case *in propria persona*.) In Maria Edgeworth's *Patronage* (1814), for example, the woman's letter is stripped of all power and exposed as an impostor; at the same time, Edgeworth questions the need to dismiss the woman's letter. *Patronage* freely offers several letters written by the Percy brothers, detailing their adventures as they set up careers in medicine, law and the army. But Edgeworth does not provide the responses of their mother and sisters. From the brothers' letters we know that the women write often and dutifully, but we do not read their (evidently entertaining) letters. The novel withholds other letters as well: the secret diplomatic correspondence, letters of court intrigue and forged letters which activate half the plot. The parallel suppression is significant.

Edgeworth pulls together the two "unseens" – women's letters and political letters – and exposes their taboo connection. In the resolution of the novel's political sub-plot, we discover that treasonous letters, attributed to the powerful Lord Oldborough, have in fact been forged by two women who had ventured too far into the business of buying and selling political influence.[12] Ingeniously, the female criminals had learned to copy the minister's seal with a wad of bread.[13] In the logic of the novel, the intrusion of the domestic into the political, effected through bread and letters, becomes a crime worse than mere treason. By implication, women writing letters, despite all their political savvy, seem no better than forgers. Better to have their letters remain dutiful but invisible, like those of the Percy women. This moral, however, seems too extreme even for Edgeworth. After all, the novelist is as ingenious as her villainesses. To Lady Jane Granville, the novel's mouthpiece of "fashion," is given the shrewd last word on the future of women and letters:

This is the last confidential letter I shall ever be able to write to you – for a married woman's letters you know, become like all the rest of her property, subject to her husband. Excepting the secrets of which she was possessed before marriage, which do not go into the common stock, if she be a woman of honour.[14]

Perhaps the very invisibility of a woman's letters, their exclusion from common stock and public visibility, invites fictions of treachery, forgery and subversion of the status quo. When the novel silences the woman letter-writer, it may well be promoting the fear of unsanctioned or undomesticated secrets.

Forgotten or repudiated letters hold stories that are not necessarily "feminine," but have been feminized in order to be discounted. Elizabeth Gaskell's *Cranford* (1853) helps articulate this crucial dilemma. Due to the exigencies of "personal economies" in Cranford, we find the narrator and Miss Matty burning bundles of old family letters. As the two women, young and old, remark on the changes in epistolary style and on the fate of the family, we catch a glimpse of England's recent political past: the letters explicitly cover the period from 1774 to 1824, the years of revolution in America and Europe, of constant warfare with France, and of troubled British expansion in India. Simultaneously, we read a history of the post in England. Gaskell's narrator alludes to various changes in the life of letters: from the mail coach to the railway and to other, more efficient, "overland routes" through the empires; from wafer seals to the new gummed envelopes and notepaper; from the old parliamentary "franking" allowance to the penny post reform of 1838–40. Nonetheless, these family letters, which figure the intersection of personal and political history, of emotional and economic communication, are rendered unfamiliar, antiquated and expendable – like the women of Cranford. Because they do not fit the current "economy" of Miss Matty's household, the letters, with all their emotional power and binding force, are sacrificed to the flames.[15] With the loss of the letter, the private and the public part company. And the woman writer must imagine alternative means to send a "letter to the World / That never wrote to [her]."

Having discarded the epistolary formulae of the past, nineteenth-century fiction was beginning to write its own history or elegy of letters. On the one hand it was a history which would distinguish – and leave separate – the two realms of world affairs and private, domestic concerns.[16] On the other, this history would forget the letter's volatile political past, its ability to build coalitions and voice individual concerns. At least, in this ritual burning, Gaskell's *Cranford* feeds both memory *and* flames. It does not forget that the letter not only tied home to empire, but also allowed the "various prolixities and redundancies" of multiple histories.[17]

I am not trying to argue that the letter in nineteenth-century England was no longer a viable form of communication. This is far from the case. Rather, the fiction of this period no longer employed the epistolary mode to represent interpersonal communication; furthermore, it deliberately staged the death of the letter. At the same time, writers devised narrative structures to compensate for the imagined loss of correspondence within the world of the novel. And they began to pay strict attention to the fiction of the Post Office.

The image of the Post Office, which appears in Austen's novels, in Scott's, in Gaskell's and in Dickens', was more than a device for narrative control in the novel. It figured a general restructuring of society in the nineteenth century, a restructuring that squeezed the irregularities of correspondence out of the public sphere. In its place was erected a system of communication between the public and the private which guaranteed the radical separation of each. The individual corresponded with society, or with himself; she sent letters to the post office, not to friends or lovers. The familiar letter had become a nearly impossible fiction to sustain.

ESTABLISHING ENGLISH CORRESPONDENCE

The Post Office had the business of coordinating communication and exchange within the British Empire, but also of organizing a national fiction of correspondence. Whereas the novels often tested the letter's role within conflicting fictions – domestic and national, feminine and political, emotional and commercial – the nineteenth-century British Post Office resolved these conflicts by means of a hierarchy of concordant fictions, within which "English" correspondence was ideologically defined and confined. Remarkably, the story of traitorous correspondence and partisan activity was written out of this official version. With the Postal Reform Act of 1839, which introduced the penny post, this hierarchy became law. Queen Victoria, in her speech to Parliament, made its structure explicit:

I trust that the Act ... will be a relief and encouragement to trade; and that, by facilitating intercourse and correspondence, it will be productive of much social advantage and improvement.[18]

The penny post changed more than the price of postage throughout Great Britain. In announcing the reform, the queen was endorsing a revision of correspondence authored by imperial interests and social engineers.

Victoria's language is inflected with the booming optimism of the father of the modern Post Office, Rowland Hill. When Rowland Hill (later Sir Rowland Hill, Postmaster-General from 1840 to 1864) published his pamphlet, "Post Office Reform: Its Importance and Practicality" in 1837, he successfully articulated a new ideology of the mail. Under Hill's Benthamite system, all letters are equal and equally subject to the same central authority. All letters bear the

same stamp, all distances pay the same fee; all distribution travels in
and out of one London office, not three; and all mail lines journey
directly into and out of the capital. The cross-lines established in the
mid-1700s, as well as the private carriers which had proliferated in
the more remote regions, are all gradually eliminated.[19] The Royal
Mail is now recognized as the British Post Office, conceived as a
public service for private individuals, rather than as a taxable
privilege giving access to the public sphere.

This leveling transforms the postal service into an ideological
vehicle of "progress" for both political economy and national
education. To a certain degree, the fiction of progress is underwritten
by letters. When Hill reports to Parliament on the early effects of the
postal reform, he presents statistics on deliveries and revenues, but
saves his best material for last:

I am now in the possession of various letters [presenting one] showing some
important benefits to commerce arising from the facility of communication
and easy transmission of...light goods; others [showing] great advantages
to literature, science and friendly union, evinced by the transmission of
scientific specimens, evinced, too, by the productions of works and
formations even of large societies, to the existence of which...the establishment of the penny rate was an essential condition; and others again,
telling of pains relieved, affections cultivated, and mental efforts encouraged
by correspondence, to which the former rates would have acted as absolute
prohibition.[20]

Hill then reads aloud from selected letters, all applauding the social
benefits of increased correspondence due to the lower rates and more
efficient service. One significant aspect of Hill's report on the Post
Office is the clear structure of priorities: correspondence means
commerce first; education, science and culture second; affective ties
and personal needs third. This structure echoes in Victoria's speech
(though she is more concerned with "relief" to trade than to
individuals) and in contemporary debates on the issue of postal
reform, where the "enhancement of commerce" through an improved postal system would eventually "accelerate" the "education
of the people," "promot[e] friendly intercourse amongst all classes"
and "help scattered kin to maintain contact with each other."[21]

The reformers thus sought to institutionalize, on a national level,
the rhetoric contained in a century's worth of letter-writing manuals,
but with this significant innovation: the new Mail would dissolve the
carefully marked differences between social groups and individual

purposes. The Mail would become a *Universal Letter-Writer* which recognized few, if any, boundaries.[22] A second notable aspect of Hill's report, then, is his confident approval of "large societies" brought together via correspondence: at a safe distance from the paranoia of the turn of the century, the rhetoric of national reform imagines no organized opposition to its progress.

Perhaps most curious is the story Hill creates from the actual letters he presents. In its structure and use of letters, his story mirrors the novels of the period. Despite his own repeated emphasis on benefits to national economy and commerce, Hill substantiates his report with an odd epistolary account of individual women and workers. He reads a letter from the Edinburgh Educational Society detailing the effects of the postal reform on a middle-aged woman, whose four children live and work "at a considerable distance from her":

Allured by the cheap postage, and the laudable desire of being able to reply to the letters of her children, she resolved, at the age of forty-five, to learn to write... [V]ery few of the scholars have made greater progress than this energetic woman.[23]

Another letter, from J. S. Henslow, a schoolteacher in Suffolk, assures us that "the penny postage is an important addition to the comforts of the poor labourer":

[I]ndeed, I know that the pens of my schoolchildren are already put into requisition by their parents. [Improved delivery to small villages] would greatly accelerate the development of country letter-writers.[24]

A number of other letters attest to the increased enrollment of working-class students in writing courses. Hill finishes this litany with a flourish, citing a report by a Prussian traveler on the virtues of the British system:

[B]y the reduction of the postage on letters, [the British Government] has brought the use and advantage of education home to the common man, for it no longer costs him a day's wages to communicate with his family. This great moral improvement in the condition of the lower class extends the influence of advice, admonition, and family affection among them... This measure will be the great historical distinction of the reign of Victoria I. Every mother in the kingdom, who has children earning bread at a distance, lays her head upon the pillow at night with a feeling of gratitude for this blessing.[25]

It is perhaps enough to recognize that Hill's story, extracted from letters about working-class letter-writers, neither includes nor cites

actual letters written by members of the working class. Instead,
educators and social commentators have translated the letters of the
underprivileged into the language of progress and economics. The
very desires and affections of these parents become the fictions of
reform, sent in letters to the Postmaster-General, then delivered to
the halls of Parliament.

But these domesticated desires and affections are also scripted as
the products of the postal system itself: the mail brings families
together, "extends" affect and moral influence, injects the desire to
communicate. "Advice, admonition and family affection" become
commodities sold by the Post Office for a mere penny. Only quiet
hints remind us that economic conditions and "commerce" have
split apart the very families which "correspondence" will now heal.
And of course, in the progress of Hill's own rhetoric, it is ultimately
lower-class families and women whose "want of desire" for such
commodities and such healing needs reform.[26]

By fostering a new letter-writing campaign, the post would,
according to Hill, encourage the formerly disenfranchised to enlist in
the social, economic and political system. Lower rates and "more
efficient" financial management would then give the Post Office
"the new and important character of a powerful engine of civilization."[27] Civilization would come "home to the common man"
through the penny post.

All exchange would be the same, and all would be public. The Post
Office reforms carried out in mid-century gave the institution itself
nearly unlimited access to private communication and exchange.
Throughout this period, the Post tightened its hold on the empire's
channels of information and commerce. Private messengers became
increasingly restricted, while postal "services" expanded to include
package transport and book delivery, as well as personal financial
services, including public welfare distribution, life insurance and a
savings bank.[28] The Post Office introduced Victorian England to its
first public enterprise and, in the process, established a civil service
which eventually employed more people than any private concern in
the entire world.[29] Its only rivals for influence and geographical
extension were the army and navy. Indeed, the postal system
imagined itself as an efficient model for the British empire, coordinating communication and commercial exchange, and setting the
standard for "ordering and controlling a massive workforce."[30]
Simultaneously, England could imagine itself primarily as a network

of communication and exchange, its other functions governed by that image.

But of course, the Post Office was not the British empire, nor could it successfully streamline all forms of communication within the empire. Behind the reform of epistolary fictions hides that supposedly dead letter, and with it, the letter's tendency to individuate and decentralize established systems of meaning. Even as Hill promoted postal "facilities for the collection and diffusion of information," radiating from London, another image of the letter circulated throughout the countryside. What Nancy Armstrong and Thomas Laqueur have written about working-class literacy in general can be related to letter-writing in particular:

New forms of literacy seemed to intrude upon the cultural stage brandishing a double-edged sword ... If education helped to produce a more tractable working class, working-class radicalism was predicated on literacy too – that is, on political pamphlets, on alternative programs for education, and even on a literature that spoke to their needs and desires than to those of their employers.[31]

The working-class correspondence societies gave voice to those needs and desires in the 1790s. But the threatening or "incendiary letters" of agricultural revolt in the first half of the nineteenth century, of "Captain Ludd," "Captain Swing" and "Rebecca," spoke even more vociferously.[32]

Against the Postmaster-General's collection of letters about working-class correspondence we can set a number of letters from the impoverished and nearly illiterate section of the population of Great Britain. E. P. Thompson provides copies of criminal or incendiary letters from the mid-eighteenth century up to the first decades of the nineteenth century, most of which addressed social or economic grievances.[33] The following anonymous letter, written in 1800 in Essex, was addressed to "Mister," at Deanes Church, but appears to have been copied and sent to several parishes in the area as part of a neighborhood letter-writing campaign:

Now Jantleman this is to let you know in all Parts that we have suffered hungary for sumtime and we have bore it paceantly but you still keep starfing us more and more but with great reaserlusen we will not bear it longer ... if you do not chuse to lower things so eveary wone may live and in a shoart Time for all warking Hands are sworn true to each other the hole Kingdom through ... for the damd Farmers and Factors an like wise mellers an Shopkeepers for thay are worse then the head Jantleman and we mean to set out with a great reaserlusen to destroy all them kind of men for wel will burn and disstroay eveary thing we come at…Jantlemen you have brought all this on yourselves. We mean to behave well to eveary minester that will read this in the church if he is not a ded man by night or by day we by all means disstroay the King and Parlement.[34]

Another letter, written in Salisbury in 1839, directs "A PROC-LAMATION OF BLOOD AND FIRE!" to "All Churches, States and People, on the Sea Sand," reminding them that Samson burned the Philistines' fields and warning:

so now the Gentiles and the Heathen starve the poor, why marvel ye if every man turns after Samson, "for these are the days of vengeance, when all shall be fulfilled".[35]

The letter is signed by "Mahershalalhashbaz, Sec.," "Jesus Christ," and "Cholera, Blood, Fire, and Co. Extra Executors." As a final touch, "Earthquakes, Panics, and Co." are added as "Witnesses."

Letters such as these – some tied to rocks and thrown through windows, some nailed to church doors, some signed in blood, some left at the site of destroyed grain bins – were common throughout England, in agrarian communities as well as industrial centres. Written on behalf of the poor, the working-man, and the disenfranchised, the incendiary letters typically threatened machine-breaking, massive strikes, arson and murder, if justice continued to ignore the needs of the suffering. Not surprisingly, a marked increase in epistolary activity can be charted in the years of greatest political instability – in years of extreme famine (1766–7, 1795–6 and 1800–2); in the years of Luddite revolt (1812–14); and in the most difficult years of the continental wars (1795–6, 1800–2, 1811–12).

These letters give the historian a rare example of the language of protest from the otherwise inaccessible "voice of the poor." As the century moved on, it became clear that the voice was not only anonymous, but also collective – therein lay its power. One letter from 1794, reprinted by Thompson, bears the signature of "The Monster"; another, from 1816, is signed by "The voice of the Multitude."[36]

At the same time that reformers were writing to Rowland Hill to applaud the increased enrollment in writing classes, organized groups of protesters were transforming the power of letters into the fires of revolt. Under the banner of "Captain Ludd," in the 1810s, weavers and "mechanics" in the north of England waged a "war of nerves" and threatening letters were vital to their campaign.[37] During the 1830s and 1840s, the mythical "Captain Swing" and his anonymous troops sent fierce letters, threatening to destroy machinery, maim cattle and burn buildings. These letters, as well as the similarly volatile "Rebecca" letters circulating in Wales at this period, waged a desperate guerrilla war against a new social order based on industrial capitalism. In rural England and Ireland, the names of Swing and Ludd united an invisible army; in Wales, Rebecca's followers disguised themselves in women's clothes and fought as her "daughters." Not only did these rebels overturn the very notions of identity and property, but they also challenged any idea that letter-writing promoted "family affections" and Hill's goals of "civilization." Other desires were produced through these clandestine liaisons, and other models of British society. A few more examples will demonstrate both the marginal literacy and lyrical wit of these "vexatious" letters:

J. Sutter:
> Revenge for thee is on the wing
> From thy determined
> > Capt. Swing
J. Deary mind your yards be not of a fire dam you D.

Sir
> Your name is down amongst the Black hearts in the Black Book and this is to advise you and the like of you... to make your wills
> Ye have been the Blackguard Enemies of the People on all occasions, Ye have not yet done
> > as ye ought
> > – Swing[38]

Sir,
> mind yourself for as sure as this letter will come to your hand I and my dutiful daughters from 5 to 10 hundred of us will visit your habitation... in a few days and you will do well to prepare a secure place for your soul we will do well with your body your flesh we will give to the Glausevin hounds and your bones we will burn.
> take the hint in time, lo, I tell you fairly.

> > I remain your faithful Servant,
> > Rebecka Dogood[39]

The rhetoric of reform, which insisted upon the interdependence of laissez-faire capitalism and widespread literacy, sounds anxious and reactionary when juxtaposed to the language of Swing and Rebecca. The story of letters written by these outlaws reveals that the letter had not lost its dangerous double-edge. In fact, the letter could imagine a death sentence quite different from that of Derrida's post. Despite the Post Office's progressive ideology, which aimed to domesticate the individual voice and facilitate the movements of commerce, anonymous and collective voices from the margins could still be heard, breaking through the too-economical definitions of correspondence.

I point to the phenomenon of incendiary letters in the British countryside in order to underscore what the reform of the postal system was meant to erase: unregulated communication between distinct social groups, collective expression of special interests, and threats to property and the status quo. The Post Office offered the fiction that all members of society could communicate equally well with all other members, *if* they submitted to the efficient machinery of the public service. If all eyes were turned toward the central system as the source and destination of personal correspondence, the beginning and end, then the opportunities for collusion or private liaisons would cease. Alternative fictions would be incommunicable.

"THE ENGLISH MAIL COACH" AND THE INCOMMUNICABLE

But when we turn our eyes askance, and look around and outside the imperial mail coach, we can see again the force of that "vexatious" letter of unregulated and much too private communication. So we turn to De Quincey's apocalyptic "English Mail Coach" (1850), which drives through his imagination bearing the "secret" or "dread word" of the Post Office's institutional power; what he calls elsewhere "the burden of the Incommunicable."[40] For De Quincey, the sanctity of this "Incommunicable" guarantees a vision of catholic, eternal harmony, complete with military triumph, cathedral choirs and the sacrifice of a young girl. But despite the thunderous progress of De Quincey's prose, we might halt to examine this contradiction: why invest a mail coach with something that cannot be communicated? What are the silences which fuel the "Incommunicable?" "The English Mail Coach" careens through history, converting the volatile past of the letter into a harmonious vision of future redemption.[41] Around the edges of the coach, however, and in its traces, we read the threats of political insurrection,

unsupervised intercourse and female imagination which had marked
the history of the letter in English literature – the very history the
mail coach wants to erase.

The celebration of the "Incommunicable," the "secret word –
Waterloo and Recovered Christendom" requires the excommuni-
cation of discordant voices. De Quincey transfers the disturbing work
of the eighteenth-century letter to a post-Waterloo fiction of the
"post-office service," a "mighty orchestra,"

> where a thousand instruments, *all disregarding each other*, and in danger of
> discord, yet all obedient as slaves to the supreme baton of some great leader,
> terminate in a perfection of harmony like that of the heart, veins, and
> arteries.[42]

But look at what falls out along the roadside of De Quincey's
narrative. There are no actual letters in "The English Mail Coach,"
only representations of "exchanges" which introduce the "danger of
discord" amidst that "mighty orchestra." And these exchanges
adopt progressively less political, more private guises. The opening
section, "The Glory of Motion," is rife with references to the politics
of revolution. Veiled threats to the coach appear in forms which
indicate England's domestic troubles First, another coach – a
"plebeian wretch," "a beast from Birmingham" – challenges the
supremacy of the Royal Mail. "For some time this Birmingham
machine ran along by our side – a piece of familiarity that seemed to
us sufficiently jacobinical."[43] Later De Quincey compresses into
anecdote the incendiary violence which threatened the countryside
even as he wrote. "Jack," an "obstinate sailor" (possibly fleeing
empressment) takes a "forbidden seat" on the outside of the coach,
in order to "exchange yarns" with the guard. "No greater offence
was then known to the coaches," fumes the narrator, than this extra-
official communication which "makes light of the law and the
lawgiver." Predictably, this making light, unlike Gaskell's version in
Cranford, signals Promethean insolence: ashes from Jack's pipe
inadvertently set flame to the mail bags, thus threatening "a
revolution in the republic of letters."[44]

As the narrative continues, the veiled threats change their dress
from that of class to that of gender. At one point the narrator
remembers his roadside dalliances with Miss Fanny of the Bath
Road, a mail coachman's granddaughter; but he recalls that the
"crocodile" coachman was always ready to regulate their encounters

and to interfere. "Timed, in reality, by the General Post Office," the narrator was able "to make love for seven years... and yet never to compromise" himself – or his progress. "Had it not been for the Bath and Bristol mail," De Quincey insists, he might have succumbed to the charms of the many "Fannies of our island."[45] He concludes that any man who feels so tempted "ought to be made a ward of the General Post Office, whose severe course of timing and periodical interruption might intercept many a foolish declaration."[46]

More than sexual timing and foolish declarations of love are at stake in these anecdotes. De Quincey produces a suspicion of human contact outside the official lines of communication, outside the predictable schedules of the English mail coach. As the mail coach runs its course, we learn the dangers of such mistiming and of clandestine intercourse. The most disturbing encounter in the essay, the one which reverberates and echoes in the narrator's dreams, occurs when "a frail, reedy gig," carrying two young lovers, crosses the path of the galloping coach. The scene seems far removed from the political and sexual politics of the earlier encounters, but in fact, it serves as their culmination.

The lovers' wagon recalls, in fact, that Birmingham machine and its radical politics; in the lovers' murmurs are heard the whispers of conspiracy. Both narrator and mail coach interrupt the private conversation. The narrator imposes the first intervention – "Ah, young sir! What are you about?" – and proceeds to protest that, given that no one would be "likely to overhear your conversation – is it, therefore, necessary that you should bring your lips to hers?" The jocular remark about this innocent intercourse is brutally reiterated by the mail coach itself. With the "ravings of hurricanes," the coach collides with the tiny carriage, killing the young woman within:

from the manly tenderness of this flattering, whispering, murmuring love, – suddenly, as from the woods and fields, – suddenly as from the chambers of the air opening in revelation, – suddenly as from the ground yawning at her feet, leaped upon her, with the flashing of cataracts, Death the crownéd phantom, with all the equipage of his terrors, and the tiger roar of his voice.[47]

By a series of narrative transpositions, the silent woman figures all the obstructions which have stood in the path of the mail coach. And by the mail coach's "fiercest of translations," this figure receives the death sentence, and "stands before the judgement seat of God." Thus

De Quincey sweeps a history of "vexatious letters" out of history. Moreover, this figure of a "helpless girl" is "swept into [his] dreams forever" – underwriting the magnificent "Dream-Fugue" which culminates the essay.[48] In this way, De Quincey asserts the solitary superiority of his dreaming, "the one great tube through which man communicates with the shadowy," over dangerous, foolish and ultimately feminized correspondence.[49]

De Quincey's "English Mail Coach" allows us to follow the stages necessary to convert the fiction of a dangerously politicized letter into a fiction of "helpless" femininity, at odds with the inexorable movements of nation and progress. Moreover, the image of the "General Post Office" offers the structure for "translating" correspondence with radical otherness into a vision of undifferentiated privacy. Finally, the mail coach, the fatal machinery of the Post Office, services "a world – in which every man, the very meanest, is a solitary presence, and cannot admit the fellowship even of that one amongst his fellow creatures whom he loves the most and perhaps regards as his other self."[50] The path of "The English Mail Coach" traces not only the victory of "Waterloo" and "Empire," but the defeat of "fellowship" with this "other self."

Notes

INTRODUCTION: THE PUBLIC LETTER, OR *LA LETTRE PERFIDE*

1 Erica Rand, in "Depoliticizing Women: Female Agency, the French Revolution, and the Art of Boucher and David," *Genders*, 7 (1990), 47–68, offers another reading of politics and feminization in David's painting. Although we concur in the general effect of *Marat Assassiné*, my disagreement with Rand's notion of depoliticization should become clear in the course of this chapter.

2 Anita Brookner, *Jacques-Louis David* (London: Chatto & Windus, 1980), p. 115.

3 Corday used this letter to gain an audience with Marat. For Baudelaire's discussion of the murder, see Brookner, *David*, p. 118.

4 Robert Rosenblum, *Transformations in Late Eighteenth-Century Art* (Princeton: Princeton UP, 1967), p. 84.

5 Ibid., p. 84.

6 On the formal traditions underscoring David's achievement, see ibid., pp. 50–106; Brookner, *David*, p. 112; and Ronald Paulson, *Representations of Revolution, 1789–1820* (New Haven: Yale UP, 1983), p. 14. All three critics explicitly point to the *pietà*.

7 "One aspect of sentimentalism is the attempt to express religious values – 'a transcendent, religious consciousness' – in a medium and sensibility – 'fundamentally secular and empiricist' – that are in a significant measure resistant to the transcendental absolutism of the religious metaphysics." Michael Bell, *The Sentiment of Reality* (London: G. Allen & Unwin, 1983), p. 16. Bell argues that this tension is most obvious in the novel's death scenes, especially religious death scenes, as in *Clarissa* or *Julie*.

8 David explicitly referred to Rousseau's notion of "L'Etre Supreme," as found in *Julie ou la Nouvelle Héloïse* (Paris: Garnier-Flammarion, 1967), in his preparation for Robespierre's great festival in 1793, the same year as the *Marat*. And he confessed that the idea for a figure in his *Death of Socrates* had been given him "by the supreme novelist" of *Clarissa*. Brookner, *David*, pp. 168 and 85.

9 Michael Fried, *Absorption and Theatricality* (Berkeley: University of California Press, 1980), pp. 172–4, discusses the erotics of Greuze's *The*

Kiss (fig. 3), with special reference to the letter's role in establishing the theme of sensual abandon.

10 Marat is not the only revolutionary martyr "feminized" by David. The paintings of Bara, a young soldier, and of Lepeletier display "the dead raped-murdered body, the 'heroic corpse'...idealized and classicized (increasingly...feminized) into a Christ that retains vestiges of the sexuality of Lucretia but also inevitably recalls the bodies of the sons of Brutus [from David's 'Lictors Returning to Brutus the Bodies of his Sons']." Paulson, *Representations of Revolution*, p. 34.

11 Ibid., pp. 25–6.

12 For an account of the reverberations of Corday's act, see J. M. Thompson, *The French Revolution*, rev. ed. (London: Basil Blackwell Ltd., 1985), pp. 367–75. According to Thompson, Corday "had rendered political assassination, for once, almost respectable; and she had made herself immortal" (p. 368). Erica Rand complicates Thompson's analysis: "Virtually all who judged her, no matter what the verdict, saw her act as a violation of gender norms. People either saw a woman and could not see a political actor, or saw a political assassin and could not quite call her a woman." Rand, "Depoliticizing Women," p. 56. See also Michael Marrinan, "Images and Ideas of Charlotte Corday: Texts and Contexts of an Assassin," *Arts* 54, no. 8 (April 1980), 158–61. In any case, the immediate politics of Corday's act were cast in terms of gender and virtue, not in terms of Montagnards and Girondins.

13 Brookner, *David*, p. 112.

14 In the public display David mounted for Marat's funeral, the artist was careful to elevate the corpse on a pedestal several meters high – exposed to view, but inaccessible. On David's public pageants, and their influence on his painting, see Norman Bryson, *Tradition and Desire: From David to Delacroix* (Cambridge: Cambridge UP, 1984), p. 85. David reinforces the hero's inaccessibility by withholding from view the pages under Marat's arm, evidently his "derrières pensées pour le salut du public". Brookner, *David*, p. 114, quoting David's own description of the painting.

15 Of the *Marat*, Ronald Paulson writes, "Also in the background of Marat's corpse (offstage) is the woman who speaks for human feelings. In some strange way, Charlotte Corday merges the chorus-for-mercy with the raped, violated figure for whom it mourns." Paulson, *Representations of Revolution*, p. 34. Paulson also mentions the recurrence of latent female imagery in several of David's major works, including *The Oath of the Horatii*, the *Brutus* and *Paris and Helen*. In all of these, David is following an accepted tradition in historical painting, where the woman is sacrificed to "Honor and Duty," to nation and law (pp. 29–30). See also Rosenblum, *Transformations*, pp. 65–77; and Brookner, *David*, p. 83. Erica Rand's reading is similar to mine, suggesting that David inscribes Corday's letter into the less threatening economy of the banknotes, evidence of Marat's charity. Thus "instead of being a Girondin in the

guise of a Montagnard [Corday's ploy in her letter], Corday seems to be a bad woman disguised as a good woman." But that inscription is not erasure. I cannot subscribe to Rand's (admittedly qualified) statement that the "painting's internal discourse can be completely understood without reference to contemporary politics." As she herself notes, the Parisian public was all too well aware of the exercise of female political power. Rand, "Depoliticizing Women," p. 57.

16 Burke, *Reflections on the Revolution in France* (Garden City, NY: Doubleday Inc., 1973), Prefatory Notice, n. p.

17 Elizabeth C. Goldsmith, introduction, in Goldsmith, ed., *Writing the Female Voice: Essays on Epistolary Literature* (Boston: Northeastern UP, 1989), p. xii.

18 Patricia Meyer Spacks, "Female Resources: Epistles, Plot and Power," in ibid., p. 75.

19 See Rand, "Depoliticizing Women," pp. 55–8.

I HISTORY AND THE FICTION OF LETTERS

1 For analyses of this version of the epistolary genre, see Howard Anderson and Irvin Ehrenpreis, *The Familiar Letter in the Eighteenth Century* (Lawrence: University of Kansas Press, 1966); Bruce Redford, *The Converse of the Pen: Acts of Intimacy in the Eighteenth-Century Familiar Letter* (Chicago: Chicago UP, 1986); and Elizabeth Goldsmith, "Authority, Authenticity, and the Publication of Letters by Women," in Goldsmith, ed., *Writing the Female Voice: Essays in Epistolary Literature* (Boston: Northeastern UP, 1989), pp. 46–59.

2 Jerome Christensen, *Practicing Enlightenment: Hume and the Formation of a Literary Career* (Madison: University of Wisconsin Press, 1987), p. 190.

3 Ibid., p. 195.

4 Ibid., p. 183.

5 Ibid., pp. 195, 199.

6 David Hume, "Of Simplicity and Refinement in Writing," quoted in Christensen, *Practicing Enlightenment*, p. 115.

7 Jacques Derrida, "Envois," in *The Post Card: From Socrates to Freud and Beyond*, trans. Alan Bass (Chicago: University of Chicago Press, 1987), p. 48.

8 Ibid., p. 144.

9 See especially Christensen, "The Example of the Female," in *Practicing Enlightenment*, pp. 95–6n. Moving from Hume's plan in *A Treatise on Human Nature* for "castrating my work," Christensen explores the gendering implications of Hume's representation of publication as feminization in style and form (not content). He quotes from Hume's letters: "Had I a Son I shou'd warn him as carefully against the dangerous Allurements of Literature as James did his Son against those of Women."

10 Stuart Hall, "Signification, Representation, Ideology: Althusser and

the Post-Structuralist Debates," *Studies in Mass Communication*, 2 (1985), 95.

11 The combined effects of the expiration of the Licensing Act in 1695 and the establishment of a standard copyright in 1710 made eighteenth-century London booksellers free from governmental restrictions and gave them preference over provincial printers. The creation of a unified British postal system in 1711 consolidated the London publishers' power over the literary marketplace: "no business in the mid-eighteenth-century exemplified so fully the integration of the product with the means of production and distribution as did the publishing industry." In 1774, the neat system faltered when the publishers lost this support and parallel identification with the state. The House of Lords refused to back the Conger in its demand for certified common law rights. Christensen, *Practicing Enlightenment*, pp. 188, 195.

12 See J. Ann Hone, *For the Cause of Truth: Radicalism in London 1796–1821* (Oxford: Clarendon Press, 1982), pp. 360–2; and Albert Goodwin, *The Friends of Liberty: The English Democratic Movement in the Age of the French Revolution* (Cambridge: Harvard UP, 1979), pp. 224–7, and 268–358, for examples of the ingenuity and political savvy of radical groups in the 1790s, which were operating under restriction or censure by the Pitt ministry.

13 Eric Batstone, Anthony Ferner and Michael Terry, *Consent and Efficiency: Labour Relations and Management Strategy in the State Enterprise*, Warwick Studies in Industrial Relations (Oxford: Basil Blackwell, 1984), p. 123.

14 Howard Robinson, *The British Post Office: A History* (Princeton: Princeton UP, 1948), pp. 126–40.

15 Ibid., p. 140.

16 Samuel Richardson, *Clarissa*, ed. John Butt, 4 vols. (New York: E. P. Dutton, 1962), vol. IV, pp. 328, 334–7.

17 The "utmost confusion" attached itself to the attack on Palmer. Response to his plans for making the mail coach "the swiftest conveyance in England" could not avoid this expression: 'correspondence will be thrown into the utmost confusion," if the coaches do not pause more often; the changes "will fling the whole commercial correspondence of the country into the utmost confusion, and ... raise such a clamour as the Postmaster will not be able to appease." *Report of the Committee of the House of Commons on Mr. Palmer's Agreement for the Reform and Improvement of the Post Office and Its Revenues. 1797* (London: n. p., 1797–8), pp. 117–20.

18 Robinson, *British Post Office*, pp. 150–5 and Rowland Hill, *First-Third Reports from the Select Committee on Postage: Together with the Minutes of Evidence and Appendix* (London: 1838), pp. 87–8.

19 Stuart Hall writes: "Often ideological struggle consists of attempting to wish some new set of meanings for an existing term or category, of dis-articulating it from its place in a signifying structure." Hall, "Signifi-cation," 111. I am proposing that the genre of the letter and the idea of correspondence were subject to just such a struggle.

20 Linda S. Kauffman, *Discourses of Desire: Gender, Genre, and Epistolary Fictions* (Ithaca: Cornell UP, 1986), pp. 26–7, 21. The letter also serves as the repository of feminine desire in literature, the "reading of a bodily residue." Peggy Kamuf, *Fictions of Feminine Desire: The Disclosures of Héloïse* (Lincoln: University of Nebraska Press, 1987), pp. xi–xix. In a related use of letter imagery, see Luce Irigaray's explanation of the "enveloping and enveloped body" in "Sexual Difference," in Toril Moi, ed. and trans., *French Feminist Thought: A Reader* (New York: Blackwell, 1987), p. 155.

21 See, for instance, the essays in Elizabeth Goldsmith, ed., *Writing the Female Voice*.

22 A collection of essays generated by and including Lacan's discussion of Edgar Allen Poe's "The Purloined Letter" is John P. Muller and William J. Richardson, eds., *The Purloined Poe* (Baltimore: The Johns Hopkins UP, 1988).

23 Linda Kauffman, *Discourses of Desire*, pp. 314–15, quotes from Gregory L. Ulmer's review-essay of Derrida's *The Post Card*: "The Post-Age," *Diacritics* 11 (Fall 1981), 39–56.

24 Hall, "Signification," 94–5.

25 Ibid., 95.

26 Kamuf, *Fictions of Feminine Desire*, p. ix.

27 Walter Scott, *The Journal of Sir Walter Scott*, ed. W. E. K. Anderson (London, 1972). For Scott's dismissal of epistolary narrative, see *Redgauntlet: A Tale of the Eighteenth Century*, ed. Kathryn Sutherland (New York: Oxford UP, 1985), pp. 141–2.

28 Ruth Perry, *Women, Letters, and the Novel* (New York: AMS Press, 1980), pp. xiii.

29 Janet Gurkin Altman, *Epistolarity: Approaches to a Form* (Columbus: Ohio State UP, 1982), p. 202.

30 Shari Benstock, "From Letters to Literature: *La Carte Postale* and the Epistolary Genre," *Genre* 18 (Fall 1985), 262.

31 Richardson, "Author's Preface [1759]," *Clarissa*, p. xx. Richardson is quoting from his own novel, specifically from Belford's letter of 4 August (vol. IV, letter 81).

32 Derrida, *The Post Card*, p. 48.

33 Perry, *Women, Letters*, pp. 68–70.

34 Benstock, "From Letters to Literature," 287.

35 Jean-Jacques Rousseau, Second Preface, *Julie, ou la Nouvelle Héloïse* (Paris: Garnier-Flammarion, 1967), p. 575. All quotations from this text will be my own translations.

36 Rousseau, of course, spoke out repeatedly against the corrupting influence of the theater and public "spectacles." See his "Lettre à D'Alembert sur les spectacles," *Œuvres complètes*, ed. Bernard Gagnebin *et al.*, 12 vols. (Bruges: Editions Gallimard, 1951), vol. XI. Rousseau calls attention to his own fiction of a privatized "spectacle" in the letter-novel. He opens the First Preface with this characteristic lament/boast:

"There must be spectacles in the great cities, and novels for a corrupted populace. I have seen the habits of my age, and I have published these letters" (First Preface, *Julie*, p. 3).

37 Rousseau, "Second Preface," in *Julie*, p. 580.

38 My observations on Rousseau's construction of the ideal reader owe a great deal to Robert Darnton, "Readers Respond to Rousseau," in *The Great Cat Massacre and Other Episodes in French Cultural History* (New York: Vintage Books, 1985), pp. 215–56. Darnton remarks especially on the "familiarity" generated between the author, the reader, and the novel's own writers and readers. The source of his study is a collection of letters to Rousseau's publishers from his readers, but Darnton does not explicitly discuss the connection between these letters and the form of *Julie*.

39 Rousseau, *Julie*, pp. 580, 574.

40 Rousseau, *Les Confessions*, in *Œuvres complètes*, vol. 1, especially book 5.

41 Julie herself is sacrificed to preserve the image of domestic perfection and maternal love. The minister tells her, as she lies on her death bed: "Madam... you die a martyr's death to maternal love. May God return you to us to serve as an example." Rousseau, *Julie*, p. 546.

42 The "conventional" plot of epistolary fiction usually details the seduction and/or death of the heroine – a "dysphoric" plot, according to Nancy R. Miller; or it leads to the heroine's social redemption in marriage – a "euphoric" plot. Nancy K. Miller, *The Heroine's Text: Readings in the French and English Novel, 1722–1782* (New York: Columbia UP, 1980), p. xi. See also Perry, *Women, Letters*, pp. 129–35.

43 Robert Adams Day, *Told in Letters* (Ann Arbor: University of Michigan Press, 1966), pp. 70–2, gives extensive statistics on the popularity of the epistolary novel. Godfrey Frank Singer, in *The Epistolary Novel: Its Origin, Development, Decline, and Residual Influence* (New York: Russell & Russell, 1963), pp. 99–155, makes the point that "every author of importance in the eighteenth century used this mode at one time or another."

44 Day, *Told in Letters*, pp. 49, 71–7.

45 Ibid., p. 48.

46 Taken from *The Young Secretary's Guide* (1696), quoted in Katherine Gee Hornbeak, "The Compleat Letter-Writer in English, 1568–1800," *Smith College Studies in Modern Languages* 15, no. 3–4 (1934), 82.

47 Frank Gees Black, *The Epistolary Novel in the Late Eighteenth Century* (Eugene: University Of Oregon Press, 1940), p. 161.

48 See Perry, *Women, Letters*, p. 68, on Thomas Brown's *Letters From the Dead to the Living* and its imitators. On the *Adventures of Lucifer*, see Black, *Epistolary Novel in the Late Eighteenth Century*, p. 161. Black also cites such improbable correspondence as *Admonitions From the Dead, in Epistles to the Living* (1754); *Adventures Underground: A Letter from a Gentleman Swallowed up in an Earthquake* (1750); and *Great News from Hell; or the Devil Foiled by Bess Weatherby* (1760).

49 Black, *Epistolary Novel in the Late Eighteenth Century*, p. 161.
50 Anna Letitia Barbauld, "Tribute to Samuel Richardson," in *British Novelists*, 50 vols. (London: Home and Van Thale, n.d.), vol. I, p. xiv.
51 Day, *Told in Letters*, p. 48.
52 Ibid., p. 63.
53 Hugh Blair, *Lectures on Rhetoric and Belles Letters*, 14th ed. (London: T. Caddell *et al.*, 1825), p. 496.
54 Ibid., p. 497.
55 The preface to Mme. de Noyes' *Letters from a Lady in Paris to a Lady at Avignon* (1716), cited in Perry, *Women, Letters*, p. 76. See Perry's discussion of the stylistic change, pp. 75–8. Hornbeak, "Compleat Letter-Writer," 50–97, traces the "courtly" influences of early French letter-writing manuals and their replacement by more "up-to-date," colloquial, "bourgeois" and pragmatic letter-writers in England.
56 Alexander Pope, *The Twickenham Edition of the Poems of Alexander Pope*, gen. ed. John Butt (London: Methuen & Co., 1961), vol. IV, p. 68.
57 Edmund Burke, *Reflections on the Revolution in France* (Garden City, NY: Doubleday, Inc., 1973), p. 13.
58 Ibid., p. 15.
59 In the *Reflections*, private and public duty, personal and political feeling, all eventually merge. Burke concludes: "I have little to recommend my opinions... They come from one, almost the whole of whose public exertion has been a struggle for the liberty of others; from one in whose breast no anger durable or vehement has ever been kindled, but by what he considered as tyranny" (pp. 265–6).
60 Ibid., p. 266.
61 Ibid., p. 265.
62 Ibid., p. 13.
63 Ibid., p. 265.
64 Ibid., pp. 17–20.
65 Ibid., pp. 21–2.
66 Albert Goodwin, *The Friends of Liberty*, pp. 99–207.
67 Richard Price, "A Discourse on the Love of Our Country" (1790), in Marilyn Butler, ed., *Burke, Paine, Godwin, and the Revolution Controversy* (Cambridge: Cambridge UP, 1988), p. 32.
68 *Abstract of the History and Proceedings of the Revolution Society* (London, 1789); quoted in Goodwin, *The Friends of Liberty*, p. 110.
69 *Proceedings of the Society of the Friends of the People* (London: Mr. Westley, 1793), n.p.
70 Taken from Thomas Hardy's *History of the Origins of the London Corresponding Society* (1799), quoted in Mary Thrale, ed., *Selections from the Papers of the London Corresponding Society, 1792–1799* (Cambridge: Cambridge UP, 1983), p. 6. According to Hardy's plan, membership dues were dedicated to the costs of stationary, postage and printing.
71 E. P. Thompson, *The Making of the English Working Class* (New York: Vintage Books, 1966), pp. 17–101.

72 Thrale, *Selections from the Papers of the LCS*, p. 7.

73 Ibid., pp. xv–xxix; Goodwin, *The Friends of Liberty*, pp. 137–207.

74 The Society of the Friends of the People, founded in 1792 by Lord Lauderdale, Charles Grey and Philip Francis, was a relatively moderate reform society dedicated to "Freedom of Election...more equal Representation of the People, and...more frequent [elections]." See Goodwin, *The Friends of Liberty*, chap. 7, for a discussion of the society's unsuccessful jockeying with the LCS for leadership of the "Friends of Liberty," and for the various splinterings among the "Friends," especially in the wake of Paine's *Rights of Man*.

75 Thrale, *Selections from the Papers of the LCS*, p. 21; Goodwin, *The Friends of Liberty*, pp. 112–35.

76 Goodwin, *The Friends of Liberty*, pp. 125–35.

77 William Cobbett, *The Parliamentary History of England. from the Earliest Period to the Year 1803* (London: T. C. Hansard, 1794–5), vol. xxxi, pp. 490, 495–6. See also Goodwin, *The Friends of Liberty*, pp. 223–5, on the rhetoric of the *Patriot* and other radical periodicals and their strategies for representing the variety of their correspondents.

78 Goodwin, *The Friends of Liberty*, pp. 280–306.

79 Samuel Taylor Coleridge, "The Plot Discovered; or an Address to the People, Against Ministerial Treason" (Bristol, 1795), in *Collected Works*, ed. Kathleen Coburn and Bary Winer, Bollingen Series lxxv (London: Routledge & Kegan Paul Ltd., 1971), vol. i, pp. 288–9.

80 Lucyle Werkmeister, *A Newspaper History of England, 1792–3* (Lincoln: University of Nebraska Press, 1967), pp. 191–4, 204–83.

81 Ibid., pp. 192–3.

82 Ibid., p. 193, my emphasis.

83 Insurrection was in the air that winter: December had witnessed the "insurrection which wasn't" and the raising of the militia in London; it had heard riots threatened in Edinburgh, and seen uprisings in Cambridge and Manchester. Ibid., pp. 204–6.

84 Ibid., p. 242.

85 Ibid., p. 238.

86 Ibid., p. 243.

87 Fox's speech in Parliament, March 1793; ibid., p. 244.

88 Other civil rights in England were also suspended or severely restricted at this time. Habeas Corpus was suspended twice in four years. The "Two Acts" against Treason and Sedition, passed in 1795, limited the right to public assembly and imposed strict censorship. Right to trial was frequently denied; sudden search without warrant became routine.

89 Great Britain, *Public General Acts* (London: Charles Eyre and Andrew Stratham, 1793), vol. lxii, pp. 68–9.

90 Werkmeister, *Newspaper History*, p. 250.

91 Benstock, "From Letters to Literature," 262–5, gives the clearest description of this "tradition" in literary criticism. For recent studies which adopt and study this tradition, see not only Nancy K. Miller, *The*

Heroine's Text, but also Altman, *Epistolarity*; Kauffman, *Discourses of Desire*; and Perry, *Women, Letters*, esp. p. 131. For a more historically oriented perspective on the female voice in letters, see Kathryn Shevelow, "The Production of the Female Writing Subject: Letters to the *Athenian Mercury*," *Genre* 19 (Winter 1986), 385–407.

92 The authorship of *The Portuguese Letters* (whether male or female) and the origin of the letters (fictional or authentic) have been the subject of centuries of debate. See Kamuf, *Fictions of Feminine Desire*, pp. ix–xix, 56–66); and Nancy K. Miller, "'I's in Drag': The Sex of Recollection," *Eighteenth Century* 22 (1981), 47–57.

93 See Judith Kegan Gardiner, "The First English Novel: Aphra Behn's *Love Letters*, the Canon, and Women's Tastes," *Tulsa Studies in Women's Literature* 8, no. 2 (Fall 1989), 203. Gardiner argues that Behn's novel, a best-selling example of "women's popular erotic fiction," as well as a political "roman à clef," similarly remains "anomalous to literary history and repulsive to many critics."

94 Montesquieu, Charles-Louis de Secondat, Baron de, "Reflexions," in *The Persian Letters*, trans. C. J. Betts (Harmondsworth: Penguin Books, 1973 [orig. 1721]), p. xii.

95 Perry, *Women, Letters*, p. 93.

96 Lovelace, in *Clarissa*, for instance, employs military terminology and the language of statesmanship as metaphors for his sexual conquest.

97 Singer, *Epistolary Novel*, pp. 152–3, finds that the epistolary novel's "sudden decline" in the mid-1790s occurred "chiefly because it was overworked, not to extinction, but into sudden abeyance." Its form had become too "artificial" for contemporary tastes. Black, *Epistolary Novel in the Late Eighteenth Century*, pp. 108, 110, argues that the letter, as a "sentimental document" could not accommodate the "fact and action" which became popular in the nineteenth century: "The old epistolary exchange was cumbersome and artificial." The years from 1780–9 averaged an unprecedented eighteen letter-novels per year, with a high of thirty-four published in 1788 and twenty-six in 1789. The 1790s registered roughly fifteen per year. By the first decade of the new century the numbers had dwindled to an average of six per year (pp. 154–68).

98 See Lady Mary Wortley Montagu's highly critical "Letter to the Princess of Wales," *The Letters and Works of Lady Mary Wortley Montagu*, 2nd ed. (London: R. Bentley, 1837); and see Perry, *Women, Letters*, p. 23, on Aphra Behn's *Letters From a Young Nobleman to His Sister*, a story involving incest and regicide in the court of Charles I.

99 The original full title for *Familiar Letters on Important Occasions* (1741). See Samuel Richardson, *Familiar Letters on Important Occasions* (London: G. Routledge and Sons, 1928). The 1928 edition reprints the original title page of the 1741 edition.

100 Hornbeak, "Compleat Letter-Writer," pp. 108–10.

2 *LETTERS* OR LETTERS: POLITICS, INTERCEPTION
AND SPY FICTION

1 J. Ann Hone, *For the Cause of Truth: Radicalism in London, 1796–1821* (Oxford: Clarendon Press, 1982), p. 61. For a detailed account of Turner's activities as a government spy see W. J. Fitzpatrick, *Secret Service under Pitt*, 2nd ed. (London: 1892), especially chapters 1–3.
2 E. P. Thompson, *The Making of the English Working Class* (New York: Vintage Books, 1966), p. 485.
3 Ibid., p. 485.
4 Hone, *For the Cause of Truth*, pp. 47 and 78, cites Francis Place in claiming 1798 as the beginning of Pitt's "Reign of Terror," which lasted until 1802. But the accumulated acts of repression, dating from 1793, laid the foundation for this coordinated government intelligence network (pp. 65–78). For further discussion of this series of legislation, see J. H. Plumb, *England in the Eighteenth Century* (Harmondsworth: Penguin Books, 1950, rpt. 1973), pp. 155–94; Albert Goodwin, *The Friends of Liberty: The English Democratic Movement in the Age of the French Revolution* (Cambridge, Mass.: Harvard UP, 1979); and E. P. Thompson, *The Making of the English Working Class*.
5 See Hone, *For the Cause of Truth*, pp. 47–53; F. K. Prochaska, "English State Trials in the 1790s: A Case Study," *Journal of British Studies*, 8 (1973), 63–82; E. P. Thompson, *The Making of the English Working Class*, pp. 182–91; and *Report from the Committee on Secresy* (London: 1799).
6 For discussion of resistance to government spies and their brand of intelligence, see Hone, *For the Cause of Truth*, pp. 59–60; E. P. Thompson, *The Making of the English Working Class*, pp. 529–39; and Roger Sales, *English Literature in History, 1780–1830* (New York: St. Martin's Press, 1983), pp. 132–65.
7 Hone, *For the Cause of Truth*, p. 64.
8 From State Trials, xxv, cited in Lionel D. Woodward, *Une Amie Anglaise de la Révolution Française* (Paris: Librairie Ancienne Honoré Champion, 1930), p. 106 and note. Woodward reprints this letter with the comment: "Do these ambiguous remarks not have some connection to the project of invasion in England?" Extracts from this letter were later published in the *Anti-Jacobin*, 9 April 1798. See also a letter from William Jackson to Stone, 21 April 1794, in Woodward, *Une Amie Anglaise*, pp. 110–11n.
9 Ibid., p. 106.
10 Hone, *For the Cause of Truth*, pp. 89, 91, and 103.
11 J. H. Stone, *Copies of Original Letters Recently Written by Persons in Paris to Dr. Priestley in America, Taken on Board a Neutral Vessel*, 2nd ed., (London: J. Wright, 1798). The editor is not named.
12 Ibid., pp. v and viii.
13 William Cobbett ("Peter Porcupine"), *Remarks on the Explanation Lately Published by Dr. Priestley, Respecting the Intercepted Letters of his Friend and Disciple, J. H. Stone* (London: J. Wright, 1799), pp. 6–7.

14 Ibid., p. 9; my emphasis.

15 Ibid., p. 8.

16 Ibid., p. 4.

17 See previous chapter. For an intelligent introduction to the political psychology of conspiracy theories in this period, see Lynn Hunt, *Politics, Culture, and Class in the French Revolution* (Berkeley: University of California Press, 1984), pp. 38–45. On contemporary reaction to the ministerial sighting of plots, and on their link to the LCS, see Hone, *For the Cause of Truth*, pp. 42–50; Thompson, *The Making of the English Working Class*, p. 183; and *Report from the Committee on Secresy*.

18 Cobbett, *Remarks*, p. 17.

19 For this insight, I am indebted to Jerome Christensen's subtle discussion of the symbiosis of the British Post Office and the publishing cartel, both centered in London, in the mid- to late-eighteenth century. Christensen, *Practicing Enlightenment: Hume and the Formation of a Literary Career* (Madison: University of Wisconsin Press, 1987), pp. 175–95. Christensen dates the collapse of this partnership around 1774, but I am suggesting an analogous partnership in the 1790s between the print culture and the Pitt ministry's idea of the British nation. In this latter case, the partnership grows primarily out of coercion – that is, the government's severe regulation of the publication and dissemination of information. But the ideological alliance is forged in these prefaces and commentaries as well: the editors aim to regulate readers' understanding and use of written material. Thus they work to neutralize and even redirect potentially subversive writing, such as Stone's.

20 Cobbett, *Remarks*, p. 12; my emphasis.

21 Stone, *Original Letters*, pp. vi, viii; my emphasis.

22 *The Whole Official Correspondence Between the Envoys of the US and Mons. Talleyrand, on the Subject of the Disputes Between the Two Countries* (London: John Stockdale, 1798), p. 3. The two envoys named are John Adams and Thomas Pickering, Secretary of State.

23 Stone, *Original Letters*, pp. vi, vii.

24 Ibid., p. vii.

25 Cobbett, *Remarks*, p. 24.

26 Ibid., p. 25.

27 Stone, *Original Letters*, p. 16n.

28 Louis Althusser, "Ideology and Ideological State Apparatuses," *Lenin and Philosophy and Other Essays*, trans. Ben Brewster (New York and London: Monthly Review Press, 1971), pp. 170–1 and 170n., describes the "subject in law" in the course of explaining the category of the subject of ideology: "There is no ideology except for concrete subjects, and this destination for ideology is only made possible by the subject: meaning, *by the category of the subject* and its functioning... [W]ith the rise of bourgeois ideology, above all with the rise of legal ideology (which borrowed the legal category of 'subject in law' to make an ideological notion: man is by nature a subject), the category of the subject... is the

constitutive category of all ideology, whatever its determination."
Simply put, the seditious spy must be constituted as a subject in law in
order to establish a law "beyond dispute" – an ideology of the British
nation.

29 Stone, *Original Letters*, p. viii.
30 Ibid., p. vi.
31 Ibid., pp. 16 and 28.
32 Cobbett, *Remarks*, p. 39.
33 Nor was this the first time that Stone's correspondence had produced
double meanings. A few months before the appearance of the "Intercept[e]d Letters," The *Anti-Jacobin* produced a pamphlet which
reprinted a 1790 letter from Stone to Priestley, "found in [Priestley's]
house, and sent up to Government." The *Anti-Jacobin, Jacobinism
Displayed, in an Address to the English People* and *New Lights on Jacobinism,
with an Appendix Containing an Account of Voltaire's Behaviour on His Death-
Bed, and a Letter from J. H. Stone (Who Was Tried for Sedition) to His Friend
Dr. Priestley, Disclosing the Principles of Jacobinism*, 2nd ed., 2 vols.
(Birmingham: E. Piercy, 1798), vol. II, pp. 4–5. This letter, "Disclosing
the Principles of Jacobinism," was offered as "proof, that the *illuminati*
were carrying on their diabolical plots in England," although the letter
predates any real tensions between England and France. The *Anti-
Jacobin* did not hesitate to weave this epistle into the history of an esoteric
(and paradoxically aristocratic) conspiracy propagated by the Abbé
Barruel and others. Like Cobbett, the *Anti-Jacobin* read all correspondence as "dark conspiracy." The downfall of the civilized nations of
Europe would be the result of "a plot carried on principally by
correspondence," a correspondence which must, therefore, be "brought
to light." In the process, this pamphlet, like Cobbett's, glossed the
"enigmatical [i.e. allegorical] language" of the conspirators (vol. II, pp.
4–5). Moreover, interception and publication would succeed where the
law had failed: "As government had this letter in their possession, it is
unaccountable that it was not produced in evidence at Mr. Stone's trial"
(vol. II, p. 45). Through "the ample freedom of the British Press!"
announces the *Anti-Jacobin*, Stone's letter is finally given a history and
deposited into the public account.
34 Cobbett, *Remarks*, pp. 38–41; my emphasis.
35 Ibid., p. 23.
36 The *Anti-Jacobin, Jacobinism Displayed*, vol. II, pp. 41–2; my emphasis.
37 Marilyn Butler, Introduction to Priestley's *Letters to Burke*, in *Burke,
Paine, Godwin and the Revolution Controversy*, ed. Marilyn Butler (Cambridge: Cambridge UP, 1984), p. 84. *The Letters to the Rt. Hon. Edmund
Burke* were a response to Burke's own *Reflections On The Revolution in
France*, also written under the guise of a letter.
38 Butler, *Burke, Paine, Godwin*, p. 84; see also Joseph Priestley, *The
Theological and Miscellaneous Works of Joseph Priestley*, ed. John Towell
Rutt (London: 1817–32), vol. X. Priestley was fond of using the

epistolary form to engage individuals in public debate. See, for example, his *Letters to a Philosophical Unbeliever* (1780), written to David Hume, and his *Letter to the Rt. Hon. William Pitt* (1797), for repeal of the Test and Corporation Acts. The *Letters to Burke* (1791), however, led the government to suspect the scientist-scholar as an increasingly dangerous figure. Priestley's later epistolary publications, *An Appeal to the Public, on the Subject of the Riots in Birmingham* (1791) and *Letters to the Inhabitants of Northumberland* (1799) carry a new tone of defensiveness and, significantly, imagine a general rather than an individual recipient for the epistle.

39 Joseph Priestley, "Letter VI: Of the Interference of the State in Matters of Religion in General," *Letters to the Right Hon. Edmund Burke*, in Butler, ed., *Burke, Paine, Godwin*, p. 85; his emphasis.

40 Ibid., p. 85.

41 For Priestley's account of this event, see *Memoirs of Dr. Joseph Priestley, to the Year 1795* (London: 1806), vol. II. For Priestley's role among the radical intellectuals and in the public eye, see Joseph O. Baylen and Norbert J. Goddman, ed., *Biographical Dictionary of Modern British Radicals* (Sussex: Harvester Press and New Jersey: Humanities Press, 1979), vol. I, pp. 396–401.

42 Cobbett, *Remarks*, p. 14.

43 Stone, *Original Letters*, p. 35.

44 Ibid., p. vii.

45 Ibid., p. 16.

46 Ibid., p. 16n.

3 HELEN MARIA WILLIAMS AND THE LETTERS OF HISTORY

1 J. H. Stone, *Copies of Original Letters Recently Written by Persons in Paris to Dr. Priestly in America, Taken on Board a Neutral Vessel*, 2nd ed. (London: J. Wright, 1798), p. vii.

2 Robert D. Mayo, *The English Novel in the Magazines, 1740–1815* (Evanston, Ill.: Northwestern UP, 1962), p. 259.

3 Hester Thrale Piozzi, "To Penelope Pennington," 4 November 1793, in *The Intimate Letters of Hester Piozzi and Penelope Pennington, 1788–1821*, ed. Oswald Knapp (London: George Allen, 1914), p. 92. Cited in Lionel Woodward, *Une Amie Anglaise de la Révolution Française* (Paris: Librairie Ancienne Honoré Champion, 1930), p. 88.

4 William Wordsworth, *The Poems*, The Yale Edition, ed. John O. Hayden, 2 vols. (New Haven and London: Yale UP, 1977), vol. I, pp. 47 and 923n.

5 Letitia Hawkins, *Letters on the Female Mind*, 2 vols. (London: Hookham & Carpenter, 1793), vol. II, pp. 182–3.

6 Ibid., vol. I, p. 23.

7 The comments from Richard Polwhele's *The Unsex'd Female*, from Horace Walpole and the *Gentleman's Magazine*, are all cited in Janet Todd's Introduction to Helen Maria Williams' *Letters from France*, ed.

with intro. by Janet Todd, 8 volumes in 2 (1795 and 1796, photorpt., Delmar, NY: Scholars' Facsimile and Reprints, Inc., 1975), vol. I, p. 7. William Beloe's remark appears in his work, *The Sexagenarian* (1817), cited in Gina Luria's introduction to Williams' novel, *Julia*, ed. with intro. by Gina Luria, 2 vols. (1790, rpt. New York and London: Garland Publishing, Inc., 1974), vol. I, p. 13. There are few other extended discussions of Williams' work or life. Woodward's study, *Une Amie Anglaise*, is the only biography. The *Dictionary of National Biography* refers to Williams, as do two larger studies of the period: John G. Alger, *Englishmen in the French Revolution* (London: 1889) and A. Mathiez, *La Révolution et les étrangers* (Paris: La Renaissance du Livre, 1918). See also B. P. Kurtz and Carrie C. Autrey, eds., *Four New Letters of Mary Wollstonecraft and Helen Maria Williams* (Berkeley: University of California Press, 1937). The first two volumes of Williams' letters sold especially well: five printings in six years, with frequent excerpts in the more popular review journals (*Monthly Review*, *Quarterly Review*, *Analytic Review* and *Gentleman's Magazine*).

8 Jerome McGann, "Introduction: A Point of Reference," in *Historical Studies and Literary Criticism*, ed. Jerome McGann (Madison: University of Wisconsin Press, 1985), p. 14. McGann describes the "incommensurates" of a text as those "details, persons, events which the work's own (reflected) conceptual formulas and ideologies must admit, but which they cannot wholly account for." They draw our attention to "the socially located tensions and contradictions, as well as the responses to such things, which poetry [or the work of art] imitates and participates in."

9 Hevda Ben-Israel, *English Historians on the French Revolution* (London: Cambridge UP, 1968), p. 12. According to Janet Todd, *British Women Writers: A Critical Reference Guide* (New York: Continuum, 1989), pp. 720–1, Williams "perceived events in sentimental and personal terms... Her judgements remained spontaneous and emotional." M. Ray Adams, "Helen Maria Williams and the French Revolution," in *Studies in the Literary Backgrounds of English Radicalism* (Lancaster, Pa.: Franklin and Marshall Press, 1947), pp. 87–8, disparages Williams as well: "[S]eeing life about her steadily and seeing it whole was precluded by her disposition... We may as well, then, not labor the point of her reliability as a historian."

10 Hawkins, *Letters on the Female Mind*, vol. I, pp. 21–3.

11 Letitia Hawkins' full title is: *The Female Mind: Its Powers and Pursuits, Addressed to Miss Helen Maria Williams, with Particular Reference to her Letters from France*; see vol. I, pp. 21–3. Later critics tend to agree with Hawkins that the politics in Williams' sentimental letters give evidence of some dysfunction: "With her it [the revolution] was not so much a matter of intellectual conviction as it was of emotional contagion." M. R. Adams, "Helen Maria Williams," pp. 88–9.

12 Jean Rousset, *Forme et signification* (Paris: Corti, 1962), p. 77; and Janet Gurkin Altman, *Epistolarity: Approaches to a Form* (Columbus: Ohio State

UP, 1982), p. 179. Rousset refers to this "literature of the cardio-gramme," as "the direct registering of the heart." The letter form is "an apt instrument for translating the fluctuations, incoherences, contra-dictions of passion thus conceived." Elsewhere, he refers to the "epistolary sequence" as "a privileged instrument" for probing "the awakening and the vibrations of sensibility, caprice, and emotion" (p. 68). Altman repeats Rousset's notion, but transforms his clinical "instrument" into a writing "instrument." For her, the letter becomes "an apt instrument for transcribing the sudden switches and inconsis-tencies [of] a love affair" (p. 179).

13 Svetlana Alpers, *The Art of Describing : Dutch Art in the Seventeenth Century* (Chicago: University of Chicago Press, 1984), pp. 192–207.

14 Ibid., p. 196.

15 I am indebted to Michael Fried's discussion of Greuze's and others' work in this genre in *Absorption and Theatricality* (Berkeley: University of California Press, 1980), p. 144.

16 J. M. Thompson, *The French Revolution*, rev. ed. (London: Basil Black-well, 1985), p. 139. For a more detailed account of the *lettre de cachet* in the *ancien régime*, see F. Funck-Brentano, *Les Lettres de cachet* (Paris: 1926).

17 J. M. Thompson, *The French Revolution*, p. 139, reports that Louis XV is said to have signed 150,000 *lettres de cachet*, mainly concerned with "moral delinquencies." The writers Mirabeau and Voltaire were among the recipients. Under Louis XVI, this expedient of justice was less frequent: roughly 14,000 *lettres* were issued in the 1780s, aimed primarily at the intelligentsia and the aristocracy.

18 The *Letters Written…to a Friend* constitute the first volume of letters. Later volumes followed in the years 1791, 1793 (2 volumes), 1795 (2 volumes), and 1796 (2 volumes). All eight volumes are reprinted as *Letters from France*, ed. Janet Todd, 2 vols. I indicate the reprint volume number first, followed by the original volume number and the original page: e.g. (1:1:21).

19 For more on the symbolic power of "the language of ritual and the ritual of language," see Lynn Hunt's chapter on "The Rhetoric of Rev-olution," in *Politics, Culture, and Class in the French Revolution* (Berkeley: University of California Press, 1984), pp. 19–51. On the symbolic importance of revolutionary oath-taking, see Jean Starobinski, *1789: The Emblems of Reason*, trans. Barbara Bray (Charlottesville: University of Virginia Press, 1982), pp. 66–7.

20 Jean Starobinski, *Jean-Jacques Rousseau: Transparency and Obstacle*, trans. Arthur Goldhammer (Chicago: University of Chicago Press, 1988). See also François Furet, *Penser la Révolution Française* (Paris: 1978), pp. 86, 103. Hunt elaborates on the political uses of transparency, in *Politics, Culture, and Class*, pp. 44–6. For another, more detailed version of use of Rousseauian concepts by revolutionaries and their opponents, see Carol Blum, *Rousseau and the Republic of Virtue* (Ithaca: Cornell UP, 1989).

21 The association between letters and dramatics is nearly a commonplace in criticism of the epistolary mode. See John Preston, *The Created Self: The Reader's Role in Eighteenth-Century Fiction* (New York: Barnes and Noble, Inc., 1970), pp. 2–3 and Frank Gees Black, *The Epistolary Novel in the Late Eighteenth Century* (Eugene: University of Oregon Press, 1940), pp. 50–1. Black notes that "the epistolary method demands very much the same versatility, command of varied styles, detachment and imaginary identification of author with character as successful play writing." Janet Todd makes a point about Williams' use of spectacle, similar to my own, in *Sensibility: An Introduction* (New York: Methuen, 1986), pp. 130–6: "[Williams] rapturously converted the French ceremonies and revolutionary festivals into enactments of the sentimental fictions she also wrote." Rousseau, with whose writings Williams was well acquainted, connects the 'theatrical" mode especially to women in his *Lettre à M. d'Alembert sur les spectacles*, ed. M. Fuchs (Geneva and Lille, 1948). For a subtle discussion of the ideologies and contradictions at work in this letter, see Fried, *Absorption and Theatricality*, pp. 167–8.

22 Mona Ozouf, *La Fête révolutionnaire, 1789–1799* (Paris: Gallimard, 1976), is the definitive study of revolutionary spectacles; see also Hunt, *Politics, Culture and Class*, p. 55.

23 William Wordsworth, *The Prelude, 1799, 1805, 1850*, ed. Jonathan Wordsworth, M. H. Abrams and Stephen Gill (New York: W. W. Norton & Company, Inc., 1979), p. 316. (1805 version, Bk. ix, lines 88–95.)

24 These terms derive from Vivienne Mylne, *The Eighteenth-Century French Novel: Techniques of Illusion* (Manchester: Manchester UP, 1965), pp. 150–1, and François Jost, "L'Evolution d'un genre: le roman epistolaire dans les Lettres Occidentales," in *Essais de la Littérature comparée* (Urbana: University of Illinois Press, 1968), vol. II, pp. 124–5. Frances Burney's *Evelina* (1778) stands as the epitome of this type in English fiction; in non-fiction, most travel letters or journalistic "foreign correspondence" would qualify as memoir-letters. See also Michael Bell, *The Sentiment of Reality* (London: G. Allen & Unwin, 1983), p. 16.

25 The allusion is to Burney's *Evelina, or a Young Woman's Entrance Into the World*.

26 Mylne, *Eighteenth-Century French Novel*, p. 152.

27 From the personal correspondence of both Hester Thrale Piozzi and Anna Seward, respectively; cited in Woodward, *Une Amie Anglaise*, pp. 88–9.

28 For similar statements, see also 1:1:60 and 1:1:222. Williams' apology for turning from the "annals of the imagination" to the "prose" of political writing is clearly a pose. In fact, Williams had first come to the attention of London literary circles as the author of politically charged poems: *Ode on the Peace* (1783); *Peru* (1786), and *The Slave Trade* (1788).

29 Mary Ann Doane, "Film and the Masquerade: Theorizing the Female

Spectator," *Screen*, no. 3/4 (Sept.–Oct. 1982), 74–87, offers an excellent analysis of why, in a society which "sees" through a patriarchal lens, the female spectator has difficulty separating herself from the spectacle: "For the female spectator there is a certain over-presence of the image – she *is* the image. Given the closeness of this relationship, the female spectator's desire can only be described in terms of a certain narcissism – the female look demands a becoming. It thus appears to negate the very distance or gap specified…as the essential precondition of voyeurism" (78).

30 Hunt, *Politics, Culture, and Class*, p. 64.

31 Ibid., p. 65.

32 On the revolutionaries' use of female Liberty, see Maurice Agulhon, *Marianne into Battle: Republican Imagery and Symbolism in France, 1789–1880*, trans. Janet Lloyd (Cambridge: Cambridge UP, 1981), pp. 11–37; and Lynn Hunt, "Engraving the Republic: Prints and Propaganda in the French Revolution," *History Today*, 30 (1980), 11–17.

33 Williams' Salon in Paris was frequented by Wollstonecraft, Paine, Joel Barlow, as well as the leading French moderates (Verniaud, the Rolands and Brissot), General Miranda, the writer Bernardin de Saint-Pierre, and the renowned journalist Rabaut Saint-Etienne. Woodward, *Une Anglaise Amie*, pp. 47–86. Clearly, Williams' actual associates were much closer to the center of power than were the "people" with whom she associates in her letters.

34 Hunt, *Politics, Culture, and Class*, p. 60.

35 Rousseau, Second Preface, *Julie, ou la Nouvelle Héloïse* (Paris: Garnier-Flammarion, 1967), p. 585.

36 Luce Irigaray, *This Sex Which Is Not One*, trans. Catherine Porter (Ithaca: Cornell UP, 1985), p. 76. This notion of "playful" female mimesis has been elaborated by recent feminist film theory, and I am indebted to the following articles for helping me articulate this idea with respect to Williams' *Letters*: Doane, "Film and the Masquerade"; Joan Riviere, "Womanliness as Masquerade," in Hendrik M. Ruitenbeek, ed., *Psychoanalysis and Female Sexuality* (New Haven: College and University Press, 1966); and Mary Russo, "Female Grotesques: Carnival and Theory," in Teresa de Lauretis, ed., *Feminist Studies/Critical Studies* (Bloomington: Indiana UP, 1986).

37 Irigaray, *This Sex*, p. 76.

38 For a discussion of the "friendly societies" in England and the political debate circling around the definition of "friends' correspondence," see the introduction.

39 Bruce Redford, *The Converse of the Pen: Acts of Intimacy in the Eighteenth-Century Familiar Letter* (Chicago: Chicago UP, 1986), pp. 9–10. Redford cites Northrop Frye's *Anatomy of Criticism* (Princeton: Princeton UP, 1957; 1981), p. 58. Redford's formulation is not unique. Consider Shari Benstock's assertion that "the letter contains both the word and the world; it substitutes the word for the world, substitutes writing for

living." Benstock, "From Letters to Literature: *La Carte Postale* and the Epistolary Genre," *Genre*, 18 (Fall, 1985), 262.

40 Frye, *Anatomy of Criticism*, p. 58.

41 Redford, *Converse of the Pen*, pp. 1–12. Compare Edmund Burke's admission, in *Reflections on the Revolution in France* (Garden City, NY: Doubleday Inc., 1973), p. 13, that the letter form cannot adequately contain his thoughts on the Revolution, that his own letter frame refuses a sense of order amidst the chaos: "the matter gaining upon him, [the author] found that what he had undertaken not only far exceeded the measure of a letter, but that its importance required rather a more detailed consideration." Despite the apology, Burke does present his *Reflections* under the guise of a (rather excessive) letter. See discussion in the introduction.

42 Doane, "Film and Masquerade," p. 78.

43 Samuel Richardson, *Clarissa*, ed. John Butt, 4 vols. (New York: E. P. Dutton, 1962), vol. IV, letter 81.

44 Irigaray, quoted in Doane, "Film and Masquerade," pp. 78–9.

45 Irigaray, "Sexual Difference," in Toril Moi, ed. and trans., *French Feminist Thought: A Reader* (Oxford: Basil Blackwell, 1987), p. 122.

46 Richardson finds the "events" of the epistolary plot "hidden in the Womb of Fate." Samuel Richardson, "Author's Preface" [1759], in *Clarissa*, ed. George Sherburn (Boston: Houghton Mifflin, Co., 1962), vol. I, p. xx. Richardson is quoting from his own novel, specifically from Belford's letter of August 4 (vol. IV: letter 81).

47 "The mother woman [as envelope] remains the *place separated from its 'own' place*, a place deprived of a place of its own. She is or ceaselessly becomes the place of the other who cannot separate himself from it. Without her knowledge or volition, then, she threatens by what she lacks: a 'proper' place." Luce Irigaray, "Sexual Difference," p. 122.

48 The "Memoir of Mons. du F." was the most popular portion of the first volume, and was frequently reprinted in the journals. It was published separately in 1790, under the title *The Unfortunate Young Nobleman* (London: R. Harrild and John Choppell, 1790). William Wordsworth evidently drew on the "Memoir" for his own poem, *Vaudracour and Julia* (published in 1820, but taken from the 1805 version of *The Prelude* (bk. IX:555–934).) See William Wordsworth, *The Poems*, vol. I, p. 1007n. and Deborah Kennedy, "Revolutionary Tales: Helen Maria Williams' *Letters from France* and William Wordsworth's 'Vaudracour and Julia,'" in the *The Wordsworth Circle* (June 1990), 109–14.

49 This anecdote about the "rising flood," is set, significantly, in Orléans, cradle of the monarchy and of the royalty party. Williams' subtle allegory calls attention to the spreading influence of the Parisian revolutionaries.

50 On the September prison massacres and the massacres at Orléans, which so appalled Williams and her colleagues, see J. M. Thompson, *The French Revolution*, pp. 134–51.

51 Barbara Johnson, *The Critical Difference* (Baltimore: Johns Hopkins UP, 1980), p. 124.

52 Advertisement to the first edition, *Letters from France*, vol. III, n.p.

53 The original edition makes no mention of any of the three letter-writers' names. Janet Todd, Introduction, ibid., p. 5, speculates that Stone and Christie are the collaborators. Both men were known to be friends, as well as especially close acquaintances of Williams, sharing her political sympathies. Stone was reputed to have dealings with the French military (mainly as a gun-runner to rebel groups in Ireland); Christie was a seasoned journalist.

54 Anna Seward, *The Letters of Anna Seward Written Between the Years 1784–1807* (Edinburgh: A. C. Constable, 1811), vol. III, p. 332.

55 Newspaper reports and parliamentary debate made explicit the connection between the ministry's opposition to the Society of Friends and the introduction of this bill and proclamation (Werkmeister, *Newspaper History*, pp. 80–4; J. Anne Hone, *For the Cause of Truth: Radicalism in London, 1796–1821* (Oxford: Clarendon Press, 1982), pp. 11–41).

56 As Commander-in-Chief of the French armies, General Dumouriez was well known to the British reading public. News of Dumouriez's stunning victories in Holland and his subsequent defection to the Austrians filled the London newspapers throughout March and April 1793. See J. M. Thompson, *The French Revolution*, pp. 338–43 and Werkmeister, *Newspaper History*, pp. 257–9. James Gillray's cartoons of the general and his treachery had made Dumouriez's image indelible. *The Works of James Gillray* (London: Henry G. Bohn, 1851; republished New York: Benjamin Blom, Inc., 1968). See especially plate 45.

57 Todd, Introduction, *Letters from France*, p. 5.

58 For the amount of government-sponsored interference in the domestic mail serice, the extent of government secret intelligence, and public awareness of this intervention, see Howard Robinson, *The British Post Office: A History* (Princeton: Princeton UP, 1967), pp. 120–5; Hone, *For the Cause of Truth*, pp. 74–82; and Werkmeister, *Newspaper History*, pp. 252–3.

59 In another episode, when the hero Beaurepaire commits suicide, a letter of comfort is sent to his wife by the president of the National Assembly. This official letter, given in volume III without translation, leaves no room for the woman's sorrow: her loss is "a public loss"; recognition of the public good should console her grief. Moreover, *la patrie*, not satisfied with the husband alone, now claims this widow's son: "may he live long for her!" (1:3:158). Of course, we read no transcription of the woman's response.

60 Rousset, *Form et significance*, pp. 79–80.

61 Ibid., p. 74.

62 Jacques Derrida, for example, makes this point an underlying theme in "Les Envois." He writes about the letters of Plato as inevitable frauds, *because* they are letters: "And the Frenchman adds calmly: 'These

epistles have often created confusion, and criticism has occasionally had difficulty undoing the subterfuge.' You don't say. They not only allege that they know how to distinguish between the authentic and the simulacrum, they do not even want to do the work, the simulacrum should point itself out, and say to them: 'here I am, look out, I am not authentic!'... what above all throws them off the track in their hunt is that the epistolary simulacrum cannot be stabilized, installed in a certain place, and especially that it is not necessarily, and completely, intentional." From *The Post Card: From Socrates to Freud and Beyond*, trans. Alan Bass (Chicago: University of Chicago Press, 1987), p. 89.

63 Helen Maria Williams, *Souvenirs* (Paris: 1828), p. 82, quoted in Woodward, *Une Amie Anglaise*, p. 189. My translation.

64 *Souvenirs*, p. 81; in Woodward, *Une Anglaise Amie*, p. 100.

65 Woodward, *Une Anglaise Amie*, p. 105.

66 Ibid., p. 105.

67 This letter, translated by Williams and included in her *Letters*, was sent by seventy-three members of the National Assembly, accusing Robespierre's faction (the "Mountain") of severe injustice. The letter was considered to be one of the provocations leading to the September massacres three months later.

68 On Mme. Roland and her influence on her husband, and on the Girondin party, see J. M. Thompson, *The French Revolution*, pp. 295 and 320–3; and Gita May, *Madame Roland and the Age of Revolution* (New York: Columbia UP, 1970).

69 Ben-Israel, *English Historians*, p. 18 and Todd, introduction, *Letters from France*, pp. 8–9. The *Dictionary of National Biography* sums up the conventional assessment of Williams' talents: "She freely wrote her impressions of the events which she witnessed or heard of, impressions frequently formed on very imperfect, one-sided, and garbled information, travestied by the enthusiasm of a clever, badly educated woman... And in fact her writings are very much what might be expected of a warm-hearted and ignorant woman. The honesty with which she wrote carried conviction to many of her readers; and there can be little doubt that her works were the source of many erroneous opinions." Cited in Luria, Introduction, *Julia*, pp. 10–11.

70 Rousset, *Forme et signifiance*, p. 87.

71 After the 1740s, this movement was always mediated in England by the institution of the Post Office. In fiction, similar institutions – prisons, wars, convents and parents – usually stood as the obstructing and regulating agencies.

4 MARY WOLLSTONECRAFT AND THE BUSINESS OF LETTERS

1 For example: Carol H. Poston, Introduction to Mary Wollstonecraft, *Letters Written During a Short Residence in Sweden, Norway and Denmark*, ed. Carol Poston (Lincoln: University of Nebraska Press, 1976), p. xx,

describes the *Letters* as "quite possibly the perfect fusion of the personal and intellectual selves of Mary Wollstonecraft"; see also Mary Poovey, *The Proper Lady and the Woman Writer: Ideology as Style in the Works of Mary Wollstonecraft, Mary Shelley, and Jane Austen* (Chicago: University of Chicago Press, 1984), pp. 82–94 and Per Nystrom, *Mary Wollstonecraft's Scandinavian Journey*, Acts of the Royal Society of Arts and Letters of Gothenburg, *Humaniora*, no. 17 (1980), pp. 34–6. Poston's edition serves as the text for this chapter; when citing, I refer to it in the text as *LWS*.

2 Nystrom, *Scandinavian Journey*, pp. 16–32.

3 Lucyle Werkmeister, *A Newspaper History of England, 1792–3* (Lincoln: University of Nebraska Press, 1967), p. 349; see also my introduction.

4 Great Britain, *Public General Acts* (London: Charles Eyre & Andrew Strahan, 1793), vol. LXII, p. 68.

5 Richard Holmes, introduction to Mary Wollstonecraft and William Godwin, *A Short Residence in Sweden, and Memoir of the Author of "A Vindication of the Rights of Woman"* (Harmondsworth: Penguin Books, 1987), p. 22.

6 Holmes, Introduction to Wollstonecraft and Godwin, *Residence in Sweden*, p. 23.

7 Ibid., pp. 22–3; see also Nystrom, *Scandinavian Journey*, pp. 20–6.

8 For other explanations of Wollstonecraft's role as Imlay's "agent," see Poston, introduction to *Letters Written...in Sweden*, pp. ix–xi; William Godwin, *Memoirs of Mary Wollstonecraft*, ed. W. Clarke Durant (London: Constable & Co., Ltd., 1927; rpt. 1978), pp. 84–6; Ralph M. Wardle, *Mary Wollstonecraft: A Critical Biography* (Lawrence, Kansas: University of Kansas Press, 1951), p. 225; and Claire Tomalin, *The Life and Death of Mary Wollstonecraft* (New York: Harcourt, Brace, Jovanovich, 1974), pp. 179–80. Each of these gives a slightly different motivation for Imlay's mission. Tomalin also suggests that Wollstonecraft took along work to do for her publisher, Joseph Johnson (ibid., p. 179n.).

9 Mary Wollstonecraft, *The Collected Letters*, ed. Ralph M. Wardle (Ithaca: Cornell UP, 1979), pp. 328–9.

10 For notes on the contemporary political situation in the three Scandinavian countries, see Nystrom, *Scandinavian Journey*, pp. 16–7 and 34–44; and Moira Ferguson and Janet Todd, eds., *Mary Wollstonecraft* (Boston: G. K. Hall & Company, 1984), pp. 96–103.

11 *LWS*, p. 154; also Nystrom, *Scandinavian Journey*, pp. 16–18; 37–9.

12 The letter-writer includes several oblique attacks against men, especially regarding their treatment of women as domestic servants (*LWS*, p. 26). Elsewhere, a bitter passage about husbands abusing wives concludes with a deft deferral: "but this does not come home" (*LWS*, p. 104). We should recall that Wollstonecraft is performing unpaid "offices" for Imlay in Scandinavia, and she does so as his "wife." See Tomalin, *Life and Death*, p. 180.

13 Poston, Introduction to *Letters Written...in Sweden*, pp. xii, xvi; and Wardle, *Mary Wollstonecraft*, pp. 250–7. Wardle writes that "she wrote

what amounted to twenty-five personal essays...each letter contained digressions into the endless number of topics which occupied *her fertile mind*"; but also that "Experience had confirmed what she had long felt: that it was futile to ignore *the claims of the heart*; and in this book, *the heart had its say*" (pp. 250, 254; my emphasis). Notable exceptions to this approach include Richard Holmes, Introduction to Wollstonecraft and Godwin, *Residence in Sweden*, and Nystrom, *Scandinavian Journey*.

14 Poovey, *Proper Lady*, p. 83; my emphasis.

15 The details of her suicide attempts become public knowledge only after Wollstonecraft's death, and the subsequent publication of William Godwin's *Memoirs of Mary Wollstonecraft* (1798). See pp. 81–94 of Godwin's *Memoirs* for his elaborate discussion and defense of Wollstonecraft's despair.

16 *Collected Letters*, pp. 323–4; Wardle, *Mary Wollstonecraft*, p. 248.

17 On the transition from journal to published *Letters*, see *Collected Letters*, p. 306. In his biography, Wardle glosses over the existence of the journal and tends to conflate the *Letters from Sweden* with the personal letters written to Imlay during the trip (Wardle, *Mary Wollstonecraft*, pp. 227–54). Sylva Norman, in her introduction to Mary Wollstonecraft, *Letters Written*, ed. Sylva Norman (Fontwell, Sussex: Centaur Press, Ltd., 1970), p. iii, does note that Wollstonecraft begins to keep a journal at Tonsberg, Norway, well into her journey.

18 Wardle, Preface to *Collected Letters*, p. 19.

19 *Collected Letters*, p. 293.

20 Ibid., p. 312.

21 Ibid., p. 304.

22 Ibid., p. 309.

23 Ibid., pp. 291, 301, 302, 307, 310, and 314.

24 Ibid., p. 298.

25 Ibid., p. 297.

26 Ibid., p. 298.

27 Jean-Jacques Rousseau, *Les Rêveries d'un promeneur solitaire* (Paris: Garnier-Flammarion, 1964), p. 65; all translations are my own.

28 Elsewhere, however, Wollstonecraft translates the terms of botany into her own brand of anthropology, again converting Rousseau's escapism into social concern (*LWS*, p. 37).

29 Rousseau, *Reveries*, pp. 99–100.

30 *LWS*, p. 141; Rousseau, *Reveries*, p. 166.

31 Rousseau, *Reveries*, p. 166.

32 Ibid., pp. 134–5.

33 Ibid., pp. 40–1.

34 These works are all included in Wollstonecraft's *Posthumous Works by the Author of a Vindication of the Rights of Woman*, ed. William Godwin, 2 vols. (London: J. Johnson, 1798; facsimile rpt. Clifton, NJ: Augustus M. Kelley Publishers, 1975). For evidence of her investment in education, see Wollstonecraft's introduction and chapter 12, "A National Edu-

cation," in *A Vindication of the Rights of Woman* (1792, rpt. New York: W. W. Norton and Company, 1975); and her "Review of Catherine Macauley's *Letters on Education*," in *A Wollstonecraft Anthology*, ed. Janet Todd (New York: Columbia UP, 1990), p. 115. For further discussion, see Janet Todd, introduction to Mary Wollstonecraft's *An Historical and Moral View... of the French Revolution*, ed. Janet Todd (1795; facsimile rpt., Delmar, NY: Scholars' Facsimiles and Reprints, 1975), p. 8; and Ferguson and Todd, eds., *Mary Wollstonecraft*, pp. 80–8.

35 *An Historical and Moral View*; and Todd and Ferguson, eds., *Mary Wollstonecraft*, pp. 81–2. Nystrom, *Scandinavian Journey*, pp. 43–4, attributes this change to the influence of Godwin's *Political Justice*.

36 See also *Historical and Moral View*, p. 519 and "Letter on... French Character," in *Posthumous Works*, vol. II, pp. 48–50.

37 Poston, Introduction to *Letters Written... in Sweden*, p. xi.

38 In an analogous passage, the author observes the impotent king of Denmark, a "puppet... moved by the strings" of his ambitious Minister of Finance, Count Bernstorff. "He is merely a machine of state," laments the traveler; a representative cipher, "to subscribe the name of king to the acts of government..." and ensure the value of state currency (*LWS*, p. 154).

39 Godwin, *Memoirs*, p. 84.

40 At the end of the book, the letter-writer recounts several pleasant conversations with friends and fellow travelers. These points of connection with others reinforce a sense that the nominal "you" is countered by a "we" and "us" which exclude him. See, for example, *LWS*, pp. 189–90.

41 Marilyn Butler, ed., *Burke, Paine, Godwin, and the Revolution Controversy* (Cambridge: Cambridge UP, 1988), pp. 1–8.

42 Olympe De Gouges began her public career as an actress and playwright. But during the Revolution she turned to publishing political pamphlets, many of them addressed as open letters to "Le Peuple Français." See Leonora Cohen Rosenfield, "The Rights of Women in the French Republic," *Studies in Eighteenth-Century Culture* 7 (1978), 117–37. Rosenfield describes the career of De Gouges at some length, highlighting her "Declaration des Droits de la Femme et la Citoyenne" (1791), a feminist version of France's "Droits de l'Homme."

43 Quoted from C. Monsalet, *Les Oubliés et les dédaignés*, in Rosenfield, "Rights of Women," p. 23. Note that in the letter to Robespierre, Olympe De Gouges employs the familiar, or "tu" (thou) form of address.

44 Michael Bell, *The Sentiment of Reality* (London: G. Allen & Unwin, 1983), p. 15.

45 Bruce Redford, *Converse of the Pen: Acts of Intimacy in the Eighteenth-Century Familiar Letter* (Chicago: University of Chicago Press, 1986), pp. 9–10.

46 Ibid., p. 6; also pp. 44–5; 133–5.

47 For other Shakespearean echoes, see the following pages: *King Lear*:

LWS, pp. 144 and 154; *Macbeth*: *LWS*, pp. 180 and 19 ; *A Midsummer Night's Dream*: *LWS*, pp. 13–14 and 40; *Romeo and Juliet*: *LWS*, p. 84; *The Tempest*: *LWS*, pp. 23–4, 107, 156, 164–5. Other plays cited include Wycherly's *The Country Wife* (*LWS*, p. 1 1), and Dryden's *The Indian Queen* (*LWS*, pp. 81–2).

48 *Historical and Moral View*, p. 26. Wollstonecraft makes this assertion with some disapproval of the French, speculating that Louis's wars had become "theatrical productions," and adventures "pursued by the idle."

49 Notice that she mentions none of Shakespeare's Roman history plays or pseudo-classical comedies, but concentrates on *Hamlet*, *Macbeth*, *King Lear*, and the magical world of *The Tempest*. For the republican celebration of classical mythology and history (of Rome's republic) see Marilyn Butler, *Romantics, Rebels, and Reactionaries: English Literature and Its Background, 1760–1830* (Oxford: Oxford UP, 1981), pp. 18–20, 37; and Lynn Hunt, *Politics, Culture, and Class in the French Revolution* (Berkeley: University of California Press, 1984), pp. 19–119.

50 See *LWS*, p. 166 for Pope, and pp. 93 and 183 for Chaucer and Dryden; biblical references occur on pp. 20, 53, 58, 7 , and 104; snatches of popular rhymes and literature can be found on pp. 45 74, 97, 119, and 194.

51 *LWS*, p. 152n.; also Nystrom, *Scandinavian Journey*, pp. 40–1.

52 In the actual letters to Imlay, Marguerite is treated quite kindly. Wollstonecraft mentions her with affection and gratitude. See *Collected Letters*, pp. 267, 305, 307, and 316.

53 Wollstonecraft did herself spend time in these positions, both as a governess/servant to the wealthy Lord Kingsborough's family, and as the daughter of a bourgeois, mercantile family. See Tomalin, *Life and Death*, chapters 1 and 3.

54 I borrow the term "actor-magician" from Bruce Redford, *The Converse of the Pen*, pp. 6–7: "The letter-writer is an actor, but a *magician*-actor who works on his audience by sustaining the illusion of physical presence."

55 Ferguson and Todd, eds., *Mary Wollstonecraft*, p. 94, point to the strong parallels between this oft-excerpted passage and Samuel Taylor Coleridge's poem, "Frost at Midnight" (1798), especially lines 4–19 and 44–7.

56 Charlotte Brunsdon, "It is Well Known that by Nature Women Are Inclined To Be Rather Personal," in *Women Take Issue: Aspects of Women's Subordination*, Women's Studies Group (Birmingham: Centre of Contemporary Studies, 1978), p. 25.

57 Norman, Introduction to Mary Wollstonecraft, *Letters Written*, p. v; also Wardle, *Mary Wollstonecraft*, p. 257.

58 Wollstonecraft, *Vindication*, p. 10; my emphasis.

59 *Collected Letters*, pp. 219–20.

60 *Historical and Moral View*, p. 2.

61 Ibid., p. 21.
62 Ibid., p. 18.
63 See *LWS*, pp. 23 and 192 for other references to the "trickiness" of commercial dealings. On p. 164, Wollstonecraft reports a curious anecdote about a street play in which a magician, disguised as a tinker, tricks the local farmers out of their produce.
64 Wardle, *Mary Wollstonecraft*, p. 256.
65 *Collected Letters*, p. 164.
66 Jon P. Klancher, *The Making of English Reading Audiences, 1790–1832* (Madison: University of Wisconsin Press, 1987), p. 41; Butler, *Romantics, Rebels*, pp. 71–3.
67 Mitzi Myers, "Mary Wollstonecraft's *Letters Written…In Sweden*: Towards Romantic Biography," *Studies in Eighteenth-Century Culture*, 8 (1979), p. 170.
68 Klancher, *English Reading Audiences*, p. 41.
69 "Are Mental Talents Productive of Happiness?" in ibid., p. 40.
70 Brunsdon, "It is Well Known that by Nature Women are Inclined To Be Rather Personal," p. 23.
71 See statistics in Wardle, *Mary Wollstonecraft*, p. 257, of the book's popularity in the journals, and abroad. See also her letter to Imlay, July 1795: "I have begun writing [the *Letters*]," she writes Imlay, "which will, I hope, discharge all of my obligations of a pecuniary kind. I am lowered in my own eyes, on account of not doing it sooner" (*Collected Letters*, p. 306).
72 Jerome McGann, *The Romantic Ideology* (Chicago: University of Chicago Press, 1983), p. 1.
73 *Monthly Review*, 20 (1796), 251.
74 *British Critic*, 7 (1796), n.p.
75 *Monthly Mirror*, 1 (1796), 285–6.
76 *Monthly Review*, 20 (1796), 251.
77 *Monthly Mirror*, 1 (1796), 287.
78 *Analytic Review*, 23 (1796), 236.
79 *Monthly Mirror*, 1 (1796), 287.
80 Godwin, *Memoirs*, p. 6.
81 Ibid., pp. 84–5.
82 Ibid., p. 73.
83 Godwin, Preface to *Posthumous Works*, n.p.
84 *Analytic Review*, 33 (1798), n.p.
85 *Monthly Mirror*, 13 (1798), 287–8.
86 Tomalin, *Life and Death*, pp. 221–4.
87 See "The Visions of the Daughters of Albion" (1793), and "Mary" (n.d.), in *The Complete Poetry and Prose of William Blake*, ed. David V. Erdman, rev. ed. (Berkeley: University of California Press, 1982), pp. 45–50, 487–8.
88 Nystrom, *Scandinavian Journey*, p. 35.
89 Mary Hays, "Memorial for Mary Wollstonecraft Godwin," *Gentleman's*

Magazine, 67 (1797), 894; and Richard Polwhele, *The Unsex'd Females: A Poem*. ed. with intro. by Gina Luria (London: Caddell and Davies, 1798; rpt. New York: Garland Publishing, Inc., 1974), pp. 26–8.

90 Poston, introduction to *Letters Written…in Sweden*, p. xvi.

91 Wardle, *Mary Wollstonecraft*, pp. 255–6.

92 "To William Godwin," *Collected Letters*, p. 395.

5 JANE AUSTEN AND THE LOOK OF LETTERS

1 *Jane Austen's Letters to Her Sister Cassandra and Others*, ed. with intro. R. W. Chapman, 2nd ed. (London: Oxford UP, 1952) is the most complete collection of Austen's extant letters. No letters written prior to 1796 survive, although Austen surely wrote many during her teenage years. Chapman's efforts have assembled 149 letters and notes from Jane Austen's pen, but he acknowledges the teasing gaps in the collection – notably, any correspondence with Austen's "favorite" brother, Henry.

2 Bruce Redford, *The Converse of the Pen: Acts of Intimacy in the Eighteenth-Century Familiar Letter* (Chicago: University of Chicago Press, 1986), p. 10, describes the eighteenth-century's "sense of vocation" for letter-writing as "a campaign for intimacy with the other." Redford analyzes epistolary writing from "within," and thereby offers a picture of epistolary discourse which directly opposes the one I perceive in writers such as Wollstonecraft and Austen. According to Redford, epistolary discourse "fashions a distinctive world at once internally consistent, vital and self-supporting … coherence replaces correspondence as the primary standard of judgement. Such letters achieve, in Northrop Frye's words, "a centripetal structure of meaning" that coexists with a centrifugal movement outward into historical circumstance." In my study, and particularly in my study of Jane Austen, I emphasize the "correspondence" over the "coherence" of letters, the centrifugal over the centripetal, and the social over the "reinforced self-projection" which Redford stresses (pp. 9–10).

3 Caroline Austen, *Reminiscences of Caroline Austen*, ed. Deirdre Le Faye (1897, rpt. Basingstoke: Jane Austen Society, 1986), p. 7.

4 James Austen-Leigh, "A Memoir of Jane Austen." reprinted in Jane Austen, *Persuasion*, ed. D. W. Harding (Baltimore: Penguin Books, 1965), p. 312.

5 Caroline Austen, *Reminiscences*, p. 7.

6 Mary Poovey, *The Proper Lady and the Woman Writer: Ideology as Style in the Works of Mary Wollstonecraft, Mary Shelley, and Jane Austen* (Chicago: University of Chicago Press, 1984), pp. 173, 209–10.

7 For an outline of the debate and record of Jane Austen's correspondence, see Jo Modert, "Letters/Correspondence" in J. David Grey, ed., *The Jane Austen Companion* (New York: Macmillan Publishing Company, 1986), pp. 271–7; and R. W. Chapman's introduction to Austen's

Letters. Austen's niece, Caroline Austen, is the source of the story of Cassandra's letter purge.

8 Chapman, Introduction to Austen's *Letters*, pp. xl–xliii. Examples of the same sort of cross-reading abound. The letters' "incompleteness and opacity," for example, only reinforce "the notorious instability of her novelistic irony," writes Mary Poovey in *The Proper Lady*, p. 173. And whereas the letters "displayed none of that zeal for documentation so common at the time," yet her novels "clearly and brilliantly record economic and social change in southern English village life," Marilyn Butler, "History, Politics and Religion," in Grey, ed., *Jane Austen Companion*, p. 202. Accusations of "triviality" in the letters provoke a defensive admiration of their "expressive *awareness* of social triviality," an awareness which, we learn, the novels substantiate. Alistair Duckworth, responding to E. M. Forster, in "'Spillikins, Paper Ships, Riddles, Conundrums, and Cards': Games in Jane Austen's Life and Fiction," in John Halperin, ed., *Jane Austen Bicentenary Essays* (Cambridge and New York: Cambridge UP, 1975), p. 282. See also Henry Austen, "Biographical Notice of the Author," in *The Works of Jane Austen*, ed. R. W. Chapman, with further revisions by B. C. Southam, 6 vols. (London: Oxford UP, 1975), vol. v, pp. 3–10.

9 Poovey, *The Proper Lady*, p. 173. Chapman, in his introduction to Austen's *Letters*, p. xliii, is best at this epistolary elitism: "But the enchantment which enthusiasts have sometimes found in these letters will not be universally admitted. It will be admitted by those only in whose own experience little things...are inseparable from the deeper joys, and even from the deeper sorrows of life; and by those only who find wisdom and humanity in this correspondence, as well as – or in despite of – its devotion to minutiae."

10 Quoted in Modert, "Letters/Correspondence," p. 227.

11 Henry Austen, "Biographical Notice," in *Works*, vol. v, p. 8.

12 Quoted in Modert, "Letters/Correspondence," p. 274.

13 M. J. Daunton, *The Royal Mail: The Post Office Since 1840* (London: The Athlone Press, 1985), pp. 6–8.

14 For this reflection on the exchange of signs and commodities, I am indebted to Andrew H. Miller's "The Fragments and Small Opportunities of *Cranford*," in "No Silent Thing Without a Voice," unpublished Ph.D. thesis, Princeton University, 1991.

15 Marilyn Butler also discusses this aspect of the letters and its significance in her introduction to *Jane Austen: Selected Letters 1796–1817*, ed. R. W. Chapman (Oxford: Oxford UP, 1985).

16 Butler, "History, Politics, Religion," p. 193.

17 *Mansfield Park*, in *Works*, vol. iii, pp. 303–8, 375–6, 393–5. All further references will appear in the text as *MP*.

18 See Patricia Meyer Spacks, "Female Resources: Epistles, Plot, and Power," in Elizabeth C. Goldsmith, ed., *Writing the Female Voice: Essays on Epistolary Literature* (Boston: Northeastern UP, 1989), pp. 68–73.

19 Poovey emphasizes the issue of propriety for Austen's work in *The Proper Lady*, chapters 6 and 7.

20 Conclusion to *Lady Susan*, in *Works*, vol. vi, p. 31 : . All further references will appear in the text as *LS*.

21 A. Walton Litz, *Jane Austen, A Study of Her Artistic Development* (London: Chatto & Windus, 1965), p. 43, 73–7; Spacks, "Female Resources," p. 74.

22 Litz, *Jane Austen, A Study*, p. 44. In this statement, I differ somewhat from Lloyd Brown, who claims in "Jane Austen and the Feminist Tradition," *Nineteenth-Century Studies* 28 (1973), that the only "real" contest in *Lady Susan* occurs between the heroine and Mrs. Vernon. In fact, Mrs. Vernon can be seen as a figure for the narrator – her interference is a failure until she abandons letter-writing and relies on "personal" supervision.

23 John Davie, Introduction in Jane Austen, *Northanger Abbey, Lady Susan, The Watsons, and Sanditon*, ed. John Davie (Oxford: Oxford UP, 1980), p. xv.

24 Of course, *Elinor and Marianne*, and *First Impressions*, composed shortly afterwards, were probably longer epistolary works, but were revised into Austen's first two published novels. The manuscripts of these works do not survive. "Love and Friendship," which still exists in manuscript, is better characterized as a burlesque of epistolary form. According to B. C. Southam, it was written several years before *Lady Susan*, when Austen was not yet fifteen years old. See Southam, *Jane Austen's Literary Manuscripts* (London: Oxford UP, 1954), pp. 1–19.

25 The surviving manuscript is written on paper marked "1805." Some scholars hypothesize that the conclusion was added at this later date. See Davie, Introduction, *Northanger Abbey*, p. xiv; and Mary Lascelles, *Jane Austen and Her Art* (Oxford: Oxford UP, 1963), pp. 13–14. See Southam's meticulous discussion of the dating of *Lady Susan* in *Jane Austen's Literary Manuscripts*, pp. 45–7. He discounts the late addition of the conclusion, but admits that "certain features of *Lady Susan* might well lead us to suppose it a work of some maturity." See also Litz, *Jane Austen, A Study*, p. 17, and Poovey, *The Proper Lady*, pp. 174–5, who argue for a 1794–5 date of composition.

26 Warren Roberts, in *Jane Austen and the French Revolution* (New York: St. Martin's Press, 1979), Poovey, in *The Proper Lady*, and Litz, in *Jane Austen, A Study*, all connect the character of Lady Susan with Eliza de Feuillide, Austen's reckless French cousin and eventual sister-in-law. Southam traces the history of this association and cautiously delineates the dangers of over-stressing the likeness. See Southam, *Jane Austen's Literary Manuscripts*, pp. 140–2.

27 Howard Robinson, *The British Post Office: A History* (Princeton: Princeton UP, 1948), pp. 141–58.

28 Ibid., pp. 152–5.

29 Poovey, *The Proper Lady*, p. 175.

30 Litz, *Jane Austen, A Study*, p. 41.
31 Hannah More, in her *Strictures on the Modern System of Female Education* (1799), describes an ideal not far from Lady Susan's plans for her daughter: "[Women] should be led to distrust their own judgement; they should learn not to murmur at expostulation; they should early acquire a submissive temper and a forebearing spirit." See *The Works of Hannah More*, 7 vols. (London: H. Fisher, R. Fisher & P. Jackson, 1834), vol. I, pp. 152–3.
32 I am indebted here to the extensive discussion of eighteenth-century female conduct books in Poovey, *The Proper Lady*, pp. 30–5.
33 Spacks, "Female Resources," p. 74.
34 Litz, *Jane Austen, A Study*, pp. 3–30, is very helpful on background to the juvenilia, especially in his account of "sentiment" and "sensibility."
35 "Love and Friendship," in *Works*, vol. VI, p. 78. Hereafter cited as "L&F".
36 See especially "Amelia Webster" and "Catherine" in *The Works of Jane Austen*, vol. VI, pp. 47–9 and 192–242.
37 "Henry and Eliza," in *Works*, vol. VI, p. 66.
38 Southam, *Jane Austen's Literary Manuscripts*, pp. 52–62.
39 Susan Pepper Robbins, "The Included Letter in Jane Austen's Fiction," unpublished Ph.D. thesis, University of Virginia, 1976, p. 30, writes that in *Sense and Sensibility*, "the letter [serves] as a model of shattered relationships and the new privacy that results."
40 Dorrit Cohn, in *Transparent Minds: Narrative Modes for Presenting Consciousness in Fiction* (Princeton: Princeton UP, 1978), locates Austen as "one of the first" to use *style indirect libre*, or what he calls "the narrated [interior] monologue," "frequently and extensively" in fiction (p. 113). For a brief account of the differences between epistolary style and Austen's use of *style indirect libre*, see David Lodge, "Jane Austen's Novels: Form and Structure," in Grey, ed., *Jane Austen Companion*, pp. 175–7.
41 Tony Tanner, *Jane Austen* (Cambridge: Harvard UP, 1986), p. 84.
42 *Sense and Sensibility*, in *Works*, vol. I, pp. 160–1. Hereafter cited as *S&S*.
43 "Amelia Webster," in *Works*, vol. VI, p. 48.
44 *Pride and Prejudice*, vol. II, in *Works*, pp. 47–50. Hereafter cited as *P&P*. Other notable examples of the "look" of letters include Frank Churchill's "handsome" correspondence in *Emma*, and Lucy Steele's note, which Mrs Jennings proclaims "as pretty a letter as I ever saw, and does Lucy's head and heart great credit" (*S&S*, p. 277).
45 Walter Scott, *The Heart of Midlothian* (London: J. M. Dent & Sons, Ltd., 1978), pp. 290–1.
46 Samuel Richardson, *Clarissa*, ed. John Butt, 4 vols. (New York: E. P. Dutton, 1962), vol. IV, p. 431.
47 Samuel Richardson, *Selected Letters*, ed. John Carroll (Oxford: Clarendon Press, 1964), p. 289.
48 John Preston, *The Created Self: The Reader's Role in Eighteenth Century*

Fiction (New York: Barnes and Noble, Inc., 1970), pp 63, 66. Preston suggests that epistolary writing, by its very nature, represents an "estrangement and alienation." The "tragedy" of its form, depicted in Richardson's *Clarissa*, lies in the fact that it "affirms the reality of what it must exclude," i.e. "the whole experience of love" – or union (pp. 80–1, 86). For further discussion of the letter as artifact in *Clarissa*, see Terry Castle, *Clarissa's Ciphers* (Ithaca: Cornell UP, 1982), pp. 119–23; and Robert Paulson, *Emblem and Expression* (Cambridge: Harvard UP, 1975), p. 51.

49 See Robert Darnton, "Readers Respond to Rousseau," in *The Great Cat Massacre and Other Episodes in French Cultural History* (New York: Vintage Books, 1985), pp. 215–55; and "Five Steps Toward a History of Reading," in *The Kiss of Lamourette: Reflections on Cultural History* (New York: W. W. Norton, Inc. 1990), pp. 154–87; and Svetlana Alpers, *The Art of Describing: Dutch Art in the Seventeenth Century* (Chicago: University of Chicago Press, 1984), pp. 192–207.

50 Darcy's letter begins by explaining that the reputation of his "character required it to be written and read." Elizabeth "must, therefore, pardon the freedom with which I demand your attention; your feelings, I know, will bestow it unwillingly, but I demand it of your justice." The letter proceeds to refute "two offences" which Elizabeth had "laid to the charge" of Mr. Darcy (*P.&P*, p. 196).

51 Robbins, "The Included Letter," p. 25.

52 Tanner discusses Marianne's reaction to this impasse quite eloquently, although he does not link the episode to the history of epistolary fiction (*Jane Austen*, pp. 75–102).

53 Ian Watt, *The Rise of the Novel* (Berkeley: University of California Press, 1964), p. 208.

54 In this I cannot agree with Robbins, who maintains that Elinor's view does replace the view of the "World." Robbins, "The Included Letter," p. 19.

55 Tanner, *Jane Austen*, p. 84.

56 Georg Lukács, *The Historical Novel*, trans. Hannah and Stanley Mitchell (London: Merlin Press, 1965), pp. 300–22.

57 Tanner, *Jane Austen*, p. 12.

58 Raymond Williams provides a short history of the concept of "society" in the English language, and its movement away from the interpersonal into the institutional, in *Keywords: A Vocabulary of Culture and Society*, rev. ed. (New York: Oxford UP, 1983), pp. 291–5. "The interest of the word," writes Williams, "is partly in the often difficult relationship between the generalization and the abstraction. It is mainly in the historical development which allows us to say 'institutions and relationships,' and we can best realize this when we remember that the primary meaning of *society* was companionship or fellowship" (p. 291). The "decisive transition" toward an abstract notion of society, according to Williams, began in the eighteenth century (p. 293).

59 Robbins discusses this point at some length in "The Included Letter," pp. 109–14.

60 For examples, see Darcy's letter, as well as Mr. Collins' letters, in *Pride and Prejudice*; Lucy Steele's announcement of her marriage in *Sense and Sensibility*; and Edmund's and Lady Bertram's letters in *Mansfield Park*. *Mansfield Park* introduces a suspicion of the letter's news-bearing function, however. Mary Crawford's long letters to Fanny Price "supply matter for reflection...[but] leave everything in greater suspense than ever" (*MP*, p. 417). When Mary writes to dispel any rumors about her brother's behavior, a newspaper report corrects her letter, and provides the damning information (*MP*, pp. 439–40). Austen obviously reconsiders the effectiveness of "news" letters during Fanny's exile in Portsmouth; that reconsideration spills over into *Emma*.

61 From a letter to Anna Austen, in Austen, *Collected Letters*, p. 401.

62 Tanner, *Jane Austen*, p. 122.

63 *Emma*, in *Works*, vol. IV, pp. 18, 119–20, 265–7, 297.

64 David Monaghan, *Jane Austen; Structure and Social Vision* (London: The Macmillan Press, 1980), p. 2. See also Raymond Williams, *The Country and the City* (New York: Oxford UP, 1973).

65 Monaghan, *Structure and Social Vision*, p. 2.

66 Robinson, *The British Post Office*, pp. 213–17.

67 Walter Scott, *The Antiquary*, Waverley Novels Border Edition, ed. Andrew Lang, 24 vols. (London: John C. Nimmo, 1898), vol. III, p. 179.

68 Ibid., chapters 38–43.

69 Ibid., p. 187.

70 Ibid., pp. 187–8.

71 Ibid., chapter 43.

72 Robinson, *The British Post Office*, pp. 213–17; see also Daunton, *The Royal Mail*, chapter 1.

73 An interesting comparison to Austen's use of the local post office would, again, be Scott's *The Antiquary*. The deleterious and supervisory manner of the women in the local post office lead the main characters to resort to secret correspondences and, consequently, dangerous affairs.

74 Robinson, *The British Post Office*, pp. 126–40.

75 Scott, *The Antiquary*, p. 181.

76 For more on blackmail, see Alexander Welsh's study, *George Eliot and Blackmail* (Cambridge: Harvard UP, 1985).

77 At one point, after listening to Mrs. Elton go on about "our dear Jane," Emma explodes in private: "The kindness and protection of Mrs. Elton! 'Jane Fairfax and Jane Fairfax!' Heavens! Let me not suppose that she dares go about Emma Woodhouse-ing me!" (*Emma*, p. 284).

78 Lawrence Stone, in *The Family, Sex, and Marriage in England 1500–1800* (New York: Harper & Row, 1979), pp. 246–8, discusses at length this strain upon the nuclear family during Jane Austen's lifetime. "The series of developments from the sixteenth to the eighteenth centuries," writes Stone, "...had the effect of stripping away from a marriage one by one

many of those external economic, social and psychological supports which normally serve as powerful reinforcing agencies to hold together the nuclear family." Furthermore, "this erosion of outside supports involved a reduction of sociability, of contacts and emotional ties with persons outside the nuclear group...the conjugal family turned more in upon itself" (pp. 246–8).

79 The bitter paradox of Jane's remarks appears more blatantly in the *1797 Report of the Committee of the House of Commons on...the Post Office and Its Revenues* (London: 1797): the committee members could declare that the current postal service was "almost as perfect as could be" in terms of commercial correspondence, and, at the same time, admit that the safety of letters was "unattainable by any means; at least, any means in command to the Post Office" (pp. 116, 120).

80 See Stuart Tave, *Some Words of Jane Austen* (Chicago: University of Chicago Press, 1973), on the repetition of "intensive words" in *Emma*: "These words are repeated in the mouths of almost everybody, but always with a different slant of intention, a different degree of irony or earnestness. In the process, they accumulate depth...These 'intensive words' run through [*Emma*], accumulating resonance far beyond their meaning in any one syntactical arrangement."

81 Elizabeth Deeds Ermarth, *Realism and Consensus in the English Novel* (Princeton: Princeton UP, 1983), p. 157.

82 Lodge, "Jane Austen's Novels," p. 175.

83 Besides the endings to *Sense and Sensibility* and *Pride and Prejudice*, which I have already mentioned, Austen questions the letter's efficacy in *Northanger Abbey*. Note her narratorial assertion of power in the final chapters: "I leave it to my reader's sagacity to determine how much of all this it was possible for Henry to communicate.. and what portion must yet remain to be told in a letter from James. I have united for their ease what they must divide for mine" (*NA*, vol. v, p. 247).

84 Lodge, "Jane Austen's Novels," pp. 172–5.

85 In this paragraph I draw much assistance from Robbins, "The Included Letter," pp. 109–14, with a rather less pessimistic slant.

86 The best of these can be found in Tanner, *Jane Austen*, pp. 241–3; Litz, *Jane Austen, A Study*, pp. 158–9; Southam, *Jane Austen's Literary Manuscripts*, pp. 88–95; and Susan Morgan, *In the Meantime: Character and Perception in Jane Austen's Fiction* (Chicago: University of Chicago Press, 1980), pp. 177–85.

87 Southam, *Jane Austen's Literary Manuscripts*, p. 95.

88 Monaghan, *Structure and Social Vision*, pp. 144–5.

89 *Persuasion*, in *Works*, vol. v, p. 237.

90 Duckworth, "Spillikins," p. 181; Monaghan, *Structure and Social Vision*, p. 145.

91 Butler, "History, Politics, Religion," p. 193.

92 Susan Morgan makes a similar point, in *In the Meantime*, p. 19.

93 On the correlation between *Persuasion* and a Wordsworthian sense of

time and memory, see Gene W. Ruoff, "Anne Elliot's Dowry," in Harold Bloom, ed., *Jane Austen*, Modern Critical Views Series (New York: Chelsea House Publishers, 1986), pp. 63–5.

94 Monaghan, *Structure and Social Vision*, p. 15.

95 Litz, *Jane Austen, A Study*, pp. 152–9.

96 For this strain of criticism on *Persuasion* see Ruoff, "Anne Elliot's Dowry"; Litz, *Jane Austen, A Study*; and Poovey, *The Proper Lady*.

97 The one, telling exception to this "angle of vision" occurs in chapter 7, when we peek for a moment into Wentworth's view of things: "He had thought her wretchedly altered, and, in the first moment of appeal, had spoken as he felt. He had not forgiven Anne Elliot. She had used him ill; deserted and disappointed him; and, worse, she had shewn a feebleness of character in doing so...She had given him up to oblige others. It had been the effect of over-persuasion. It had been weakness and timidity...Her power with him was gone for ever." (*Persuasion*, p. 61). This exception is discussed at some length by Wayne Booth, *The Rhetoric of Fiction* (Chicago: University of Chicago Press, 1961), p. 251.

98 See Tanner's extended treatment of this issue, in *Jane Austen*, pp. 240–2.

99 Ibid., p. 241.

100 Quoted in Litz, *Jane Austen, A Study*, p. 154.

101 Tanner, *Jane Austen*, p. 229.

102 M. M. Bakhtin, *The Dialogic Imagination*, ed. Michael Holquist and trans. Michael Holquist and Caryl Emerson (Austin: University of Texas Press, 1983). See also Litz, *Jane Austen, A Study*, pp. 152–3; and Lodge, "Jane Austen's Novels," p. 172.

103 Poovey, *The Proper Lady*, p. 224.

104 Tanner, *Jane Austen*, p. 221.

6 THE LETTERS OF *FRANKENSTEIN*

1 Mary Shelley, *Frankenstein, or the Modern Prometheus*, ed. James Rieger (New York: Bobbs-Merrill Company, Inc., 1974), p. 50. All subsequent citations will be from Rieger's edition, and will be noted as *F* in the text.

2 See Mary Poovey's discussion of this "propriety" in *The Proper Lady and the Woman Writer; Ideology as Style in the Works of Mary Wollstonecraft, Mary Shelley, and Jane Austen* (Chicago: University of Chicago Press, 1984), esp. pp. 114–42.

3 Mikhail Bakhtin, "Discourse in the Novel," in *The Dialogic Imagination*, ed. Michael Holquist and trans. Michael Holquist and Caryl Emerson (Austin: University of Texas Press, 1983), pp. 259–422.

4 For other recent approaches to *Frankenstein* which touch on this discussion, see Marc A. Rubenstein, "'My Accursed Origin': The Search for the Mother in *Frankenstein*," *Studies in Romanticism* 15 (1976), 165–94; Anne K. Mellor, "Possessing Nature: The Female in *Frankenstein*," in Mellor, ed., *Romanticism and Feminism* (Bloomington: Indiana UP, 1988), pp. 220–32, and *Mary Shelley: Her Life, Her Fiction, Her*

Monsters (Oxford: Oxford UP, 1989); and George Levine and U. C. Knoepflmacher, eds., *The Endurance of Frankenstein* (Berkeley: University of California Press, 1979). Essays in this collection that stress the radical themes of *Frankenstein* are U. C. Knoepflmacher, "Thoughts on the Aggression of Daughters"; Kate Ellis, "Monsters in the Garden: Mary Shelley and the Bourgeois Family"; Peter Dale Scott, "Vital Artifice: Mary, Percy and the Psychopolitical Integrity of *Frankenstein*"; and Peter Brooks, "Godlike Science / Unhallowed Arts: Language, Nature and Monstrosity." Rubenstein's questions about the novel's unsettling form are echoed by my own.

5 Readers who have skillfully examined the question of authority in this text are Rubenstein, "'My Accursed Origin'"; Poovey, *The Proper Lady*; and Frank Randel, "*Frankenstein*, Feminism, and the Intertextuality of Mountains," *Studies in Romanticism* 23 (1984), 515–23.

6 Author's introduction to the third edition (1831) in *Frankenstein*, ed. James Rieger, p. 222.

7 Ibid., p. 229.

8 Ibid., p. 227.

9 Ibid., p. 229.

10 Brooks, "Godlike Science," p. 214.

11 Ibid., p. 218.

12 Ibid., p. 220.

13 In one sense, Walton provides the response of the Wedding Guest to the Ancient Mariner's tale, which Coleridge's poem never gives: "Even now, as I commence my task, his full-toned voice swells in my ears; his lustrous eyes dwell on me ... I see his thin hand raised in animation, while the lineaments of his face are irradiated by the soul within. Strange and harrowing must be his story..." (*F*, p. 233).

14 Brooks, "Godlike Science," p. 220.

15 Terry Castle, in *Clarissa's Ciphers* (Ithaca and London; Cornell UP, 1982), p. 156. Castle writes of the epistolary form in *Clarissa* reacting against the constraints and intentions of its author or "editor" and displaying the "fictional history of its own production." In the epistolary novel, according to Castle, "The reader can never really penetrate the textual surface, being constantly reminded of that activity of production, which supposedly, yet improbably, brings it into production. One cannot escape into a world of experience 'beyond' the world of correspondence ... [the epistolary form] confirms its own denatured status. This fact has disturbed some readers; particularly those whose critical lights lead them in a continual search after 'Story' – an experiential realm somewhere beyond, or in spite of textual surface" (p. 156). In one sense, I am arguing that the monster embodies the epistolary form, and runs away with it.

16 Julia Kristeva, *Desire in Language: A Semiotic Approach to Literature and Art*, ed. Leon S. Roudiez, trans. Thomas Gora, Alice Jardine, and Leon Roudiez (New York: Columbia UP, 1980), pp. 126–7. In Kristeva's

argument, those who place their belief in such a language place their belief in the one, the individual, the unique truth. For them, "language is always *one* system, perhaps even one 'structure,' always *one meaning*, and, therefore, it necessarily implies a subject... to bear witness to its history... The signifying unit remains implicit within each description of law or text... linear, unidimensional descriptions – with no analysis of the sign's density, the logical problematic of reading, etc. – but which, once technically completed, restore structural identity... or meaning."

[They express] an ideology that posits either the people or an exceptional individual as appropriating this structure or this meaning... [I]t does not lend itself to change... to shifting from one law to another, from one structure to another, from one meaning to another, except by postulating the movement of becoming, that is, of history." Kristeva's critique of "phallocentric language" places Victor Frankenstein in the company of such "exceptional individuals" as Blake's Urizen, or even Jay Gatsby, among other flawed witnesses to history.

17 Poovey, *The Proper Lady*, p. 131.
18 Kristeva, *Desire in Language*, p. 134.
19 Ibid. Brothers and sisters in Shelley's later tales contrast sharply with the pair in *Frankenstein*. In the later fiction, the sister–brother bond is either pedagogic or seductive-erotic, with the brother in the more powerful position. I am suggesting that the Walton–Saville correspondence relies on mutual trust and understanding between individuals. *Frankenstein* shows no signs that Walton patronizes his sister; nor that she "paternalizes" her brother. We do not even know which sibling is older. Similarly, the seductive-erotic element has been virtually erased by the fact that Margaret Saville is married and a mother. Walton expresses little that could be construed as seduction to incest. See especially the stories "The Brother and Sister: An Italian Story", "The Pilgrims" and "Euphrasia." An exceptional brother–sister exchange of equal power occurs in "The False Rhyme." See Mary Shelley, *Collected Tales and Stories, with Original Engravings*, ed. Charles E. Robinson (Baltimore: Johns Hopkins UP, 1976).
20 Kristeva, *Desire in Language*, pp. 130–40.
21 Marc Rubenstein, in "'My Accursed Origin,'" p. 169, calls these letters "the emotional, not to say the geographical center of the novel." He relates the notebook account of the monster's origin with the love letters of William Godwin and Mary Wollstonecraft, written about the time of their daughter's conception. Rubenstein hypothesizes that the explicit eroticism and sexual references in her parents' correspondence would have disgusted the young Mary Shelley, had she read them. I would venture that the young wife and mother directed her disgust not at the lovers' letters, but rather at the more corrupt and unnatural account of conception written from the secluded "workshop of filthy creation."
22 Mary Shelley, *The Letters of Mary Wollstonecraft Shelley*, ed. Betty T. Bennet, 3 vols. (Baltimore: Johns Hopkins UP, 1980, 1983 and 1989), vol. I, p. 360.

23 Bakhtin, *The Dialogic Imagination*, p. 292.
24 Ibid., p. 263.
25 Ibid., p. 314.
26 Author's introduction, in *Frankenstein*, p. 227.
27 Lee Sterrenburg, "Mary Shelley's Monster: Politics and Psyche in *Frankenstein*," in Levine and Knoepflmacher, eds., *The Endurance of Frankenstein*, pp. 143–71.
28 Ibid., p. 171.
29 Kristeva, *Desire in Language*, p. 139.
30 Bakhtin, *The Dialogic Imagination*, p. 315.
31 Kristeva, *Desire in Language*, p. 65.
32 Just after he experiences "a light so brilliant and so wondrous that [he] became dizzy with the immensity of the prospect it illustrated," Victor denies the experience and closes its broadening landscape: "Not that, like a magic scene, it all opened upon me at once...I was like the Arabian who had been buried with the dead and found a passage to life, aided by one glimmering and ineffectual light" (*F*, p. 51).
33 In the 1818 version, Victor Frankenstein takes the journey with Elizabeth, his father and brother. Rieger's collation of the 1818 and 1831 texts, showing the many transitions from "we" to "I" in this scene, indicates Shelley's increased emphasis on isolation.
34 This mountain, like Frankenstein's monster, has no name, but stands "exactly opposite" to the fertile Montanvert, as "a bare, perpendicular rock." Frank Randel, in "*Frankenstein*, Feminism" p. 526, makes much of the verbal pun that connects Franken-stein to this "open or uncovered and auchfrichtig rock, a rock set upright or erect." He concludes, wittily: "It is an emblem of his high-mindedness but even more of the solitary and sterile existence which has become his." Randel does not mention the peculiar vulnerability of such an "open rock." This translation of the protagonist's name seems to underscore the paradoxical nature of his position: seemingly solid and singular, yet exposed to infinite influences.
35 Ibid., p. 527.
36 Randel, ibid., makes the point that "Our visually based stereotypes," like Frankenstein's, "are challenged by [the monster's] own story told in his own words." He credits Shelley with "a brilliant appropriation of the conventional romantic transition from sight to sound amidst mountain scenery."
37 Kristeva, *Desire in Language*, p. 88. Despite the adjective "poetic," Kristeva is referring specifically to the language (or "poetics") of the novel.
38 Randel, "*Frankenstein*, Feminism," p. 529.
39 For Rubenstein as well, the novel's center is diffused and infinite, but he prefers to emphasize the psychosexual symbolism. "The entire novel...is a womb," he maintains. "The mother...seems to recede into the very design of the story" ("'My Accursed Origin,'" pp. 178, 187).
40 Percy Bysshe Shelley, "Remarks on *Frankenstein*," in *Shelley's Prose, or The*

Trumpet of a Prophecy, ed. with intro. by David Lee Clark, with new preface by Harold Bloom (New York: New Amsterdam Books, 1988), p. 307.

41 The *Quarterly Review*, Jan. 1818. Quoted in R. Glynn Grylls, *Mary Shelley: A Biography* (Oxford: Oxford UP, 1938), p. 316.

42 Kristeva, *Desire in Language*, p. 132.

43 Ibid., p. 135. See Philip Stevick, "*Frankenstein* and Comedy," in Levine and Knoepflmacher, eds., *The Endurance of Frankenstein*, pp. 221–39, for an excellent study of the nonsense behind the sense of *Frankenstein*, its rhythms beyond language, and "its mythic seriousness and uncomfortable laughter" (p. 222).

CONCLUSION, OR THE DEATH OF THE LETTER: FICTION, THE POST OFFICE AND "THE ENGLISH MAIL COACH"

1 Jacques Derrida, "Envois," in *The Post Card: From Socrates to Freud and Beyond*, trans. Alan Bass (Chicago: University of Chicago Press, 1987), p. 29.

2 Lucyle Werkmeister, *A Newspaper History of England, 1793–4* (Lincoln: University of Nebraska Press, 1967), p. 244.

3 Thomas De Quincey, *The Confessions of an English Opium Eater*, in *The Collected Writings of Thomas De Quincey*, ed. David Masson, 16 vols. (Edinburg: A. and C. Black, 1889–90), vol. III, pp. 302, 308.

4 Walter Scott, *The Antiquary*, Waverley Novels Border Edition, ed. Andrew Lang (London: John C. Nimmo, 1898). See chaps. 15 and 43.

5 Caroline Lamb, *Glenarvon*, intro. James L. Ruff (1816 fascimile rpt., Delmar, NY: Scholars' Facsimiles and Reprints, 1972), p. 198.

6 Ibid., p. 200.

7 Ibid., p. 295.

8 *Pride and Prejudice*, in *The Works of Jane Austen*, ed. R. W. Chapman, with further revisions by B. C. Southam, 6 vols. (London: Oxford UP, 1975), vol. II, p. 368. Letters are similarly discounted in the final pages of Austen's *Lady Susan*, *Sense and Sensibility*, *Northanger Abbey* and *Mansfield Park*. *Emma* and *Persuasion*, as I argue elsewhere, ascribe a different, more constructive function to the letter.

9 Walter Scott, *Redgauntlet, a Tale of the Eighteenth Century*, ed. Kathryn Sutherland (London: Oxford UP, 1985), p. 141.

10 Charles Lamb, "Distant Correspondents," in *The Works of Charles Lamb*, ed. Percy Fitzgerald, 6 vols. (London and Philadelphia: J. B. Lippincott Company, 1897), vol. III, pp. 303–4.

11 For a provocative complication, see Charlotte Brontë's *Villette* (1854), where the narrator/heroine hides and buries her letters, but subsequently reports her drugged reveries. In *Glenarvon*, when the letters that "persecute" Lord Glenarvon have lost their force, their role is transferred to a series of dreams that haunt and chastise him.

12 Maria Edgeworth, *Patronage*, intro. Eva Figes (New York: Methuen, Inc., 1986), pp. 546–7.

13 Ibid., p. 538.
14 Ibid., p. 571.
15 Elizabeth Gaskell, *Cranford, and Cousin Phillis*, ed. Peter Keating (Harmondsworth: Penguin Books, 1976).
16 For an excellent account of the novel's implication in this split and the gendering of the separate spheres, see Nancy Armstrong, *Desire in Domestic Fiction: A Political History of the Novel* (New York: Oxford UP, 1987), pp. 3–27.
17 In fact, the overlapping histories and plot-lines of *Cranford*, notably the "detective" plot of locating Miss Matty's brother and the "financial" plot of the failed bank, intersect in the novel, in the form of letters to the narrator. I owe this insight to my colleague, Andrew Miller.
18 Rowland Hill, *et al.*, *Report of the Select Committee on Postage, 1843* (London: 1843), vol. III, p. 56.
19 M. J. Daunton, *The Royal Mail: The Post Office Since 1840* (London: The Athlone Press, 1985), pp. 35–6, 119–21.
20 Hill, *et al.*, *Report of the Select Committee on Postage, 1843*, p. 13.
21 William Pritchard to the Court of Common Council, 1837; quoted in Howard Robinson, *The British Post Office, A History* (Princeton: Princeton UP, 1948), pp. 244–7.
22 Letter-writers, wildly popular in the eighteenth century but on the wane in the early nineteenth, were guides to writing socially appropriate letters. They generally divided types of letters according to purpose and the gender/class/status of both writer and receiver. See Katherine Gee Hornbeak, "The Compleat Letter-Writer in English, 1568–1800," *Smith College Studies in Modern Languages* 15, no. 3–4 (1934); and Janet Gurkin Altman, "Political Ideology in the Letter Manual (France, England, New England)," in John W. Yolton and Leslie Allen Brown, eds., *Studies in Eighteenth-Century Culture* (East Lansing, Mich.: Colleagues Press, 1988), vol. XVIII, pp. 105–19.
23 Hill, *et al.*, *Report of the Select Committee 1843*, p. 14.
24 Ibid., p. 13.
25 Ibid., pp. 15–16.
26 Ibid., p. 16.
27 Hill, cited in Daunton, *The Royal Mail*, p. 16.
28 Daunton, ibid., esp. chapters 2, 3.
29 Ibid., p. xv.
30 Ibid., p. xvii, and chapter 6.
31 Armstrong, *Desire and Domestic Fiction*, pp. 16–18. Armstrong draws on the work of Thomas Laqueur's *Religion and Respectability: Sunday Schools and Working-Class Culture, 1780–1850* (New Haven: Yale UP, 1979), p. 229.
32 For background on these movements, I have drawn from E. P. Thompson, "Crimes of Anonymity," in Douglad Hay, *et al.*, eds., *Albion's Fatal Tree: Crime and Society in Eighteenth Century England* (New York; Random House, 1975); E. J. Hobsbawm and George Rudé, *Captain Swing* (New York: Random House, 1968); David J. V. Jones,

Rebecca's Children: A Study of Rural Society, Crime and Protest (New York: Oxford UP, 1989); and David J. V. Jones, *Crime, Protest, Community and Police* (London and Boston: Routledge, 1982), esp. pp. 33–61. Thompson, "Crimes of Anonymity," pp. 260–4, and David Jones, *Crime, Protest*, p. 39, mention vague statistics on the literacy or semi-literacy of most of these letter-writers.

33 E. P. Thompson, "Crimes of Anonymity," pp. 260–82.
34 Ibid., p. 331.
35 Ibid., p. 316.
36 Ibid., pp. 342–3.
37 Ibid., p. 321.
38 Hobsbawm and Rudé, *Captain Swing*, pp. 205, 210.
39 Thompson, "Crimes of Anonymity," p. 317.
40 "The English Mail Coach," in *Confessions of an English Opium Eater and Other Writings*, ed. Grevel Lindop (Oxford: Oxford UP, 1985), p. 228; and *The Confessions of an English Opium Eater*, in *Collected Writings*, vol. III, pp. 315–6. De Quincey first experiences this "burden" as a separation from specifically female understanding and discourse. The separation is predicted on the death of his sister, and manifested by his inability to "confess" to his mother. See his *Confessions* and J. Hillis Miller, *The Disappearance of God: Five Nineteenth-Century Writers* (Cambridge: Harvard UP, 1963), pp. 20–8.
41 Several very good studies explore the complex interplay between De Quincey's prose style and the headlong progress of the mail coach. See V. A. DeLuca, *Thomas DeQuincey: The Prose of Vision* (Toronto: University of Toronto Press, 1980), pp. 84–116; Robert Hopkins, "De Quincey on War and the Pastoral Design of 'The English Mail Coach,'" *Studies in Romanticism*, 6 (1967), 129–51; Robert Maniquis, "Lonely Empires: Personal and Public Visions of Thomas DeQuincey," in Eric Rothstein and Joseph Wittreich, Jr., eds., *Literary Monographs*, vol. VIII (Madison: University of Wisconsin Press, 1976), 65–77; and Arden Reed, "'Booked for Utter Perplexity' on DeQuincey's Mail Coach," *Thomas DeQuincey: Bicentenary Studies*, ed. Robert Lance Snyder (Norman, Oklahoma: University of Oklahoma Press, 1985), pp. 279–307.
42 "The English Mail Coach," *Confessions*, ed. Lindop, p. 183.
43 Ibid., p. 19.
44 Ibid., p. 189.
45 Ibid., p. 197.
46 Ibid., p. 197.
47 Ibid., pp. 223–4. For a comparable, but more critical representation of the mail coach, see the opening pages of Walter Scott's *The Heart of Midlothian* (London: J. M. Dent & Sons, Ltd., 1978). The intrusion of the coach into the rural districts of the kingdom dismays the narrator, who paints the coming of the mail coaches as a sort of military occupation: "in our village alone, three post-coaches, and four coaches with men armed, and in scarlet cassocks, thunder through the street each

day" (p. 15). But for Scott, the progress of the British mail only
endangers itself: "Now and then...the career of these dashing rivals of
Salmoneus meets with as undesirable and violent a termination as that
of their prototype – [T]he modern vehicle is smashed to pieces with the
velocity of [a ship] hurled against breakers, or rather with the fury of a
bomb bursting at the conclusion of its career through the air" (p. 16).

48 "The English Mail Coach," *Confessions*, ed. Lindop, pp. 221–4.
49 Thomas De Quincey, in *Collected Writings*, vol. VIII, p. 355.
50 De Quincey, quoted in H. A. Page, *Thomas De Quincey, His Life and
Writings*, 3 vols. (London: 1877), vol. I, p. 304.

Bibliography

Adams, M. Ray, "Helen Maria Williams and the French Revolution," in *Studies in the Literary Backgrounds of English Radicalism* (Lancaster, Pa.: Franklin and Marshall Press, 1947).

Agulhon, Maurice, *Marianne into Battle: Republican Imagery and Symbolism in France, 1789–1880*, trans. Janet Lloyd (Cambridge: Cambridge UP, 1981).

Alger, John G., *Englishmen in the French Revolution* (London: 1889).

Alpers, Svetlana, *The Art of Describing: Dutch Art in the Seventeenth Century* (Chicago: University of Chicago Press, 1984).

Althusser, Louis, *Lenin and Philosophy and Other Essays*, trans. Ben Brewster (New York and London: Monthly Review Press, 1971).

Altman, Janet Gurkin, *Epistolarity: Approaches to a Form* (Columbus: Ohio State UP, 1982).

"Political Ideology in the Letter Manual (France, England, New England)," in John W. Yolton and Leslie Allen Brown, eds., *Studies in Eighteenth-Century Culture* (East Lansing, Mich.: Colleagues Press, 1988), vol. XVIII.

Andersen, Howard, and Irvin Ehrenpreis, *The Familiar Letter in the Eighteenth Century* (Lawrence: University of Kansas Press, 1966).

Anti-Jacobin, The, Jacobinism Displayed, in an Address to the English People and *New Lights on Jacobinism, with an Appendix Containing an Account of Voltaire's Behaviour on His Death-Bed, and a Letter From J. H. Stone (who was tried for sedition) to His Friend Dr. Priestley, Disclosing the Principles of Jacobinism*, 2nd ed., 2 vols. (Birmingham: E. Piercy, 1798).

Armstrong, Nancy, *Desire in Domestic Fiction: A Political History of the Novel* (New York: Oxford UP, 1987).

Austen, Caroline, *Reminiscences of Caroline Austen*, ed. Deirdre Le Faye (1897; rpt. Basingstoke: Jane Austen Society, 1986).

Austen, Henry, "Biographical Notice of the Author," in *The Works of Jane Austen*, ed. R. W. Chapman, with further revisions by B. C. Southam, 6 vols. (London: Oxford UP, 1975), vol. V.

Austen, Jane, *Jane Austen's Letters to Her Sister Cassandra and Others*, ed. with intro. R. W. Chapman, 2nd ed. (London: Oxford UP, 1952).

Jane Austen: Selected Letters 1796–1817, ed. R. W. Chapman, with intro. by Marilyn Butler (Oxford: Oxford UP, 1985).

Northanger Abbey, Lady Susan, The Watsons, and Sanditon, ed. with intro. John Davie (Oxford: Oxford UP, 1980).

The Works of Jane Austen, ed. R. W. Chapman, with further revisions by B. C. Southam, 6 vols. (London: Oxford UP 1975).

Austen-Leigh, James, "A Memoir of Jane Austen," reprinted in Jane Austen, *Persuasion*, ed. D. W. Harding (Baltimore: Penguin Books, 1965).

Bakhtin, Mikhail M., *The Dialogic Imagination*, ed. Michael Holquist and trans. Michael Holquist and Caryl Emerson (Austin: University of Texas Press, 1983).

Barbauld, Anna Letitia, "Tribute to Samuel Richardson," in *The British Novelists*, 50 vols. (London: Home and Van Thale, n.d.).

Batstone, Eric, *et al.*, *Consent and Efficiency: Labour Relations and Management Strategy in the State Enterprise*, Warwick Studies in Industrial Relations (Oxford: Basil Blackwell, 1984).

Baylen, Joseph O. and Norbert J. Gossman, eds., *Biographical Dictionary of Modern British Radicals* (Sussex: Harvester Press and New Jersey: Humanities Press, 1979).

Bell, Michael, *The Sentiment of Reality* (London: G. Allen & Unwin, 1983).

Ben-Israel, Hevda, *English Historians on the French Revolution* (London: Cambridge UP, 1968).

Benstock, Shari, "From Letters to Literature: *La Carte Postale* and the Epistolary Genre," *Genre* 18 (Fall 1985).

Black, Frank Gees, *The Epistolary Novel in the Late Eighteenth Century* (Eugene: University of Oregon Press, 1940).

Blair, Hugh, *Lectures on Rhetoric and Belles Lettres*, 14th ed. (London: T. Caddell *et al.*, 1825).

Blake, William, *The Complete Poetry and Prose of William Blake*, ed. David V. Erdman, rev. ed. (Berkeley: University of California Press, 1982).

Bloom, Harold, ed., *Jane Austen*, Modern Critical Views Series (New York: Chelsea House Publishers, 1986).

Blum, Carol, *Rousseau and the Republic of Virtue* (Ithaca: Cornell UP, 1989).

Booth, Wayne, *The Rhetoric of Fiction* (Chicago: University of Chicago Press, 1961).

Brookner, Anita, *Jacques-Louis David* (London: Chatto & Windus, 1980).

Brooks, Peter, "Godlike Science / Unhallowed Arts: Language, Nature and Monstrosity," in Levine and Knoepflmacher, eds., *The Endurance of Frankenstein*.

Brown, Lloyd, "Jane Austen and the Feminist Tradition," *Nineteenth-Century Studies* 28 (1973).

Brunsdon, Charlotte, "It is Well Known that by Nature Women Are Inclined to Be Rather Personal," in *Women Take Issue: Aspects of Women's Subordination*, Women's Studies Group (Birmingham: Centre of Contemporary Studies, 1978).

Bryson, Norman, *Tradition and Desire: From David to Delacroix* (Cambridge: Cambridge UP, 1984).

Burke, Edmund, *Reflections on the Revolution in France,* and Thomas Paine, *The Rights of Man* (Garden City, NY: Doubleday, Inc., 1973).

Butler, Marilyn, ed., *Burke, Paine, Godwin, and the Revolution Controversy,* (Cambridge: Cambridge UP, 1988).

"History, Politics and Religion," in Grey, ed., *The Jane Austen Companion.*

Romantics, Rebels, and Reactionaries: English Literature and Its Background, 1760–1830 (Oxford: Oxford UP, 1981).

Castle, Terry, *Clarissa's Ciphers* (Ithaca: Cornell UP, 1982).

Christensen, Jerome, *Practicing Enlightenment: Hume and the Formation of a Literary Career* (Madison: University of Wisconsin Press, 1987).

Cobbett, William, *The Parliamentary History of England, from the Earliest Period to the Year 1803* (London: T. C. Hansard, 1794–5), vol. xxxi (1794–5).

("Peter Porcupine"), *Remarks on the Explanation Lately Published by Dr. Priestley, Respecting the Intercepted Letters of his Friend and Disciple, J. H. Stone* (London: J. Write, 1799).

Cohn, Dorritt, *Transparent Minds: Narrative Modes for Presenting Consciousness in Fiction* (Princeton: Princeton UP, 1978).

Coleridge, Samuel Taylor, *The Collected Works of Samuel Taylor Coleridge,* ed. Kathleen Coburn and Bary Winer, Bollingen Series lxxv (London: Routledge & Kegan Paul Ltd., 1971).

Darnton, Robert, *The Great Cat Massacre and Other Episodes in French Cultural History* (New York: Vintage Books, 1985).

The Kiss of Lamourette: Reflections on Cultural History (New York: W. W. Norton, Inc. 1990).

Daunton, M. J., *The Royal Mail: The Post Office Since 1840* (London: The Athlone Press, 1985).

Day, Robert Adams, *Told in Letters* (Ann Arbor: University of Michigan Press, 1966).

de Lauretis, Teresa, ed., *Feminist Studies/Critical Studies* (Bloomington: Indiana UP, 1986).

DeLuca, V. A., *Thomas DeQuincey: The Prose of Vision* (Toronto: University of Toronto Press, 1980).

De Quincey, Thomas, *The Collected Writings of Thomas DeQuincey,* ed. David Masson, 16 vols. (Edinburgh: A. and C. Black, 1889–90).

Confessions of an English Opium Eater and Other Writings, ed. Grevel Lindop (Oxford: Oxford UP, 1985).

Derrida, Jacques, *The Post Card: From Socrates to Freud and Beyond,* trans. Alan Bass (Chicago: University of Chicago Press, 1987).

Doane, Mary Ann, "Film and the Masquerade: Theorizing the Female Spectator," *Screen,* no. 3/4 (Sept.–Oct. 1982).

Duckworth, Alistair, "'Spillikins, Paper Ships, Riddles, Conundrums, and Cards': Games in Jane Austen's Life and Fiction," in Halperin, ed., *Jane Austen Bicentenary Essays.*

Edgeworth, Maria, *Patronage,* intro. by Eva Figes (New York: Methuen, Inc., 1986).

Ellis, Kate, "Monsters In The Garden: Mary Shelley And The Bourgeois

Family," in Levine and Knoepflmacher, eds., *The Endurance of Frankenstein*.

Ermarth, Elizabeth Deeds, *Realism and Consensus in the English Novel* (Princeton: Princeton UP, 1983).

Ferguson, Moira and Janet Todd, eds., *Mary Wollstonecraft* (Boston: G. K. Hall & Company, 1984).

Fitzpatrick, W. J., *Secret Service under Pitt*, 2nd ed. (London: 1892).

Fried, Michael, *Absorption and Theatricality* (Berkeley: University of California Press, 1980).

Frye, Northrop, *Anatomy of Criticism* (Princeton: Princeton UP, 1957; 1981).

Funck-Brentano, F., *Les Lettres de cachet* (Paris: n.p., 1926).

Furet, François, *Penser la Révolution Française* (Paris: 1978)

Gardiner, Judith Kegan, "The First English Novel: Aphra Behn's *Love Letters*. The Canon, and Women's Tastes," *Tulsa Studies in Women's Literature* 8, no. 2 (Fall, 1989).

Gaskell, Elizabeth, *Cranford, and Cousin Phillis*, ed. Peter Keating (Harmondsworth: Penguin Books, 1976).

Gillray, James, *The Works of James Gillray* (London: Henry G. Bohn, 1851; republished New York: Benjamin Blom, Inc., 1968).

Godwin, William, *Memoirs of Mary Wollstonecraft*, ed. W. Clarke Durant (1798; rpt. London: Constable & Co., Ltd., 1927).

Goldsmith, Elizabeth, "Authority, Authenticity, and the Publication of Letters by Women," in Goldsmith, ed., *Writing the Female Voice: Essays in Epistolary Literature*.

Writing the Female Voice: Essays on Epistolary Literature (Boston: Northeastern UP, 1989).

Goodwin, Albert, *The Friends of Liberty: The English Democratic Movement in the Age of the French Revolution* (Cambridge: Harvard UP, 1979).

Great Britain, House of Commons, *1797 Report of the Committee of the House of Commons on ... the Post Office and Its Revenues* (London: 1797).

Parliament of, *Public General Acts* (London: Charles Eyre and Andrew Stratham, 1793–6), vols. LXV–LXVIII.

Post Office Commissioners, *The Ninth Report of the Commissioners, Appointed to Inquire into the Management of the Post-Office Department* (London: W. Clowes and Sons, 1837).

Rpt. of the Committee of the House of Commons on Mr. Palmer's Agreement for the Reform and Improvement of the Post Office and Its Revenues. 1797 (London: n.p., 1797–8).

Report From the Committee on Secresy (London: 1799).

Grey, J. David, ed., *The Jane Austen Companion* (New York: Macmillan Publishing Company, 1986).

Grylls, R. Glynn, *Mary Shelley: A Biography* (Oxford: Oxford UP, 1938).

Hall, Stuart, "Signification, Representation, Ideology: Althusser and the Post-Structuralist Debates," *Studies in Mass Communication*, 2 (1985).

Halperin, John, ed., *Jane Austen Bicentenary Essays* (Cambridge and New York: Cambridge UP, 1975).

Hardy, Thomas, *History of the Origins of the London Corresponding Society* (1799), in Thrale, ed., *Selections from the Papers of the London Corresponding Society, 1792–1799.*

Hawkins, Letitia, *Letters on the Female Mind: Its Powers and Pursuits, addressed to Miss Helen Maria Williams, with Particular Reference to her Letters from France,* 2 vols. (London: Hookham & Carpenter, 1793).

Hay, Douglas, *et al.,* eds., *Albion's Fatal Tree: Crime and Society in Eighteenth Century England* (New York: Random House, 1975).

Hays, Mary, "Memorial for Mary Wollstonecraft Godwin," *Gentleman's Magazine,* 67 (1797).

Hill, Rowland, *First-Third Reports from the Select Committee on Postage: Together with the Minutes of Evidence and Appendix* (London: 1838).

Post Office Minutes and Reports, 2 vols. (London: Harrison & Sons, 1860).

et al., Report of the Select Committee on Postage, 1843, 3 vols. (London: 1843).

Hobsbawm, E. J. and George Rudé, *Captain Swing* (New York: Random House, 1968).

Holmes, Richard, Introduction to Mary Wollstonecraft and William Godwin, *A Short Residence in Sweden, and Memoir of the Author of "A Vindication of the Rights of Woman"* (Harmondsworth: Penguin Books, 1987).

Hone, J. Ann, *For the Cause of Truth: Radicalism in London 1796–1821* (Oxford: Clarendon Press, 1982).

Hopkins, Robert, "DeQuincey on War and the Pastoral Design of 'The English Mail Coach,'" *Studies in Romanticism,* 6 (1967).

Hornbeak, Katherine Gee, "The Compleat Letter-Writer in English, 1568–1800," *Smith College Studies in Modern Languages* 15, no. 3–4 (1934).

Hunt, Lynn, "Engraving the Republic: Prints and Propaganda in the French Revolution," *History Today,* 30 (1980).

Politics, Culture, and Class in the French Revolution (Berkeley: University of California Press, 1984).

Irigaray, Luce, "Sexual Difference," in Moi, ed. and trans., *French Feminist Thought: A Reader.*

This Sex Which Is Not One, trans. Catherine Porter (Ithaca: Cornell UP, 1985).

Johnson, Barbara, *The Critical Difference* (Baltimore: Johns Hopkins UP, 1980).

Jones, David, *Crime, Protest, Community and Police* (London and Boston: Routledge, 1982).

Rebecca's Children: A Study of Rural Society, Crime and Protest (New York: Oxford UP, 1989).

Jost, François, "L'Evolution d'un genre: le roman epistolaire dans les Lettres Occidentales," in *Essais de la littérature Comparée* (Urbana: University of Illinois Press, 1968).

Kamuf, Peggy, *Fictions of Feminine Desire: The Disclosures of Héloïse* (Lincoln: University of Nebraska Press, 1987).

Kauffman, Linda S., *Discourses of Desire: Gender, Genre, and Epistolary Fictions* (Ithaca: Cornell UP, 1986).

Kennedy, Deborah, "Revolutionary Tales: Helen Maria Williams' *Letters From France* and William Wordsworth's Vaudracour and Julia,'" *The Wordsworth Circle* (June 1990).

Klancher, Jon P., *The Making of English Reading Audiences, 1790–1832* (Madison: University of Wisconsin Press, 1987).

Knoepflmacher, U. C., "Thoughts On The Aggression Of Daughters," in Levine and Knoepflmacher, eds., *The Endurance of Frankenstein* (Berkeley: University of California Press, 1979).

Kristeva, Julia, *Desire in Language: A Semiotic Approach to Literature and Art*, ed. Leon S. Roudiez, trans. Thomas Gora, Alice Jardine, and Leon Roudiez (New York: Columbia UP, 1980).

Lamb, Caroline, *Glenarvon*, intro. by James L. Ruff (1816; facsimile rpt., Delmar, NY: Scholars' Facsimiles and Reprints, 1972).

Lamb, Charles, *The Works of Charles Lamb*, ed. Percy Fitzgerald, 6 vols. (London and Philadelphia: J. B. Lippincott Company, 1897).

Laqueur, Thomas, *Religion and Respectability: Sunday Schools and Working-Class Culture, 1780–1850* (New Haven: Yale UP, 1979).

Lascelles, Mary, *Jane Austen and Her Art* (Oxford: Oxford UP, 1963).

Levine, George, and U. C. Knoepflmacher, eds., *The Endurance of Frankenstein* (Berkeley: University of California Press, 1979).

Litz, A. Walton, *Jane Austen, A Study of Her Artistic Development* (London: Chatto & Windus, 1965).

Lodge, David, "Jane Austen's Novels: Form and Structure," in Grey, ed., *The Jane Austen Companion*.

Lukács, Georg, *The Historical Novel*, trans. Hannah and Stanley Mitchell (London: Merlin Press, 1965).

McGann, Jerome, ed. and intro., *Historical Studies and Literary Criticism* (Madison: University of Wisconsin Press, 1985).

The Romantic Ideology (Chicago: University of Chicago Press, 1983).

Maniquis, Robert, "Lonely Empires: Personal and Public Visions of Thomas DeQuincey," in Eric Rothstein and Joseph Wittreich, Jr., eds., *Literary Monographs*, vol. VIII (Madison: University of Wisconsin Press, 1976).

Marrinan, Michael, "Images and Ideas of Charlotte Corday: Texts and Contexts of an Assassin," *Arts* 54, no. 8 (April 1980).

Mathiez, A., *La Révolution et les étrangers* (Paris: La Renaissance du Livre, 1918).

May, Gita, *Madame Roland and the Age of Revolution* (New York: Columbia UP, 1970).

Mayo, Robert D., *The English Novel in the Magazines, 1740–1815* (Evanston, Ill.: Northwestern UP, 1962).

Mellor, Anne K., *Mary Shelley: Her Life, Her Fiction, Her Monsters* (Oxford: Oxford UP, 1989).

"Possessing Nature: The Female in *Frankenstein*," in Anne K. Mellor, ed., *Romanticism and Feminism* (Bloomington: Indiana UP, 1988).

Miller, Andrew H., "No Silent Thing Without a Voice," unpublished Ph.D. thesis, Princeton University, 1991.

Miller, J. Hillis, *The Disappearance of God: Five Nineteenth-Century Writers* (Cambridge: Harvard UP, 1963).

Miller, Nancy K., *The Heroine's Text: Readings in the French and English Novel, 1722–1782* (New York: Columbia UP, 1980).

"'I's in Drag': The Sex of Recollection," *Eighteenth Century* 22 (1981).

Modert, Jo, "Letters/Correspondence" in Grey, ed., *The Jane Austen Companion*.

Moi, Toril, ed. and trans., *French Feminist Thought: A Reader* (New York: Blackwell, 1987).

Monaghan, David, *Jane Austen: Structure and Social Vision* (London: The Macmillan Press, 1980).

Montagu, Mary Wortley, *The Letters and Works of Lady Mary Wortley Montagu*, 2nd ed. (London: R. Bentley, 1837).

Montesquieu, Charles-Louis de Secondat, Baron de, *The Persian Letters*, trans. C. J. Betts (1721 ed.; Harmondsworth: Penguin Books, 1973).

More, Hannah, *The Works of Hannah More*, 7 vols. (London: H. Fisher, R. Fisher & P. Jackson, 1834).

Morgan, Susan, *In the Meantime: Character and Perception in Jane Austen's Fiction* (Chicago: University of Chicago Press, 1980).

Muller, John P. and William J. Richardson, eds., *The Purloined Poe* (Baltimore: The Johns Hopkins UP, 1988).

Myers, Mitzi, "Mary Wollstonecraft's *Letters Written...In Sweden*: Towards Romantic Biography," *Studies in Eighteenth-Century Culture*, 8 (1979).

Mylne, Vivienne, *The Eighteenth-Century French Novel: Techniques of Illusion* (Manchester: Manchester UP, 1965).

Norman, Sylva, Introduction in Mary Wollstonecraft, *Letters Written,... From Sweden*, ed. Sylva Norman (Fontwell, Sussex: Centaur Press, Ltd., 1970).

Nystrom, Per, *Mary Wollstonecraft's Scandinavian Journey*, Acts of the Royal Society of Arts and Letters of Gothenburg, *Humaniora*, no. 17 (1980).

Ozouf, Mona, *La Fête révolutionnaire, 1789–1799* (Paris: Gallimard, 1976).

Page, H. A., *Thomas De Quincey, His Life and Writings*, 3 vols. (London: 1877).

Paine, Thomas, *The Rights of Man*, in Edmund Burke, *Reflections on the Revolution in France*, and Thomas Paine, *The Rights of Man* (Garden City, NY: Doubleday, Inc., 1973).

Paulson, Robert, *Emblem and Expression* (Cambridge: Harvard UP, 1975). *Representations of Revolution, 1789–1820* (New Haven: Yale UP, 1983).

Perry, Ruth, *Women, Letters, and the Novel* (New York: AMS Press, 1980).

Piozzi, Hester Thrale, *The Intimate Letters of Hester Piozzi and Penelope Pennington, 1788–1821*, ed. Oswald Knapp (London: George Allen, 1914).

Plumb, J. H., *England in the Eighteenth Century* (1950; rpt. Harmondsworth: Penguin Books, 1973).

Polwhele, Richard, *The Unsex'd Females: A Poem*, ed. with intro., Gina Luria (London: Caddell and Davies, 1798; rpt. New York: Garland Publishing, Inc., 1974).

Poovey, Mary, *The Proper Lady and the Woman Writer: Ideology as Style in the Works of Mary Wollstonecraft, Mary Shelley, and Jane Austen* (Chicago: University of Chicago Press, 1984).

Pope, Alexander, *The Twickenham Edition of the Poems of Alexander Pope*, gen. ed. John Butt (London: Methuen & Co., 1961).

Preston, John, *The Created Self: The Reader's Role in Eighteenth-Century Fiction* (New York: Barnes and Noble, Inc., 1970).

Priestley, Joseph, *Memoirs of Dr. Joseph Priestley, to the year 1795*, 2 vols. (London: 1806).

The Theological and Miscellaneous Works of Joseph Priestley, ed. John Towell Rutt, 12 vols. (London: 1817–32).

Prochaska, F. K., "English State Trials in the 1790's: A Case Study," *Journal of British Studies*, 8 (1973).

Rand, Erica, "Depoliticizing Women: Female Agency, the French Revolution, and the Art of Boucher and David", *Genders*, 7 (1990).

Randel, Frank, "*Frankenstein*, Feminism, and the Intertextuality of Mountains," *Studies in Romanticism* 23 (1984).

Redford, Bruce, *The Converse of the Pen: Acts of Intimacy in the Eighteenth-Century Familiar Letter* (Chicago: Chicago UP, 1986)

Reed, Arden, "'Booked for Utter Perplexity' on DeQuincey's Mail Coach," *Thomas DeQuincey: Bicentenary Studies*, ed. Robert Lance Snyder (Norman, Oklahoma: University of Oklahoma Press, 1985).

Richardson, Samuel, "Author's Preface" [1759], in *Clarissa*, ed. George Sherburn (Boston: Houghton Mifflin, Co., 1962).

Clarissa, ed. John Butt, 4 vols. (New York: E. P. Dutton, 1962).

Familiar Letters on Important Occasions (London: G. Routledge and Sons, 1928).

Selected Letters, ed. John Carroll (Oxford: Clarendon Press, 1964).

Riviere, Joan, "Womanliness as Masquerade," in Hendrik M. Ruitenbeek, ed., *Psychoanalysis and Female Sexuality* (New Haven: College and University Press, 1966).

Robbins, Susan Pepper, "The Included Letter in Jane Austen's Fiction," unpublished Ph.D. thesis, University of Virginia, 1976.

Roberts, Warren, *Jane Austen and the French Revolution* (New York: St. Martin's Press, 1979).

Robinson, Howard, *The British Post Office: A History* (Princeton: Princeton UP, 1948).

Rosenblum, Robert, *Transformations in Late Eighteenth-Century Art* (Princeton: Princeton University Press, 1967).

Rosenfield, Leonora Cohen, "The Rights of Women in the French Republic," *Studies in Eighteenth-Century Culture* 7 (1978).

Rousseau, Jean-Jacques, *Julie, ou la Nouvelle Héloïse* (Paris: Garnier-Flammarion, 1967).

Lettre à M. d'Alembert sur les spectacles, ed. M Fuchs (Geneva and Lille, 1948).

Œuvres complètes, ed. Bernard Gagnebin *et al.*, 12 vols. (Bruges: Editions Gallimard, 1951).

Les Rêveries d'un promeneur solitaire (Paris: Garnier-Flammarion, 1964).

Rousset, Jean, *Forme et signification* (Paris: Corti, 1962).

Rubenstein, Marc A., "'My Accursed Origin': The Search for the Mother in *Frankenstein*," *Studies in Romanticism* 15 (1976).

Ruoff, Gene W., "Anne Elliot's Dowry," in Bloom, ed., *Jane Austen*, Modern Critical Views Series.

Russo, Mary, "Female Grotesques: Carnival and Theory," in de Lauretis, ed., *Feminist Studies/Critical Studies*.

Sales, Roger, *English Literature in History, 1780–1830* (New York: St. Martin's Press, 1983).

Scott, Peter Dale, "Vital Artifice: Mary, Percy and the Psychopolitical Integrity of *Frankenstein*," in Levine and Knoepflmacher, eds., *The Endurance of Frankenstein*.

Scott, Walter, *The Antiquary*, Waverley Novels Border Edition, ed. Andrew Lang, 24 vols. (London: John C. Nimmo, 1898), vol. III.

  The Heart of Midlothian (London: J. M. Dent & Sons, Ltd., 1978).

  The Journal of Sir Walter Scott, ed. W. E. K. Anderson (London, 1972).

  Redgauntlet, A Tale of the Eighteenth Century, ed. Kathryn Sutherland (London: Oxford UP, 1985).

Seward, Anna, *The Letters of Anna Seward Written Between the Years 1784–1807* (Edinburgh: A. C. Constable, 1811).

Shelley, Mary, *Collected Tales and Stories, with Original Engravings*, ed. Charles E. Robinson (Baltimore: Johns Hopkins UP, 1976).

  Frankenstein, or the Modern Prometheus, ed. James Rieger (New York: Bobbs-Merrill Company, Inc., 1974).

  The Letters of Mary Wollstonecraft Shelley, ed. Betty T. Bennett, 3 vols. (Baltimore: Johns Hopkins UP, 1980, 1983 and 1989).

Shelley, Percy Bysshe, "Remarks on *Frankenstein*," in *Shelley's Prose, or The Trumpet of a Prophecy*, ed. with intro. David Lee Clark, with new preface by Harold Bloom (New York: New Amsterdam Books, 1988).

Shevelow, Kathryn, "The Production of the Female Writing Subject: Letters to the *Athenian Mercury*," *Genre* 19 (Winter, 1986).

Singer, Godfrey Frank, *The Epistolary Novel: Its Origin, Development, Decline, and Residual Influence* (New York: Russell & Russell, 1963).

Society of the Friends of the People, *Proceedings of the Society of the Friends of the People* (London: Mr. Westley, 1793).

Southam, B. C., *Jane Austen's Literary Manuscripts* (London: Oxford UP, 1964).

Spacks, Patricia Meyer, "Female Resources: Epistles, Plot and Power," in Goldsmith, ed., *Writing the Female Voice: Essays on Epistolary Literature*.

Starobinski, Jean, *1789: The Emblems of Reason*, trans. Barbara Bray (Charlottesville: University of Virginia Press, 1982).

  Jean-Jacques Rousseau: Transparency and Obstacle, trans. Arthur Goldhammer (Chicago: University of Chicago Press, 1988).

Sterrenburg, Lee, "Mary Shelley's Monster: Politics and Psyche in *Frankenstein*," in Levine and Knoepflmacher, eds., *The Endurance of Frankenstein*.

Stevick, Philip, "*Frankenstein* and Comedy," in Levine and Knoepflmacher, eds., *The Endurance of Frankenstein.*

Stone, J. H., *Copies of Original Letters Recently Written by Persons in Paris to Dr. Priestley in America, Taken on Board a Neutral Vessel,* 2nd ed. (London: J. Wright, 1798).

Stone, Lawrence, *The Family, Sex, and Marriage in England 1500–1800* (New York: Harper & Row, 1979).

Tanner, Tony, *Jane Austen* (Cambridge: Harvard UP, 1986).

Tave, Stuart, *Some Words of Jane Austen* (Chicago: University of Chicago Press, 1973).

Thompson, E. P., "Crimes of Anonymity," in Douglas Hay, *et al.*, eds., *Albion's Fatal Tree: Crime and Society in Eighteenth Century England.*

The Making of the English Working Class (New York: Vintage Books, 1966).

Thompson, J. M., *The French Revolution,* rev. ed. (London: Basil Blackwell Ltd., 1985).

Thrale, Mary, ed., *Selections from the Papers of the London Corresponding Society, 1792–1799* (Cambridge: Cambridge UP, 1983).

Todd, Janet, *British Women Writers: A Critical Reference Guide* (New York: Continuum, 1989).

Sensibility: An Introduction (New York: Methuen, 1986).

Tomalin, Claire, *The Life and Death of Mary Wollstonecraft* (New York: Harcourt, Brace, Jovanovich, 1974).

Ulmer, Gregory L., "The Post-Age," *Diacritics* 11 (Fall 1981).

Wardle, Ralph M., *Mary Wollstonecraft: A Critical Biography* (Lawrence: University of Kansas Press, 1951).

Watt, Ian, *The Rise of the Novel* (Berkeley: University of California Press, 1964).

Welsh, Alexander, *George Eliot and Blackmail* (Cambridge: Harvard UP, 1985).

Werkmeister, Lucyle, *A Newspaper History of England, 1792–3* (Lincoln: University of Nebraska Press, 1967).

The Whole Official Correspondence Between the Envoys of the U.S. and Mons. Talleyrand, on the Subject of the Disputes Between the Two Countries (London: John Stockdale, 1798).

Williams, Helen Maria, *Letters from France,* ed. with intro. by Janet Todd, 8 volumes in 2 (1795 and 1796; photorpt., Delmar, NY: Scholars' Facsimiles and Reprints, Inc., 1975).

Julia, ed. with intro. by Gina Luria, 2 vols. (1790; rpt., New York and London: Garland Publishing, Inc., 1974).

The Political and Confidential Correspondence of Lewis XVI, with Observations on Each Letter, 3 vols. (London: G. & J. Robinson, 1803).

Souvenirs (Paris: n.p., 1828).

The Unfortunate Young Nobleman (London: R. Harrild and John Choppell, 1790).

Williams, Raymond, *The Country and the City* (New York: Oxford UP, 1973).

Keywords: A Vocabulary of Culture and Society, rev. ed. (New York: Oxford UP, 1983).

Wollstonecraft, Mary, *The Collected Letters*, ed. Ralph M. Wardle (Ithaca: Cornell UP, 1979).

Four New Letters of Mary Wollstonecraft and Helen Maria Williams, eds. B. P. Kurtz and Carrie C. Autrey (Berkeley: University of California Press, 1937).

An Historical and Moral View ... of the French Revolution, ed. with intro., Janet Todd (1795; facsimile rpt., Delmar, NY: Scholars' Facsimiles and Reprints, 1975).

Letters Written During a Short Residence in Sweden, Norway and Denmark, ed. Carol Poston (Lincoln: University of Nebraska Press, 1976).

Posthumous Works by the Author of a Vindication of the Rights of Woman, ed. William Godwin, 2 vols. (London: J. Johnson, 1798; facsimile rpt. Clifton, NJ: Augustus M. Kelley Publishers, 1975).

A Vindication of the Rights of Woman with Strictures on Political and Moral Subjects (1792; rpt. New York: W. W. Norton and Company, 1975).

A Wollstonecraft Anthology, ed. with intro. by Janet Todd (New York: Columbia UP, 1990).

Woodward, Lionel-D., *Une Amie Anglaise de la Révolution Française* (Paris: Librairie Ancienne Honoré Champion, 1930).

Wordsworth, William, *The Poems*, Yale Edition, ed. John O. Hayden, 2 vols. (New Haven and London: Yale UP, 1977).

The Prelude, 1799, 1805, 1850, ed. Jonathan Wordsworth, M. H. Abrams and Stephen Gill (New York: W. W. Norton & Company, Inc., 1979).

Index

826.09
F

DATE DUE